Graham Greene

THE POWER AND THE GLORY

Graham Greene

THE POWER AND THE GLORY

[Edited with Introduction, Author's Information, Complete Text, Summary and Analysis and Study Questions]

Mansi Sachdeva
B.A. English (Hons), Delhi University;
M.A., M. Phil. (English), IGNOU

ANMOL PUBLICATIONS PVT. LTD.
NEW DELHI - 110 002 (INDIA)

ANMOL PUBLICATIONS PVT. LTD.

H.O.: 4374/4B, Ansari Road, Darya Ganj,
New Delhi-110 002 (India)
Ph.: 23278000, 23261597

B.O.: No. 1015, Ist Main Road, BSK IIIrd Stage
IIIrd Phase, IIIrd Block
Bangalore - 560 085 (India)
Visit us at: www.anmolpublications.com

First Published, 2009

PRINTED IN INDIA

Printed at Balaji Offset Press, Delhi.

Contents

Preface

Henry Graham Greene, OM (October 2, 1904- April 3, 1991) was a prolific English novelist, playwright, short story writer and critic whose works explore the ambiguities of modern man and ambivalent moral or political issues in a contemporary setting. Greene was born in Berkhamsted, Hertfordshire, the fourth of six children- his younger brother Hugh was later to become the Director-General of the BBC, and older brother Raymond was an eminent doctor and mountaineer.

The novel Power and the Glory starts with a priest, waiting for a boat that will take him out of the capital city. He is on the run from the police because religion has been outlawed in his state and he is the last remaining clergyman. While talking to a man named Mr. Tench, he is summoned to a dying woman's house and misses his boat.

Author

Chapter 1

Introduction

Graham Greene

Henry Graham Greene, OM was a prolific English novelist, playwright, short story writer and critic whose works explore the ambiguities of modern man and ambivalent moral or political issues in a contemporary setting. Although Greene objected strongly to being described as a mere "Catholic novelist", his religion informs most of his novels, and many of his best works (e.g. Brighton Rock, The Heart of the Matter and The Power and the Glory) are explicitly Roman Catholic in content and preoccupations.

Greene was born in Berkhamsted, Hertfordshire, the fourth of six children- his younger brother Hugh was later to become the Director-General of the BBC, and older brother Raymond was an eminent doctor and mountaineer. Their parents, Charles Henry Greene and Marion nee Raymond, were first cousins and members of a large and influential family which included the owners of the Greene King brewery, and various bankers and businessmen. Charles Greene was "second master" at Berkhamsted School, where the headmaster was Dr Thomas Fry (who was married to another cousin of Charles).

In 1910, Charles Greene succeeded Dr Fry as headmaster of the school, and Graham attended the school as a pupil. Bullied and profoundly unhappy as a boarder, Greene made several attempts at suicide (some of them purportedly by playing Russian roulette- though Michael Shelden's biography of Greene persuasively discredits the truth of these incidents), and in 1921 at the age of seventeen he underwent six months of psychoanalysis in London to deal with depression. After this he returned to the school as a day boy, living with his family. Schoolfriends included Claud Cockburn and Peter Quennell.

He went to Balliol College, Oxford, and his first work was published in 1925, while he was an undergraduate, but it was not widely praised.

Early Career

After graduation, Greene took up a career in journalism, firstly in Nottingham (a city which recurs in his novels as an epitome of mean provincial life), and then as a subeditor on The Times. While in Nottingham he started a correspondence with Vivien Dayrell-Browning, a Roman Catholic who had written to correct him on a point of Catholic doctrine. Greene converted to the faith in 1926, and the couple were married the following year. They had two children, Lucy and Francis. In 1948 Greene left Vivien for Catherine Walston, but they remained married.

Novels and Other Works

Greene's first published novel was The Man Within in 1929, and its reception emboldened him to give up his job at The Times and work full-time as a novelist. However, the following two books were not successful (Greene disowned them in later life), and his first real success was Stamboul Train in 1932- as with several of his subsequent books, this was also adapted as a film .

His income from novels was supplemented by freelance journalism, including book and film reviews for The Spectator, and co-editing the magazine Night and Day, which closed down in 1937 shortly after Greene's review of the film Wee Willie Winkie, starring a nine-year-old Shirley Temple, caused the magazine to lose a libel case. Greene's review claimed that Temple displayed "a certain adroit coquetry which appealed to middle-aged men", and is now seen as one of the first criticisms of the sexualisation of young children by the entertainment industry. His fiction was originally divided into two genres: thrillers or mystery/suspense books, such as Brighton Rock, that he himself cast as "entertainments" but which often included a notable philosophical edge, and literary works such as The Power and the Glory, on which his reputation was thought to be based.

As his career lengthened, however, Greene and his readers both found the "entertainments" to be of nearly as high a value as the literary efforts, and Greene's later efforts such as The Human Factor, The Comedians, Our Man in Havana and The Quiet American combine these modes into works of remarkable insight and compression.

Writing Style

Greene's novels are written in a contemporary, realistic style, often featuring characters troubled by self-doubt and living in seedy or rootless circumstances. The doubts were often of a religious nature, echoing the author's ambiguous attitude to Catholicism (by the end of his life he seems to have lost his faith, but still considered himself a Catholic).

Unlike other "Catholic writers" such as Evelyn Waugh and Anthony Burgess, Greene's politics were essentially left-leaning, though some biographers believe politics mattered little to him. In his later years he was a strong critic of what he saw as American imperialism, and he supported the Cuban leader Fidel Castro, whom he had met.

Travel

Throughout his life, Greene was obsessed with travelling far from his native England, to what he called the "wild and remote" places of the world. His travels provided him with opportunities to engage in espionage on behalf of the United Kingdom (in Sierra Leone during the Second World War, for example). Greene had been recruited to MI6 by the notorious double agent Kim Philby. He reworked the colorful and exciting characters and places he encountered into the fabric of his novels. A 1938 trip to Mexico to see the effects of a campaign of forced anti-Catholic secularisation was funded by the Roman Catholic Church. This resulted in the factual The Lawless Roads (published in America as Another Mexico), and the fictional The Power and the Glory, often considered to be Greene's finest novel. Ironically, the novel was condemned by the Vatican in 1953.

"There is so much weariness and disappointment in travel that people have to open up- in railway trains, over a fire, on the decks of steamers, and in the palm courts of hotels on a rainy day. They have to pass the time somehow, and they can pass it only with themselves. Like the characters in Chekhov they have no reserves – you learn the most intimate secrets. You get an impression of a world peopled by eccentrics, of odd professions, almost incredible stupidities, and, to balance them, amazing endurances."

Graham Greene, The Lawless Roads (1939)

Many of his books have been filmed, most notably 1947's Brighton Rock, and he also wrote several original screenplays, most famously for the film The Third Man.

Trivia

Greene greatly enjoyed parody. In 1949, when the New Statesman publication held a contest for parodies of Greene's distinctive writing style, he submitted an entry under a pseudonym and won second prize. The resulting work, The Stranger's Hand, was later finished by another writer and brought to the screen by Italian film director, Mario Soldati. In 1965, Greene entered a similar New Statesman parody contest, again under a pseudonym, and won an honorable mention.

Final Years

Greene moved to Antibes in 1966, to be close to Yvonne Cloetta, whom he had known for several years, and this relationship endured until his death. In the last years of his life, Greene lived in the small resort city of Vevey, on Lake Geneva in Switzerland. In 1981 he was awarded the Jerusalem Prize, given to writers concerned with 'the freedom of the individual in society'. One of his final works, J'Accuse-The Dark Side of Nice, , concerns a legal matter that he and his family were embroiled in while he lived in Nice. This led to a libel case in France, which he lost. On his death in 1991 at the age of 86, he was interred in the nearby cemetery in Corsier-sur-Vevey.

October 2004 saw the publication of the third and final volume of The Life of Graham Greene by Norman Sherry, Greene's official biographer. The writing of this biography created a story in itself in that Sherry followed in Greene's footsteps, even coming down with diseases that Greene had come down with in the same place. Sherry's work reveals that Greene continued to submit reports to British intelligence until the end of his life. This has led scholars and Greene's reading public to entertain the provocative question, "Was Greene a novelist who was also a spy, or was his lifelong literary career the perfect cover?"

English novelist, short-story writer, playwright and journalist; whose novels treat moral issues in the context of political setitbusngs. Greene is one of the most widely read novelist of the 20th-century, a superb storyteller. Adventure and suspense are constant elements in his novels and many of his books have been made into successful films. Greene was a candidate for the Nobel Prize for Literature several times, but he never received the award.

Graham Greene was born born on October 2, 1904 in Berkhamsted, Hertfordshire, to Charles Henry and Marion Raymond Greene, the fourth of six children. His father had a poor academic record but became the headmaster of Berkhamsted School, following Dr. Thomas Fry. Greene was educated at Berkhamstead School and Balliol College, Oxford. Graham's brothers included Hugh, who went on to become a Director General of the BBC, and Raymond, an accomplished mountaineer involved in the 1931 Kamet and 1933 Everest expeditions. One of Marion's distant cousins happened to be a person called R. L. Stevenson.

He wrote quite regularly in Student Magazines, and was an editor of The Oxford Outlook. His first work, a collection of apparently forgettable poems, Babbling April, was published during his last year at Oxford. It was followed by two novels in the style of Joseph Conrad. After graduation, he worked briefly for the Notitbusngham Journal. He was baptized a Catholic in February 1926. In March, he returned to London, as the Sub Editor for The Times.

Greene married Vivienne (later Vivien) Dayrell-Browning in October 1927. Vivien Greene gave birth to a daughter in December 1933, six months after they had moved again, this time to Oxford.

His first novel, The Man Within, came out in 1929, to public and critical acclaim. A lucrative contract with Heinemann followed, for his next three novels, enabling him to resign from The Times, and devote more time to his novels. The Name of Action and Rumour at night fall, his next two books, did not do very well. The Greenes moved to the Cotswolds in 1931, and he had begun work on what was to establish him as a significant literary figure. Stamboul Train went on to become a commercial success, and a film .

Greene received numerous honours from around the world, and published two volumes of autobiography, A sort of life , Ways of escape , and the story of his friendship with Panamanian dictator General Omar Torrijos.

As a writer Greene was very prolific and versatile. He wrote five dramas and screenplays for several films based on his novels. In the 1930s and early 1940s he wrote over five hundred reviews of books, films, and plays, mainly for The Spectator. His film criticism career actually stretched back to his Oxford days, with an "Outlook" article in 1925. He also had written a few essays on films for The Times.

It's a Battlefield was published in early 1934. Greene started travell -ing extensively in 1934 - brief trips to Germany, Latvia and Estonia preceding an arduous journey overland through Liberia, in the company of his cousin Barbara, which was chronicled in Journey without Maps. He returned in April 1937; England made Me, written before he had left, was published soon after. A Gun for Sale came next, in 1936. Francis Greene was born in September 1936.

Greene's religious convictions did not become overtly apparent in his fiction unti Brighton Rock , which depicted a teenage gangster Pinkie with a kind of demonic spirituality. In the same year, Greene made a trip to Mexico, to investigate into alleged atrocities against the Catholics. The result of the journey was two books, The Lawless Roads in March 1939, and The Power And The Glory, perhaps his finest book, in September 1939. The latter won for him his first major literary prize, The Hawthornden.

The Confidential Agent included a strange piece of Anti-Semitic characterization, in which the mysterious Forbes/ Furstein, a rich Jew, plans to destroy traditional English culture from within. However, in 1981 the author was invited to Israel and awarded the Jerusalem Prize.

Religious themes were explicit in the The Power And The Glory, The Heart of the Matter , a story of a man trapped between the emotional demands of two women, which Greene characterized as "a success in the great vulgar sense of that term," and The End of the Affair , which established Greene's international reputation. This novel was partly based on Greene's affair with Catherine Walston, whom he had met in 1946. She was married to one of the richest men in England, Henry Walston, a prominent supporter of the Labour Party. Catherine was the mother of five children. Greene's relationship with her continued over ten years and produced a book, After Two Years , which was printed 25 copies. Most of the copies were later destroyed.

During World War II Greene worked "in a silly useless job" as he later said in an intelligence capacity for the Foreign Office in London, directly under Kim Philby, a future defector to the Soviet Union. One mission took Greene to West Africa, but he did not find much excitement in his remote posting - "This is not a government house, and there is no larder: there is also a plague of house-flies which come from the African bush lavatories round the house," he wrote to London. Greene returned to England in 1942. His old friend, Philby, Greene met again in the late 1980s in Moscow. After the war he travelled widely as a free-lance journalist, and lived long periods in Nice, on the French Riviera. With his anti-American comments, Greene gained access to such Communist leaders as Fidel Castro and Ho Chi Minh, but the English writer Evelyn Waugh, who knew Greene well, assured in a letter to his friend that the author 'is a secret agent on our side and all his buttering up of the Russians is "cover". Greene left the Service in May 1944, and joined the Political Warfare Executive, editing a literary magazine intended for France. After the War, Greene was commissioned to write a film treatment based on Vienna, a city occupied by the Four Powers at the time. He collaborated with Carol Reed in writing The Third Man, a skillful tale of deception and drug trafficking. The film went on to win the First Prize at Cannes in 1949.

In the 1950s Greene's emphasis switched from religion to politics. He lived at the Majestic hotel in Saigon and made trips to Hong Kong and Singapore. In 1953 he was in Kenya, reporting the Mau Mau upraising, and in 1956 he spent a few weeks in Stalinist Poland, and tried to help a musician to escape to the West.

The Asian setitbusng stimulated Greene's The Quiet American , which was about American involvement in Indochina. The story focuses on the murder of Alden Pyle . The narrator, Thomas Fowler, a tough-minded, opium-smoking journalist, arranges to have Pyle killed by the local rebels. Pyle has stolen Fowler's girl friend, Phuong, and he is connected to a terrorist act, a bomb explosion in a local café. The Quiet American was considered sympathetic to Communism in the Soviet Union and a play version of the novel was produced in Moscow.

Our Man in Havanna was born after a journey to Cuba, but Greene had the story sketched already much earlier. On one trip he asked a taxi driver to buy him a little cocaine and got boracic powder. The novel was made into a film in 1959, directed by Carol Reed. During the filming Greene met Ernest Hemingway, and was invited to his house for drinks. The Comedians depicted Papa Doc Duvalier's repressive rule in Haiti, and The Honorary Consul was a hostage drama set in Paraguay. The Human Factor stayed on the New York Times bestseller list for six months. In the story an agent falls in love with a black woman during an assignment in South Africa.

Greene died in Vevey, Switzerland, on April 3, 1991. Two days before his death Greene signed a note that authorised Norman Sherry to complete an authorised biography. The first part of the book had appeared in 1989 under the title: The Life of Graham Greene.

Selected works of Graham Greene:

Babbling April
The Name of Action (1930)
Rumour at Nightfall
It's a Battlefield
The Bear Fell Free
Journey Without Maps (1936)
A Gun For Sale / This Gun For Hire
The Lawless Roads (1939)
The Confidential Agent (1939)
The Power and the Glory
The Ministry of Fear
Nineteen Stories (1947)
The Heart of the Matter
After Two Years
The Third Man (1949)
The Little Fire Engine (1950)
The Best of Saki
The Lost Childhood
The End of the Affair
The Living Room
The Little Steamroller
The Quiet American
The Potitbusng Shed
Our Man in Havanna (1958)
The Complaisant Lover
A Burnt Out-Case (1961)
In Search of a Character (1961)
The Bodley Head Ford Madox Ford
A Sense of Reality (1963)

Carving A Statue
The Comedians (1966)
Victorian Detective Fiction (1966)
May We Borrow Your Husband? and Other
Comedies of the Sexual Life (1967)
Travels With My Aunt
The Virtue of Disloyalty
The Honorary Consul (1973)
Lord Rochester's Monkey (1974)
An Impossible Woman
The Return of A.J.Raffles
The Human Factor (1978)
Dr. Fisher of Geneva or The Bomb Party
The Great Jowett
Monsignor Quixote (1982)
The Dark Side of Nice
A Quick Look Behind (1983)
For Whom the Bell Chimes
Getitbusng to Know the General
Graham Greene Country (1986)
The Captain and the Enemy (1988)
Why the Epigraph?
The Last Word
Graham Greene: Reflections 1923-88
A World of My Own
The Graham Greene Film Reader (1993)

Chapter 2

Biography

Henry Graham Greene

English novelist, short-story writer, playwright and journalist, whose novels treat moral issues in the context of political settings. Greene is one of the most widely read novelist of the 20th-century, a superb storyteller. Adventure and suspense are constant elements in his novels and many of his books have been made into successful films. Although Greene was a candidate for the Nobel Prize for Literature several times, he never received the award.

"The main characters in a novel must necessarily have some kinship to the author, they come out of his body as a child comes from the womb, then the umbilical cord is cut, and they grow into independence. The more the author knows of his own character the more he can distance himself from his invented characters and the more room they have to grow in." (Graham Greene in Ways of Escape, 1980)

Graham Greene was born in Berkhamsted, Hertfordshire, as the son of Charles Greene and Marion Raymond Greene, a first cousin of the author Robert Louis Stevenson. Greene's father had a poor academic record but became the headmaster of Berkhamsted School, following Dr. Thomas Fry. Charles Greene had a brilliant intellect. Originally he had intended to become a barrister. However, he found that he had liking for teaching and he decided to stay at Berkhamsted. Often his history lessons were less lessons than comments on the crack-up of Liberalism. His brother Graham ended his career as Permanent Secretary at the Admiralty.

Greene was educated at Berkhamstead School and Balliol College, Oxford. He had a natural talent for writing, and during his three years at Balliol, he published more than sixty poems, stories, articles and reviews, most of which appeared in the student magazine Oxford Outlook and in the Weekly Westminster Gazette. In 1926 he converted to Roman Catholicism, later explaining that "I hand to find a religion... to measure my evil against." When critics started to study the religious faith in his work, Greene complained that he hated the term 'Catholic novelist'.

In 1926 Geene moved to London. He worked for the Times of London, and for the Spectator, where he was a film critic and a literary editor until 1940. In 1927 he married Vivien Dayrell-Browning. Greene was not a good family man. Although Greene wrote four children's books, he once stated in a letter: ''How I dislike children." After the collapse of his marriage, he had several relationships, among others in the 1950s with the Swedish actress Anita Björk, whose husband writer Stig Dagerman had committed suicide. Greene's mistresses were often married women living in different countries. During the 1920s and 1930s Greene had, according to his own private list, some sort of of relationship with no less than forty-seven prostitutes. In 1938 Greene began an affair with Dorothy Glover, a theatre costume designer; they were closely involved with each other until the late 1940s. She started a career as a book illustrator under the name 'Dorothy Craigie' and wrote children's books of her own, among them Nicky and Nigger and the Pirate (1960).

During World War II Greene worked "in a silly useless job" as he later said, in an intelligence capacity for the Foreign Office in London, directly under Kim Philby, a future defector to the Soviet Union. One mission took Greene to West Africa, but he did not find much excitement in his remote posting - "This is not a government house, and there is no larder: there is also a plague of house-flies which come from the African bush lavatories round the house," he wrote to London. Greene returned to England in 1942. After the war he travelled widely as a free-lance journalist, and lived long periods in Nice, on the French Riviera, partly for tax reasons. With his anti-American comments, Greene gained access to such Communist leaders as Fidel Castro and Ho Chi Minh, but the English writer Evelyn Waugh, who knew Greene well, assured in a letter to his friend that the author "is a secret agent on our side and all his buttering up of the Russians is 'cover'."

Greene's agent novels were partly based on his own experiences in the British foreign office in the 1940s and his lifelong ties with SIS. As an agent and a writer Greene is a link in the long tradition from Christopher Marlowe, Ben Johnson and Daniel Defoe to the modern day writers John Le Carré, John Dickson Carr, Somerset Maugham, Alec Waugh and Ted Allbeury. Greene's uncle Sir William Graham Greene helped to establish the Naval Intelligence Department, and his oldest brother, Herbert, served as a spy for the Imperial Japanese Navy in the 1930s. Graham's younger sister, Elisabeth, joined MI6, and recruited his Graham into the regular ranks of the service. His old friend, Philby, Greene met again in the late 1980s in Moscow.

Greene received numerous honours from around the world, and published two volumes of autobiography, A SORT OF LIFE , and the story of his friendship with Panamanian dictator General Omar Torrijos. - Greene died in Vevey, Switzerland, on April 3, 1991. In the service the priest declared, "My faith tells me that he is now with God, or on the way there." Two days before his death Greene signed a note that gave his approval to Norman Sherry to complete an authorized biography. The first part of the book appeared in 1989.

As a writer Greene was very prolific and versatile. He wrote five dramas and screenplays for several films based on his novels. The Third Man (1949) was developed from a single sentence: "I had paid my last farewell to Harry a week ago, when his coffin was lowered into the frozen February ground, so that it was incredulity that I saw him pass by, without a sign of recognition, among the host of strangers in the Strand." To do research for the film, Greene went to Vienna, where a reported told him about the black market trade in watered-down penicillin. With the £9,000 he had received from Alexander Korda, he bough a yacht and a villa in Anacapri. Later he portryed Korda in LOSER TAKES ALL (1955) - he was Dreuther, the business tycoon.

In the 1930s and early 1940s he wrote over five hundred reviews of books, films, and plays, mainly for The Spectator. Greene's film reviews are still worth reading and often better than the films he praised or slashed. Hitchcock's "inadequate sense of reality" irritated Greene, he compared Greta Garbo to a beautiful Arab mare, and gave a warm welcome to a new star, Ingrid Bergman. When Hitchcock had troubles with the screenplay of I Confess (1953), Greene refused to help the director, saying he was interested in adapting only his own stories for the screen. In the story a priest is wrongfully accused of a murder. Although Greene knew that some critics considered his novels entertainment, his own models were Henry James, Joseph Conrad, and Ford Madox Ford. In his personal library was a large collection of James's work.

Greene's first published book was BABBLING APRIL (1925), a collection of poetry. It was followed by two novels in the style of Joseph Conrad. The title for THE MAN WITHIN (1929) was taken from Sir Thomas Browne's "There's another man within me that's angry with me." Greene started to write it after an operation for appending on his sick leave from The Times. The film version of the book, starring Michael Redgrave and Richard Attenborough, was made in 1947. Greene received a letter from Istanbul in which the film was praised for its daring homosexuality. "In Stamboul Train for the first and last time in my life I deliberately set out to write a book to please, one which with luck might be made into a film. The devil looks after his own and I succeeded in both aims, though the film rights seemed at the time an unlikely dream, for before I had completed the book, Marlene Dietrich had appeared in Shanghai Express, the English had made Rome Express, and even the Russians had produced their railway film, Turksib. My film came last and was far and away the worst, though not so bad as a later television production by the BBC." (from Introduction, in Stamboul Train, 1974)

After the unsuccessful attempts as a novelist, Greene was about to abandon writing. His first popular success was STAMBOUL TRAIN (1932), a thriller with a topical and political flavour. Greene wrote it deliberately to please his readers and to attract filmmakers. One of its characters, Quin Savory, was said to be a parody of J.B. Priestley - Greene depicted nastily the writer as a sex offender. Priestley had just published a novel, which led some reviewers to compare him with Dickens. In Greene's story Savory was a popular novelist in the manner of Dickens. Next year he attacked another well-loved writer, Beatric Potter, in an article called 'Beatrix Potter: A Critical Estimate'. Also the American actress, Shirley Temple, aged nine, got her share when Greene wrote in the magazine Night and Day that "her admirers - middle-aged men and clergymen - respond to her dubious coquetry, to the sight of her well-shaped and desirable little body, packed with enormous vitality..." This time Greene had to pay for his remark.

THE CONFIDENTIAL AGENT (1939) is a problematic work about the mysterious Forbes/Furstein, a rich Jew, plans to destroy traditional English culture from within. However, in 1981 the author was invited to Israel and awarded the Jerusalem Prize. He had visited Israel in 1967 for the first time, and spent some of the time lying against a sand dune under Egyptian fire, and thinking that the Six Day War "was a bit of misnomer. The war was too evidently still in progress." Greene's religious convictions did not become overtly apparent in his fiction until THE BRIGHTON ROCK (1938), which depicted a teenage gangster Pinkie with a kind of demonic spirituality.

Religious themes were explicit in the novels THE POWER AND THE GLORY (1940), THE HEART OF THE MATTER (1948), which Greene characterized as "a success in the great vulgar sense of that term," and THE END OF THE AFFAIR (1951), which established Greene's international reputation. The story, partly based on Greene's own experiences, was about a lover, who is afraid of loving and being loved. These novels were compared with the works of such French Catholic writers as Georges Bernanos and François Mauriac. "At a stroke I found myself regarded as a Catholic author in England, Europe and America - the last title to which I had ever aspired," Greene later complained.

Greene returned constantly to the problem of grace. In his review of The Heart of the Matter George Orwell attacked Greene's concept of 'the sanctified sinner': "He appears to share the idea, which has been floating around ever since Baudelaire, that there is something rather distingué in being damned; Hell is a sort of high-class nightclub, entry to which is reserved for Catholics only." The novel was set in Sierra Leone where the author had spent a miserable period during the war. Major Scobie, the hero of the story, dies saying: 'Dear God, I love...' The rest is silence.

The End of the Affair was drew partly on Greene's affair with Catherine Walston, whom he had met in 1946. She was married to one of the richest men in England, Henry Walston, a prominent supporter of the Labour Party. Catherine was the mother of five children. Greene's relationship with Walston continued over ten years and produced another book, AFTER TWO YEARS (1949), which was printed 25 copies. Most of them were later destroyed. In The End of the Affair Catherine was 'Sarah Miles' and the writer himself the popular novelist 'Maurice Bendix', who narrates the story and tries to understand why Sarah left him. Maurice discovers that when he was injured in a bomb blast during the war, Sarah promised God that she would end the affair if Maurice is saved. Sarah dies of a pneumonia. Maurice's response to his divine rival is: "I hate you as though You existed.'

The Third Man is among Greene's most popular books. The story about corruption and betrayal gave basis for the film classic under the same title. Successful partners on The Fallen Idol (1948) and Our Man in Havanna (1960), Graham Greene and the director Carol Reed achieved the peak of their collaboration on this film. "I am getting terribly bored with... everybody except Carol who gets nicer and nicer on acquaintance," Greene wrote to Catherine Walston from Vienna in 1948. In The Third Man Holly Martin (Joseph

Cotten) arrives in Vienna to discover that his friend Harry Lime (Orson Welles) has died in a car accident. It turns out that Lime was involved in criminal activities, and Lime's girlfriend Anna Schmidt suspects that his death may not have been accidental. A porter recalls a mysterious third man at the scene of the death. One evening Martins sees a man obscured by the shadows, who suddenly disappears - he is Lime. The meet and Lime rationalizes his villainy in a speech at a fairground Ferris wheel: "In Italy for 30 years the Borgias, they had warfare, terror, murder, bloodshed. They produced Michelangelo, Leonardo Da Vinci and the Renaissance.

In Switzerland they had brotherly love, five hundred years of democracy and peace. And what did that produce. The cuckoo clock." Major Calloway (Trevor Howard) threatens to deport Anna and Martins betrays Lime to secure her freedom. In a chase through the sewers Martins kills Lime, and Anna leaves him after the funeral. - Music, composed by Anton Karas, became highly popular.

"The reader will notice many differences between the story and the film, and he should not imagine these changes were forced on an unwilling author : as likely as not they were suggested by the author. The film in fact is better than the story because it is in this case the finished state of the story." The character of Harry Lime inspired later a series on American radio, performed by Welles, short stories published by the News of the World, and the TV series of The Third Man, starring Michael Rennie. And in Peter Jackson's Heavenly Creatures (1994) Kate Winslet fantasized about Harry. Greene's ability to create debate and his practical jokes brought him often into headlines.

He recommended Vladimir Nabokov's Lolita as his 'Book of the Year' in the Sunday Times and praised the men involved in the Great Train Robbery. In a letter to the Spectator he proposed a scheme to bankrupt the British postal system. In the 1950s Greene's emphasis switched from religion to politics. He lived at the Majestic hotel in Saigon and made trips to Hong Kong and Singapore. In 1953 he was in Kenya, reporting the Mau Mau upraising, and in 1956 he spent a few weeks in

Stalinist Poland, and tried to help a musician to escape to the West. In Ways of Escape Greene told a story about the Other, who called himself Graham Greene, but whose real name was perhaps John Skinner or Meredith de Varg. In the 1950s the Other lost his passport in India, and was sentenced to two years rigorous imprisonment. A decade later he was photographed in a Jamaican paper with "Missus drink", an attractive woman. "Some years ago in Chile, after I had been entertained at lunch by President Allende, a right-wing paper in Santiago announced to its readers that the President had been deceived by an impostor. I found myself shaken by a metaphysical doubt. Had I been the impostor all the time? Was I the other? Was I Skinner? Was it even possible that I might be Meredith de Varg?"

The Asian setting stimulated Greene's THE QUIET AMERICAN (1955), which was about American involvement in Indochina. The story focuses on the murder of Alden Pyle . The narrator, Thomas Fowler, a tough-minded, opium-smoking journalist, arranges to have Pyle killed by the local rebels. Pyle has stolen Fowler's girl friend, Phuong, and he is connected to a terrorist act, a bomb explosion in a local café. The Quit American was considered sympathetic to Communism in the Soviet Union and a play version of the novel was produced in Moscow. OUR MAN IN HAVANNA (1958) was born after a journey to Cuba, but Greene had the story sketched already much earlier. On one trip he asked a taxi driver to buy him a little cocaine and got boracic powder. The novel was made into a film in 1959, directed by Carol Reed.

During the filming Greene met Ernest Hemingway, and was invited to his house for drinks. THE COMEDIANS (1966) depicted Papa Doc Duvalier's repressive rule in Haiti, and THE HONORARY CONSUL (1973) was a hostage drama set in Paraguay. THE HUMAN FACTOR (1978) stayed on the New York Times bestseller list for six months. In the story an agent falls in love with a black woman during an assignment in South Africa. The book did not satisfy Greene and he planned to leave it in a drawer - it hung "like a dead albatross" around his neck. Interested to hear what his friend Kim Philby thought of it he sent a copy to Moscow, but denied that his double agent Maurice Castle was based on Philby. TRAVELS WITH MY AUNT (1969), which was filmed by George Cukor, took the reader on on journey round the world with an odd couple, a retired short-sighted bank manager and his temperamental Aunt Augusta, whose two big front teeth gives her "a vital Neanderthal air."

Chapter 3

Major Works

One of the authors Greene admired most was R K Narayan, probably the foremost Indian writer in English. A favourite of mine, Narayan's writings always manage to evoke heart- felt longing for a return to childhood.

"Childhood is Life Under a Dictatorship."

Graham Greene was born on October 2, 1904 to Charles Henry and Marion Raymond Greene, the fourth of six children. Charles was the Head Master of Berkhamsted School. Graham's brothers included Hugh, who went on to become a Director General of the BBC, and Raymond, an accomplished mountaineer involved in the 1931 Kamet and 1933 Everest expeditions. One of Marion's distant cousins happened to be a person called R. L. Stevenson. Greene studied at the Berkhamstead School and Oxford (in Balliol) By all accounts, he had a pretty torrid time in Berkhamstead, having to balance all the time between his father and his schoolmates.

He wrote quite regularly in Student Magazines, and was an editor of The Oxford Outlook. His first work, a collection of apparently forgettable poems, Babbling April, was published during his last year at Oxford. After graduation, he worked briefly for the Nottingham Journal. He was baptized a Catholic in February 1926. In March, he returned to London, as the Sub Editor for The Times. Greene married Vivienne (later Vivien) Dayrell-Browning in October 1927. He had met her in early '25, after she had written correcting a small mistake (Greene had talked of 'worshipping' the Virgin Mary, and Vivienne felt he ought to have used the word 'venerated') in one of his Outlook articles. His first novel, The Man Within, came out in 1929, to public and critical acclaim. A lucrative contract with Heinemann followed, for his next three novels, enabling him to resign from The Times, and devote more time to his novels. The Name of Action and Rumour at Night fall, his next two books, did not do very well. The Greenes moved to the Cotswolds in 1931, and he had begun work on what was to establish him as a significant literary figure. Stamboul Train went on to become a commercial success, and a film .

"The Critic, as much as the film, is supposed to entertain... "

Around this time, Greene started reviewing for The Spectator. His film criticism career actually stretched back to his Oxford days, with an Outlook article in 1925. He also had written a few essays on films for The Times. He remained an avid film goer for a long time, so much so that he reworked the character of, after watching Anna Sten in The Crime of Dmitri Karamazov (by Feodor Ozep). In 1935, he added films to his book reviewing work at The Spectator. He continued to review films for over a decade, and is widely reg- arded one of the finest critics of his time, the Shirley Temple fiasco notwithstanding (His review of a 1937 film, Wee Willie Winkie, contained disparaging remarks about Ms. Temple's precocious body and it's alleged exploitation by Hollywood movie moghuls. The review led to a messy lawsuit, and possibly the closing down of Night and Day, for which Greene had written the piece).

Vivien Greene gave birth to a daughter in December 1933, six months after they had moved again, this time to Oxford. "Ways of Escape" It's a Battlefield was published in early 1934. Greene started travell -ing extensively in 1934 - brief trips to Germany, Latvia and Estonia preceding an arduous journey overland through Liberia, in the company of his cousin Barbara, which was chronicled in Journey without Maps.

He returned in April 1937; England made Me, written before he had left, was published soon after. A Gun for Sale came next,in 1936. Francis Greene was born in September 1936. In 1938, Brighton Rock came out. In the same year, Greene made a trip to Mexico, to investigate into alleged atrocities against the Catholics. The result of the journey was two books, The Lawless Roads in March 1939, and The Power And The Glory, perhaps his finest book, in September 1939. The latter won for him his first major literary prize, The Hawthornden; the term Greeneland first appeared, at around this time, as a description of the atmosphere in his novels, in an Arthur Calder-Marshall article for The Horizon.

The outbreak of the Second World War led to Vivien and the children evacuating to Crowborough, and later Oxford. Greene worked for the Ministry of Information, and then volunteered for the Air Raid Precautions Squad during the London Blitz. He wrote four childrens' stories during this time, illustrated by a friend, Dorothy Glover; the books were published after the War. Greene also managed to have The Confidential Agent published in September 1939. The novel was an unusual Greene offering in that it's ending was unambiguously happy.

In August, 1941, Greene joined the SIS, and was assigned to Freetown, Sierra Leone, in December. The job was by and large boring, and Greene livened it up by coming up with some innovative plans to recruit spies; one proposed a travelling brothel and another involved tricking a Left Wing official into escaping form Freetown prison with British agents, letting them cross over into Vichy Territory, and then luring him back to blackmail him into becoming a double agent. Unfortunately he did not obtain approval for these schemes. In early 1943, Greene returned to London, to a job in Section V. He was assigned to Counter Intelligence, Portugal, and reported to Kim Philby, who was then in charge of the area.

They became good friends - after Philby's defection to the erstwhile USSR, his memoirs, My Silent War, contained laudatory references to Greene and Greene wrote it's Introduction. An interesting sidelight of Greene's tenure in the SIS is the story of 'Garcia'. A double agent in Lisbon, he fed the Germans disinformation, pretending to control a ring of agents all over England, while all he was doing was inventing armed forces movements and operations from maps, guides and standard military references. Garcia was the inspiration for Wormold a character in Our Man in Havana. Greene left the Service in May 1944, and joined the Political Warfare Executive, editing a literary magazine intended for France. After the War, Greene was commissioned to write a film treatment based on Vienna, a city occupied by the Four Powers at the time. He collaborated with Carol Reed in writing The Third Man, a skillful tale of deception and drug trafficking. The film went on to win the First Prize at Cannes in 1949

Graham Greene's Works

Early Years

1925	Babbling April
1929	The Man Within
1930	The Name of Action
1932	Rumour at Nightfall
1932	Stamboul Train (Orient Express)
	Pre World War II
1934	It's a Battlefield
1935	England made Me
1936	Journey without Maps
1936	A Gun for Sale
1938	Brighton Rock
1939	The Lawless Roads (Another Mexico)
1939	The Confidential Agent
1940	The Power and The Glory
1943	The Ministry of Fear
Post	World War II
1948	The Heart of the Matter
1950	The Third Man
1951	The End of the Affair
1955	The Quiet American
1958	Our Man in Havana
1961	A Burntout Case
1963	A Sense of Reality
1966	The Comedians
1969	Travels with My Aunt
1973	The Honorary Consul
1978	The Human Factor
1980	Dr. Fischer of Geneva, or The Bomb Party

1982	Monsignor Quixote
1985	Getting to know the General
1985	The Tenth Man
1988	The Captain and the Enemy

Chapter 4

Chronology

Graham Greene Biographical Timeline

Born Henry Graham Greene on 2 October 1904, Berkhamsted, Hertfordshire, England. Grows up as shy, sensitive boy who likes reading better than sports. Several suicide attempts at school; goes into therapy at age 15.

Attends Balliol College, "drunk and debt-ridden" as he later recalls. During college edits school paper, becomes political (even joining the Communist Party for fun ; and finished a novel, Anthony Sant, before he graduated .

Works on newspapers as subeditor, 1925-28. Is urged by Vivian Dayrell-Browning to join Catholic church; does so in 1926. Marries Vivian in 1927; they have a daughter, Lucy, and a son, Francis. Quits job at London Times to become full-time writer; struggles until the popular success of Stamboul Train, "an escapist novel that was deliberately intended to please the public," the first of Greene's "entertainments."

Begins traveling all over the world, gathering material for his books. Works for the British Secret Intelligence Service in Sierra Leone during WWII.

Is separated from Vivian in 1948.

Publishes his major works: Brighton Rock (1938); The Power and the Glory (1940); The Heart of the Matter, based on his time in Sierra Leone (1948); The End of the Affair (1951); The Quiet American, set in Vietnam just as American involvement began (1955); and The Human Factor (1978). Dies in Vevey, Switzerland, on 3 April 1991. Graham Greene and Autobiographical Realism. According to Melody Yiu, Greene achieved notoriety in his personal life.... He had many extra-marital affairs, and confessed he was a bad husband and a fickle lover, although he never revealed his affairs in his two autobiographies. In 1951, the public's reaction to The End of the Affair put Greene on the cover of Time magazine over the caption "Adultery can lead to sainthood." Yiu says that Greene "took little pains to disguise the fact that the novel was based on his own affair with Lady Catherine Walston, who also did not appear disturbed by the book. The British edition of the novel is dedicated to 'C' while the American version is made out to 'Catherine'." In his autobiography, Greene says, "The main character in a novel must necessarily have some kinship to the author, they come out of his body as a child comes from the womb, then the umbilical cord is cut, and they grow into independence. The more the author knows of his own character the more he can distance himself from his invented characters and the more room they have to grow in" .

Graham Greene on The Quiet American

When my novel was eventually noticed in the New Yorker the reviewer condemned me for accusing my "best friends" (the Americans) of murder since I had attributed to them the responsibility for the great explosion — far worse than the trivial bicycle bombs — in the main square of Saigon when many people lost their lives. But what are the facts, of which the reviewer needless to say was ignorant? The Life photographer at the moment of the explosion was so well placed that he was able to take an astonishing and horrifying photograph which showed the body of a trishaw driver still upright after his legs had been blown off. This photograph was reproduced in an American propaganda magazine published in Manila over the title "the work of Ho Chi Minh" although General Thé had promptly and proudly claimed the bomb as his own. Who had supplied the material to a bandit who was fighting French, Caodaists and Communists?

Perhaps there is more direct rapportage in the The Quiet American than in any other novel I have written. I had determined to employ again the experience I had gained with The End of the Affair in the use of the first person and the time shift, and my choice of a journalist as the "I" seemed to me to justify the use of rapportage. The Press conference is not the only example of direct reporting. I was in the dive bomber (the pilot had broken an order of General de Lattre by taking me) which attacked the Viet Minh post and I was on the patrol of the Foreign Legion paras outside Phat Diem. I still retain the sharp image of the dead child couched in the ditch beside his dead mother. The very neatness of their bullet wounds made their death more disturbing than the indiscriminate massacre in the canals around.

Chapter 5

Plot Overview

At the beginning of the novel, the priest is waiting for a boat that will take him out of the capital city. He is on the run from the police because religion has been outlawed in his state and he is the last remaining clergyman. While talking to a man named Mr. Tench, he is summoned to a dying woman's house and misses his boat. He hides out in a barn on the estate of a plantation owner, befriending the owner's daughter. Forced to move on, he heads to a village in which he used to live and work as pastor. There he meets Maria, a woman with whom he has had a brief affair, and Brigida, his illegitimate daughter. He spends the night in the town and wakes before dawn to say mass for the villagers.

The lieutenant—a sworn enemy of all r eligion—arrives at the end of mass, leading a group of policemen in search of the priest, and the priest goes out to the town square to face his enemy. No one in the village turns him in, however, and the lieutenant does not realise that he has foun d the man he is looking for. Instead, the lieutenant takes a hostage, whom he says he will execute if he finds that the villagers have been lying to him about the whereabouts of the wanted man.

The priest heads to the town of Carmen, and on the way he meets a man known simply as the mestizo. Uninvited, the mestizo accompanies the priest on his journey, and it very soon becomes clear that he is an untrustworthy figure, and most likely interes ted in following the priest so that he can turn him in and collect the reward money. The priest finally admits that he is, indeed, a priest. But the mestizo, who has become feverish by the second day of their journey together, does not have the strength to follow the priest when he veers off course. The priest knows that if he enters Carmen he will surely be captured, and he lets the mestizo ride on towards the town by himself.

The priest then backtracks to the capital city. He is in disguise, wearing a drill suit, and he tries to procure a bottle of wine so he can say mass. He meets a beggar who takes him to a hotel and introduces him to a man who says he can supply him with the wine. The man arrives and sells the priest a bottle of wine and a bottle of brandy. But, taking advantage of the priest's offer to share a drink with him, the man proceeds to drink the entire bottle of wine, thwarting the priest's plan. The priest then leaves the hotel but is caught with the bottle of brandy by a state official. After a lengthy chase through the streets of the town, during which the priest unsuccessfully attempts to take refuge at the house of Padre Jose, he is caught and taken to jail. In jail he speaks with the prisoners, admitting to them that he is a priest. A pious woman, in jail for having religious articles in her home, argues with the priest. The next day, the priest is ordered to clean out the cells and, while doing so, meets the mestizo again. But the mestizo decides not to turn the priest in to the authorities. The priest has another face-to-face encounter with the lieutenant, but again goes unrecognized, and is allowed to go free.

The priest spends a night at the abandoned estate of the Fellows and then moves on to an abandoned village. He meets an Indian woman whose son has been shot and killed by the gringo, an American outlaw who is also on the run from police. He accompanies the woman to a burial ground and then leaves her there. Fatigued, and almost completely drained of the will to live, the priest staggers on, eventually coming upon a man named Mr. Lehr who informs him that he is out of danger, having crossed the border into a neighboring state where religion is not outlawed.

After spending a few days at the home of Mr. Lehr, the priest prepares to leave for Las Casas. But before he can depart, the mestizo arrives, informing him that the gringo has been mortally wounded by the police and is asking for someone to come and hear his confession. The priest, aware that he is walking into a trap, finally agrees to accompany the mestizo back across the border. There he meets the gringo, who refuses to repent for his sins and then dies. Then, as expected, the lieutenant arrives and ta kes the priest into custody. The two men have a long conversation about their beliefs and then, when the storm front clears, the lieutenant takes the priest back to the capital city for his trial.

On the night before the priest is to be executed, the lieutenant goes to the home of Padre Jose to see if he will come and hear the confession of the captured priest. Padre Jose refuses and the lieutenant returns to the police station with a bottle of bra ndy for the priest. That night, the priest tries to repent for his sins, but finds he cannot. He wakes up the next morning afraid of the impending execution.

The next day, Mr. Tench watches the execution from the window of the jefe's office. Later that night the boy hears about what happened to the priest and realizes that the man is a martyr and a hero. He dreams about him that night, and wakes up to the sound of knocking at the door. Opening the door, he finds a man seeking shelter, and when the boy learns that the man is a priest, he swings the door wide open to let him in.

Chapter 6

Character List

The Priest: Unnamed for the entirety of the novel, the priest or "the whiskey priest" as he sometimes refers to himself, is the protagonist and the character upon whom the novel's most important moral questions centre. He spends the majority of the novel on the run from the police, friendless and homeless and searching for some sense of purpose in his life. His decadent, indulgent life as a parish priest takes place before the novel begins, but it is present in his thoughts throughout the novel as a source of deep humiliation. He spends the novel pursued by the police who believe the Church exploits the poor, and tormented by his own sense of guilt. He meets his daughter, the product of a secret affair with one of his parishioners, and finds that his love for her makes it impossible for him to repent the sin of conceiving her. He often chastises himself for impulses and reactions that are very normal and very human.

The Lieutenant: A believer in the law, a staunch opponent of the Catholic Church, and the priest's pursuer. The lieutenant's hatred of the Church stems from a traumatic event in his childhood, and it is a memory he wishes to eradicate along with all vestiges of religion. He lives a modest, almost monastic life, uninterested in any kind of sensual pleasure and desiring only the attainment of his goals. His "dapper", well-kept appearance stands in striking contrast to the confusion and grime that surround him. The ruthless tactics he employs in his pursuit of the priest seem to contradict his left-wing political and social ideals. But his conversations with the priest and a few of his more generous gestures at the novel's close indicate that he is a conflicted person, capable of empathy and perhaps even change.

The Mestizo: A person the priest meets about halfway through his journey and who continues to reappear throughout the last half of the novel. The mestizo is from the very beginning an untrustworthy character who seems intent on betraying the priest. Impoverished, occasionally delirious and always calculating, the mestizo sees in the outlawed priest an opportunity to make money. His yellow eyes and fangs are noteworthy physical features that suggest menace and evil. Like Judas in the story of Christ, the mestizo becomes an unwitting participant, even catalyst, in a story about one man's path to glory.

Coral Fellows: Coral is a young American girl whom the priest meets early on in the novel when she discovers him hiding on her family's property. Independent-minded and responsible, she anchors her family emotionally and takes charge of the business when her hapless father neglects it. Although a self-professed atheist since the age of ten, Coral is deeply affected by her brief encounter with the priest, and she, in turn, remains a presence in the priest's mind during his journeys.

The boy: A youngster growing up in this violent and impoverished land. The boy listens with skepticism to stories about Juan, a martyred boy. He meets the priest in the beginning of the novel and, by the end, is impressed that the man he encountered has become a martyr for his faith. He represents the human ability to better itself by teaching its youth.

Brigida: The priest's illegitimate daughter. Brigida meets with her father briefly during his stay at her village. Mocked because of her ignominious parentage, she is less than thrilled to meet her long-lost father, and their brief exchange is a tense one. The priest worries about how she will fare in the dangerous, cruel world, and fears that her heart has already become hardened by what she has been through.

Maria: Brigida's mother and the woman with whom the priest had a brief but extremely significant affair. Maria is unhappy to see the priest return, although she helps him to escape capture when the police come to her village.

Padre Jose: The only other priest in the novel besides the protagonist. Padre Jose opted to renounce his faith rather than flee the state or face execution. Forced to marry, Padre Jose is allowed to remain in his town as a symbol of the weakness of the priesthood. He is mocked regularly by the children in his neighborhood and feels a deep and abiding sense of shame over the choices he has made.

Mr. Tench: An Englishman living in Mexico and working as a dentist. Mr. Tench is living a life of apathy and vacancy. A portrait of spiritual deadness, estranged from his wife and filled with a low-level loathing of Mexico, Tench is the first character the reader encounters.

The Gringo: An American outlaw, and the other "hunted man" in this novel. The gringo is wanted for murder. Although his reputation seems to fill people with a strange admiration, when we finally encounter him near the novel's end, he turns out to be little more than a common criminal.

Captain Fellows: Coral's father. Captain Fellows is a benign, if ineffectual, plantation owner, who tries to remain cheerful and optimistic in the face of difficult times and an isolated existence. He is unhappy when he learns that the priest is hiding in his barn, but turns a blind eye to his daughter when she insists upon assisting him. He and Mrs. Fellows leave Mexico after Coral's death.

Mrs. Fellows: Coral's mother. Mrs. Fellows is a neurotic, hysterical woman who confines herself to her bed out of fear of death.

Mr. Lehr: A German-American living in Mexico. Mr. Lehr is the first to come upon the priest after he crosses the border. A Lutheran who is mildly disapproving of Catholicism, he engages the priest in muted religious debate, but is basically a kind person living a rather easy life.

Miss Lehr: Mr. Lehr's sister who came to join her brother in Mexico after his wife died. Miss Lehr is somewhat more curious and also somewhat more naïve than her brother.

The Woman: Nameless like her son, she tries to keep her

children in touch with the Catholic faith by reading them stories of saints' lives. She is concerned that her young son, the boy, is losing interest in religion.

Juan: A young man whom we encounter in this novel only through the stories that are told about him. Juan lives his life with perfect piety and generosity, and faces death with bravery and with perfect composure.

The pious woman: A person the priest meets during his night in jail. The pious woman is too proud of herself and her convictions to be truly pious. She looks down on the priest for having sympathy for the other prisoners in the cell.

The Jefe: The lieutenant's boss. The jefe is not nearly as concerned about the capture of the priest as his crusading underling, and is content to play billiards and delegate authority.

Chapter 7

Analysis of Major Characters

The Priest

The protagonist of the story, the priest is waging a war on two fronts: haunted by his sinful past, he struggles internally with deep qualms about himself, and pursued by the authorities, he works to evade capture by the police for as long as he can. The priest is not a conventional hero: he is at times cowardly, self-interested, suspicious, and pleasure-oriented. That is to say he is human. The extraordinary hardships he has endured on the run from the government for eight years have transformed him into a much more resilient and mentally strong individual, although he still carries around with him strong feelings of guilt and worthlessness. He is self-critical almost to a fault.

What is remarkable about Greene's depiction of this person is that he refuses to spare us the priest's less-than-noble side, and yet also convincingly shows him overcoming his weaknesses and performing acts of great heroism. The most important single act comes near the end of the novel, when he decides to accompany the mestizo back across the border, to the state in which he is being hunted, in order to hear the confession of a dying man. The priest does not recognize the real value of his actions, nor does he fully comprehend what kind of impact he has had on people's lives. He tends to hear only from those people who have been hurt or disappointed by him in some way: Maria, Brigida, the pious woman. He does not see the many people whose lives have been touched merely by coming into contact with him or hearing about his death; Mr. Tench and the boy are the two most notable examples. Because this positive influence remains hidden to him, the priest does not have a true conception of the value of his life, and therefore, remains an extremely humble man to the day of his death. He also feels that he can never be truly penitent for his sexual relationship with Maria, since it produced Brigida, his daughter, whom he loves very deeply.

The Lieutenant

Driven by an obsessive hatred for the Catholic Church, the lieutenant will stop at nothing to apprehend and execute the priest, who, he believes, is the last remaining clergyman in the state. The lieutenant is a principled, disciplined man with a strong sense of justice. He is committed to political ideals that he thinks will help the poor and create equality and tolerance in the state. Unfortunately, he oftentimes allows his focus on his noble goal to obscure questions about the means he is employing to reach that goal. The most striking example of this is his decision to round up hostages and execute people if the villagers lie to him about the priest's whereabouts. As we see, the selection process is entirely arbitrary, hardly just, and extremely violent. It is easy to see why the people are as skeptical of the state as they are of the church.

But even this person is capable of change. From time to time throughout the novel he shows that he is not an unkind person. After his conversation with the captured priest, he softens considerably, trying to find someone to hear the priest's confession and bringing him a bottle of brandy to quiet his fears. The political movement to which he belongs has taught him to look at people in generalized terms: that is, all priests are bad and all those working for the lieutenant's cause are good. The priest, who proves himself to be modest, intelligent and compassionate, disrupts the lieutenant's habitual way of looking at the Catholic clergy.

By the end of the novel, he has accomplished his mission, but he feels a strange sense of emptiness and despondency. Without a target, his life has no meaning or sense of purpose and Greene suggests that lingering doubts fill the lieutenant's mind troubling him about whether he has done the right thing by killing the priest.

The Mestizo

The mestizo, who functions as a "Judas" figure of the novel, appears at significant points throughout the priest's journey. The irony is that although he means the priest nothing but harm, he actually provides opportunities for the priest to commit heroic acts. It begins with the small sacrifice after the two first meet: the priest refuses to abandon the mestizo when he falls ill, finally putting him on the back of a mule and sending him towards a town. When the mestizo tracks him down on the other side of the border, the trap he has set becomes an opportunity for the priest to turn away from the life of leisure, and recommit himself to his ideals and his duties. The mestizo, always interested in getting something for nothing, asks the captured priest to pray for him.

The priest tells him that forgiveness cannot be given out, but must be worked for, and that he had better do some true soul-searching if he is concerned about the sins he has committed. The mestizo is in many ways the mirror image of the priest: the priest has done this soul-searching but despairs over having no third-party to hear his confession. But, while the priest attempts to root out all self-interested motivations from his mind, the mestizo is concerned only with his own advantage. Nevertheless, the priest's actions towards the mestizo make the mestizo a sympathetic character.

Chapter 8

Themes, Motifs and Symbols

Themes

The Dangers of Excessive Idealism: To put it simply, an idealist is one who imagines that the world can be a much better place than it is. What could be dangerous about that? The lieutenant, in many ways, illustrates the danger. Obsessed with the way things could be, he remains mired in dissatisfaction and bitterness about the way things actually are. Although the wish to help the poor is a noble sentiment, dreams of "starting over", erasing history, and wiping out all religious belief are simply not realizable. Moreover, being unable to bring about the impossible leads the lieutenant to feelings of frustration and anger, an even more keen awareness of how imperfect the world is, and hatred for those people whom he views as obstacles to the realization of his dream. Moreover, his conviction that he knows what is best for the people is itself a form of arrogance. The priest, on the other hand, comes to accept suffering and death as a part of life; that is not to say that he does not wish to help alleviate suffering, but his faith in the next world helps him to accept the trials and hardships of this one. The Disparity Between Representation and Reality

Greene is interested in showing the gap between life as it is remembered, recorded or retold, and life as it is lived. Acts of storytelling occur quite frequently throughout the novel. The most obvious example is the story of Juan, the young martyr. One thing that becomes apparent by the novel's close is how very different Juan's story of martyrdom is from the priest's. Juan's life is characterized from start to finish by composure, loyalty and, above all, unshakeable faith. Although the priest certainly is an admirable figure, especially by the time of the novel's close, he still faces death afraid and unable to repent. But Greene is not juxtaposing the two accounts of martyrdom merely to highlight the priest's shortcomings, but rather to show that real-life differs from idealistic stories, in most cases. This theme extends beyond storytelling to other forms of representation. For example, the priest takes note of how little the gringo looks like his picture on the wanted poster in the police office, and the lieutenant fails to recognize the priest because the priest does not have the delicate hands that a stereotypical priest would have. Stories, pictures and other kinds of representation can give a misleading, exaggerated picture of a person, and Greene is interested in writing about reality as it is truly experienced, even if he himself is attempting to create that sense of unvarnished reality through his own storytelling.

The Interrelated Nature of So-called Opposites: Love and hate, beauty and suffering, good and evil are just a few of the many pairs of seeming opposites that Greene insists are not really opposites at all. In the lieutenant's case, for example, his hatred of priests originally stems from a love of and a concern for poor people. Both feelings stem from the same strong emotions—the desire to protect the innocent and the rejection of injustice in any form. The priest often discovers the beauty of life in the moments of greatest suffering and hardship. Moreover, the priest and the lieutenant, who play such opposing roles throughout the novel (i.e. the hunted and hunter, the priest-hater and the priest) come together at the end of the novel and reach a kind of qualified understanding of one another.

The Paradox of Christian Humility: One of the most knotty problems considered in this book is how difficult it is for a Christian to be truly humble. Humility is a quality that a Christian is supposed to strive to realise in his life; yet as soon that person thinks that he is succeeding in being humble, he can become proud of his success. The priest realizes that he is trapped in this quagmire, and that he originally stayed in Mexico during the persecution so that he would appear good before God and his people. Yet, in the novel, he never allows himself to remain complacent in the sacrifices he has made, or the Christian feelings he has. Despairing over his weakness and inability to be truly humble, the priest, paradoxically, attains true humility.

Motifs

Animals: There are many references to animals throughout this novel. The most striking one, perhaps, is the crippled dog that the priest discovers at the abandoned estate. In that scene the priest battles the dog over a bone with a few bites of meat on it and the implicit question is whether anything separates us from the animals. Are human beings reducible to the will to survive? It is a question of great importance to the priest, who often is at a loss to justify his desire to live (especially when he considers the pain his presence inflicts upon others). His struggle with the maimed mongrel over a morsel of meat is a pathetic scene, one in which hunger and the will to live seem to win out over human dignity, and the priest recognizes this. There are also many mentions of insects throughout the novel, notably in scenes involving the lieutenant. Greene refers to insects hurling themselves into lamps or being crushed underfoot. Pointless life careening to pointless death seems to be the import of these details, and the implicit question is whether human life is similarly futile and meaningless.

Half-things: A striking thing about this novel is the prevalence of "half-things": the mestizo is a "half-caste"; the priest despairs most often over the "half-hearted"; Padre Jose is half-priest, half-husband; Mr. Tench seems half-alive; there are dozens of examples throughout the novel. Moreover, we can see by this list alone that half-things more often than not play some detrimental role in this novel. The priest and the lieutenant are by and large, exceptions—people who refuse half-measures and instead tend towards extremes. Near the end of the novel, the mestizo exclaims to the priest, "you do nothing in moderation." Although the extremities are often dangerous—particularly in the case of the lieutenant's actions—Greene seems to suggest that it is better to live life with intensity and passionate commitment than it is to live in an indifferent or complacent fashion.

Abandonment: Many things are abandoned in this novel, and the words "abandoned" or "abandonment" crop up repeatedly. Many of the townspeople feel that the clergy has abandoned them, and the priest, in turn, feels that the people have abandoned him. Mr. Tench has abandoned his family, Captain Fellows and Mrs. Fellows abandon their house and their dog, and the priest tries to abandon the mestizo on the road to Carmen. These are just a few examples. It is an important motif, because it implicitly raises the most important question, whether human beings have been abandoned by God and left to the cruelty of nature and each other. Significantly, the greatest act of heroism in the novel—the priest's decision to return to help the gringo—is a refusal to abandon someone in need, and a refusal to abandon a dangerous and ugly world.

Symbols

Alcohol: Alcohol recurs throughout this book as a symbol with two very different meanings. On the one hand, it represents weakness for "the whiskey priest"; a mark, to him, of his unworthiness and the decadence of his former life. The authorities' attempts to rid the state of alcohol are a manifestation of the impossible and detrimental desire to purge the world of all human weakness. On the other hand, alcohol is an integral part of the Catholic mass, evidenced by the priest's persistent attempts to procure wine. As we see throughout the book, the sacred and the profane are often portrayed not as opposites, but as two halves of the same coin.

Christian Symbolism: At many points throughout the book, different characters seem to stand in for figures from the New Testament. Perhaps the most obvious example is the mestizo, whom the priest expressly refers to as "Judas." During his night in the hut with the mestizo, the priest has trouble keeping himself awake, recalling the night Jesus spends in the garden with the disciples who cannot seem to keep themselves awake. Of course, by the end of the novel, the priest's death is reminiscent of Christ's willing sacrifice and his execution at the hands of the authorities. Despite the similarities, one must pay close attention to the differences as well, since Greene is extremely careful to emphasize that his characters have the free will to decide their own paths in life, and are not merely playing out some predetermined scheme.

Children: Coral Fellows, Brigida and the boy are just a few of the children who play key roles in this novel. In a land of violence and persecution, where a sense of community seems to have all but disappeared, the question of what will become of the next generation looms large. The lieutenant seems to be motivated by a desire to help children avoid the pitfalls of his own childhood by wiping out religion. He cannot completely eradicate the memory of religion from the minds of the older generation, but perhaps the work he and his fellow officers have done will effectively rid the next generation of all religious sentiment. The priest is consumed with worry over the fate of his daughter, Brigida, fearing that she has already been altered for the worse by the cruelty of the world. Thus, children seem to symbolize both a future that is very much hanging in the balance, and a present innocence that may be threatened, or even permanently damaged, by the conflicted times in which they live.

Chapter 9

Summary and Analysis

Part I: Chapter One

Summary

The novel opens with Mr. Tench, an English dentist living and working in a small Mexican town, heading from his home to the riverside to pick up a canister of ether that he has ordered. The ships have come in, and Tench stands in the blazing Mexican sun, watching the rickety boats and continually forgetting why he has come to the river. He meets the stranger, a mysterious man who is waiting for a boat to Vera Cruz. Tench is interested in speaking with the man because he speaks English and, upon learning that the stranger has a bottle of contraband alcohol with him, becomes even more interested. Tench invites the stranger back to his house to share a drink.

At Tench's home, the two men talk and drink for some time. Tench tells his guest that he left behind a family in England, but he has given up writing letters to his wife. The stranger looks like he has not been taking good care of himself. He seems wary and somewhat anxious. He makes strange comments that make Tench pause and wonder about the man.

The men are interrupted by the boy who knocks, seeking help for a woman, his dying mother. Reluctantly, as if he had no choice, the stranger agrees to accompany the boy back to his house. He is aware that doing so will mean that he will most likely miss the boat to Vera Cruz. As he takes his leave of his host, the stranger tells him that he will pray for him.

After his guest departs, Tench discovers that the stranger has left his book behind. He opens it and finds that it is a religious book about a Christian martyr, an illegal document in this state. Unsure of what it is, but dimly aware that he shouldn't have it in his possession, Tench hides the book in a little oven. He suddenly remembers that he forgot to pick up the canister of ether, and runs down to the river only to find that the ship has left the dock and is drifting downriver. On the boat, a young girl sings a sweet, melancholy song. She feels free and happy but she does not know why. Elsewhere, the stranger, walking along with the boy, hears the boat's whistle and realizes that he has, in fact, missed it. He feels despondent at being unable to leave, and angry towards the boy and his mother for keeping him from his boat.

Analysis

The stranger is a priest, the unnamed protagonist of the novel, and Greene introduces him to us in a strange way: although he employs a third-person narrator to tell his story, he refrains from having this narrator directly tell us who this character is at first. Like Tench, we are left to observe this mysterious figure and make inferences about him based on his strange manners, his awkward behaviour, his secretive ways. As a result, we initially meet this character feeling puzzled by him, perhaps even suspicious of him, and for good reason. The novel, in many ways, is very much about the question of how people come to terms with this character, how people evaluate his choices and his attitudes. For example, what do we make of the fact that he agrees to act honorably and help the boy but only does so grudgingly once he learns that it has inconvenienced him?

Meanwhile, Mr. Tench is a portrait of mental and spiritual numbness. It is fitting, therefore, that his errand is to pick up a canister of anesthetic. Indifferent, detached, absent-minded, almost vacant, Tench is a kind of spiritual thermometer for the novel, an indicator of the general atmosphere of quietude and apathy. Tench also serves here as something of a contrast to the priest, arguing that it is useless for him to journey with the boy to visit his dying mother. She is going to die anyway, he reasons, so what would be the point? Mired in a feeling of utter futility, Tench attaches little importance to action of any kind, indicated by his inability to complete a simple errand, as well as his curious refusal to leave Mexico, a place he dislikes. Although he accompanies the boy reluctantly, the priest still feels a sense of duty and retains a feeling that his actions are of some importance and consequence.

We should not, however, make too much of the contrast between the two men: it is also important to note that, after he picks up the religious book, Tench grows "thoughtful" for a moment. Tench may be frozen, but he is not dead, and the hope that even the most callous and indifferent people are still capable of spiritual regeneration is an important idea in this novel. It is a theme that will receive much fuller treatment as the story progresses. Although Tench is not incredibly important to the plot itself, Greene occasionally returns to him briefly over the course of the novel.

In the strange scene near the end of the first chapter, the narrator suddenly shifts his focus away from Tench and trains it on a girl on the bow of the ship in a moment of foreshadowing. He says that she is happy, but that she does not pause to consider why she is happy. This novel is filled with people who are either tormented with self-doubt, anxiety, and a hyper self-consciousness, or leading lives of complacency. This girl fits in neither category, and the brief scene with her is one of the only ones in the novel where someone is actually happy. It is fitting that the figure of happiness is sailing away at the start of the novel, foreshadowing the desperate state of affairs that pervades the rest of the novel.

Part I: Chapter Two

Summary

At the police station, the lieutenant observes his squad of ragtag policemen with distaste. A stern man, he metes out punishment to a group of prisoners who have been jailed for minor offenses and waits for the jefe, or chief, to arrive. The jefe informs the lieutenant that he has spoken with the governor, who believes that there are still priests at large in the state. The lieutenant is skeptical, but the jefe produces a photograph of a plump priest cavorting with women at a first communion party. Upon seeing the photograph, the lieutenant feels anger welling up inside of him. He is outraged at the way the priests behave, or at least at the way they used to behave before Catholicism was outlawed, believing that they lead lives of indulgence and wealth while the people who they supposedly served remained in poverty and misery.

He pins the photograph to the wall next to a photograph of James Calver (who is referred to simply as the gringo throughout the novel). The gringo may be a bank robber and a murderer, the lieutenant argues, but he actually inflicts less harm on society than a priest does. The lieutenant feels that to apprehend and execute a priest is a virtuous deed because it helps to heal the entire state. Talking himself into an angry, determined state of mind, the lieutenant vows that he can catch this priest within a month. He concocts a plan to take one hostage from every town, and kill him if no one in the town comes forward to report the priest's whereabouts. After all, it would certainly be worth a few dead peasants to be able to apprehend the last priest in the state—or so the lieutenant argues. The lieutenant returns to his small, spare room, and thinks with bitterness about the beliefs that religion propagates. He thinks that there is no merciful God, that the universe is cold and dying, and that existence is purposeless.

Meanwhile, in another part of town, a woman reads to her family the story of Juan, a young boy who was murdered because he believed in God and in the Church. A boy listens to the woman read and soon we learn that this is the boy who called at Mr. Tench's house for help for his dying mother. His mother is not dying at all, it turns out, and she and her husband have a conversation about the whiskey priest, the stranger from chapter one, who has taken his leave of them. They also discuss Padre Jose, a priest who, at the state's insistence, agreed to get married and abandon the priesthood.

In yet another part of town, Padre Jose sits on his patio watching the stars and thinking despairingly about his own life. Too afraid to face execution, he opted to give in to the states' demands and leave the Church forever. Now, he thinks, he must live out the rest of his life as a symbol of cowardice and poor faith. Some children mock him as his wife calls him to bed.

Analysis

Chapter Two introduces us to three key figures: the lieutenant, the young boy, and Padre Jose.

The lieutenant is a ruthless and perhaps even hypocritical figure. He despises priests for exploiting the people, yet he lets this feeling so overwhelm him that he declares himself prepared to execute those very people in order to rid the state of priests for good. The lieutenant, however, is far from being a simple character, and it would be a mistake to view him purely in negative terms. While he avows his opposition to the priest and to the priesthood, Greene's description of him often emphasizes the subtle similarities that exist between the lieutenant and his prey. He lives an austere, almost monastic life in his bare room, and he pursues his mission with a single-minded zeal based on principles and a concern for the poor. That his zeal often leads him to commit horrific acts is undeniable but, then again, many people in the novel would argue that the problem with the clergy is that, somewhere along the line, they too lost sight of their ideals.

The lieutenant's ideals concerning order and law can be seen even in his dress. While the lieutenant professes his belief that the universe is fundamentally chaotic, his lifestyle and his meticulous concern for his appearance indicate a desire for order and structure. Greene describes the lieutenant's dress as "dapper", while the other policemen are disheveled. Indeed, he is set apart from his surroundings as well: buildings are dilapidated, the landscape is marshy, overgrown and humid.

Perhaps, then, the figure who is meant to serve as a contrast to the lieutenant is not the priest, but the hapless, incompetent and numb Mr. Tench. Unlike Mr. Tench, the lieutenant has passion and motivation. For Greene, the opposite of love is not hate, but apathy. Both love and hate signify emotional investment, a connection to and a concern about the world, even if hate is an ultimately negative concern. Apathy indicates a lack of commitment and an unconcern for life itself. Connections between the priest and the lieutenant will become clearer as the book progresses, but even in these early chapters Greene is preparing us to question the stereotypical contrasts we may be tempted to draw.

The boy and his family, whose house the priest visited after leaving Tench, serve throughout the novel as a way for Greene to explore the effects of the state's religious intolerance on a pious family. Left with only bad examples of priests for her children, the mother struggles to impart her faith to her offspring. Already it is evident that she can no longer hold her son's attention, as he expresses a lack of interest in the story of the martyred boy, Juan. Children are extremely important in this novel, and one reason is that the future of faith in the state and the response to this wave of religious persecution is uncertain. Padre Jose represents a foil for the protagonist, the nameless priest. While both begin the novel full of shame about themselves, Padre Jose's choice to live an easeful, sedentary life contrasts sharply with the arduous, wandering life chosen by the priest.

Part I: Chapter Three

Summary

Captain Fellows is an American living in Mexico with Mrs. Fellows, his wife, and his young daughter, running the "Central American Banana Company." He returns home one day and his wife informs him that his daughter, Coral Fellows is speaking with a police officer about a priest who is at large in the area. The police officer is the lieutenant from Chapter Two, who is beginning his search for the priest. After a short, tense conversation with Captain Fellows, the lieutenant departs. Coral then informs her father that she refused to allow the lieutenant to search the premises, because the priest is hiding in the barn. Shocked, Captain Fellows asks his daughter to bring him to the priest's hiding place. He tells the priest that he is not welcome, and the priest, with characteristic deference to others' wishes, says he will depart. He asks for some brandy, but Captain Fellows refuses to break the law any further than he already has.

That night, Mr. and Mrs. Fellows lie together in bed, filled with anxiety and trying to ignore the sound of Coral's footsteps as she heads to the barn to bring food to the stranger. Curious, generous, and sensitive, Coral listens carefully to the priest's description of his troubles. With innocent logic, she asks the priest why, if he is so miserable as a fugitive, he doesn't just turn himself in. He explains that it is his duty to remain free as long as he can, and that he cannot renounce his faith because it is out of his "power." The girl listens without judging, then teaches the priest how to use the Morse Code so that he can signal her if he ever returns.

The priest then makes his way to a small village where he finds a small hut to sleep in for the night. Desperately tired and wanting only to sleep, he is beset by villagers asking him to hear their confessions. After some time, he grudgingly agrees to forgo sleep and perform his priestly duties for the people. He begins to weep out of frustration and sheer exhaustion, and an old man goes outside and announces to the villagers that the priest is waiting inside for them, weeping for their sins.

Analysis

As Americans living abroad, Captain and Mrs. Fellows remain isolated, estranged from the country in which they are residing and the people among whom they live. Their detached ineffectuality is perhaps best symbolized by Mrs. Fellows' illness, which leaves her bedridden, full of neurotic anxiety and the fear of death. Lacking any sense of meaning, both are living lives of denial. Captain Fellows refuses to think about anything negative, carefully maintaining a façade of cheerful ignorance. Needing reassurance, he asks his wife, "It's not such a bad life, Trixy? Is it now? Not a bad life?" His wife, on the other hand, sees nothing but death and disease crowding around her and, in response, she retreats further into her bed and behind her mosquito netting, in a futile attempt to hide and protect herself from the dangers that are a part of life. In a darkly comic line about Mrs. Fellows, Greene emphasizes just how warped her fears have made her: "the word 'life' was taboo: it reminded you of death." Along with Mr. Tench, Captain and Mrs. Fellows are not necessarily bad, but simply people living deadened existences.

Unlike her parents, Coral is full of compassion for others and enlivened with the desire to become involved, to engage with the world around her. A professed nonbeliever who lost her faith at the age of ten, Coral instinctively practices the Christian virtues of charity, tolerance and compassion, further emphasizing Greene's point that true Christianity exists in unexpected places, within people who may not even realise how holy they are. By contrast, for the priest, holiness and virtue are qualities that require effort, sacrifice and willpower. Coral Fellows becomes a touchstone of sorts for the priest, a figure to whom his thoughts return at intermittent points throughout the novel.

The encounter with the villagers shows that religion is still very much a part of the lives of the people. However, instead of being a joyous event, the priest's arrival in the town stirs anxiety and haste.

The old man wants him to perform the necessary rituals as quickly as possible before the soldiers arrive. The priest, on the other hand, far from being happy to be able to perform his duties among willing and suppliant believers, is too overwhelmed by fatigue to be anything but irritated. Greene refuses to romanticize religious practices, showing how imperfect people are always involved in any human endeavor, even those considered to be the most sacred. This is not an argument for skepticism; on the contrary, Greene is trying to point out that, in order to believe, one must be able to see and accept things as they are.

The shortsighted Mrs. Fellows cannot accept that death is a part of life and so does not really live; in the same way, those in this novel who do not see that the wicked is part of the sacred lack true wisdom. Complete purity exists only in myths and stories, as evidenced by the old man's telling his fellow villagers that the priest is inside weeping for their sins, when, in fact, he is crying only for himself.

Part I: Chapter Four

Summary

Mr. Tench sits at his worktable, writing a letter to his wife Sylvia, with whom he has not had any contact for many years. He finds it hard to begin, his thoughts drift, and he thinks about the stranger who visited his house. Someone knocks at the door and he abandons the letter for the time being. Padre Jose walking in a graveyard, meets a group of people who are burying a little girl.

They ask him if he would say a prayer for her, but Padre Jose, aware of the danger he is in, refuses. Living under the constant surveillance of the local authorities, he knows that he cannot trust people to keep secrets, and performing such a ceremony among so many people would be dangerous indeed. The people begin to cry and plea for him to help them but, feeling disgraced and useless, Padre Jose continues to refuse their request.

A woman again reads her children the story of Juan, the young martyr. The boy, in a fit of anger, declares that he doesn't believe any of it. His mother angrily sends him out of the room. He tells his father what has transpired, and his father, rather than becoming angry at his son's unruliness, simply sighs. Not a man of much faith, the boy's father tells him that he laments the passing of the Church, since it provided a sense of community.

While teaching Coral Fellows a history lesson, Mrs. Fellows complains of fatigue and puts her book down. Coral takes the opportunity to ask her mother whether she believe in God. Her mother asks Coral to tell her with whom she has been talking to about such things. Coral then goes out to check on a banana shipment and, realizing her father has not taken care of business and is nowhere to be found, gets to work. Then, she begins to feel ill. The lieutenant finds the jefe playing billiards and asks him if he has spoken with the governor. The jefe says that the governor has authorized the lieutenant to use any means necessary to apprehend the outlawed priest, on the condition that he catch him before the rainy season begins. The lieutenant tells the jefe that he will implement his idea to take hostages from the villages, and that he will start at the priest's hometown and parish, Concepcion.

The lieutenant takes his leave of the jefe and heads towards the police station alone. Along the way, a boy throws a rock at him and, when asked what he is doing, the child answers that he was playing a game, pretending that the rock was a bomb and the lieutenant was a gringo. Pleased with this response, the lieutenant unthreateningly shows the young boy his gun, and walks away wishing that he could eliminate everything from the child's life that keeps him in ignorance. He is further charged with a sense of purpose to find and execute the priest.

Analysis

This chapter, ranging through five different scenes, observes the townspeople responding to the presence of priests in their lives. Mr. Tench is moved—although he doesn't know why—to write to his estranged wife after so many years of silence. Although Greene does not come right out and say it, one inference to be drawn is that Mr. Tench's brief encounter with the priest has somehow awakened in him a desire to set things right with his family. That he fails to write the letter here perhaps indicates that this desire has not yet taken root in him, that it is only the faint beginnings of what will undoubtedly be a long process of change his life.

The presence of Padre Jose, meanwhile, awakens hope in the funeral goers, but his refusal to get involved or take a risk makes the ceremony more traumatic than it would have been without him. It is hard to know quite what to make of this scene: on the one hand, Padre Jose does no one a service by being so cowardly, and his frightened, mousy character stands in direct opposition to the stories of brave martyrs (such as the one about the boy, Juan, a story to which the novel continually returns). At the same time, however, his chance encounter with the family at the funeral awakens in them emotions that are perhaps better and more human than the numbness they had been experiencing before his arrival.

The next two scenes involve parents instructing—or trying to instruct—children, and in both cases, the parents prove ineffectual or uninspiring. Mrs. Fellows becomes characteristically nervous when Coral questions her directly about God, and Mr. Fellows is nowhere to be found. Again, the brief, chance encounter with the priest has stirred important questions in someone. The mother reading to her children about the martyr Juan is clearly a much more admirable figure than Mrs. Fellows, and yet she also seems to be failing to engage her son.

His father, not a very religious man, makes an important point about the church's role as a key component in the fabric of the community: whether you believe in what it preaches or not, he seems to argue, it was an organization that brought people together. Many people are isolated in this novel, even people who are living in a large town, in the midst of many others. Camaraderie, fellowship, a sense of social togetherness remain largely absent from this novel, and the father, here, seems to argue for the church as a possible source of community feeling.

The lieutenant's conversation with the young boy shows him, once again, to have good intentions, motivated by the desire to rid the world of corruption and deceit. The lieutenant yearns for purity, he wishes, "to begin the world again with them, in a desert." Greene's point, however, is that purity is not a condition of this world, simply not something available to flawed human beings. As is the case so often, and as Greene emphasizes in this chapter especially, the lieutenant's obsessive pursuit of his impossible end can lead him to resort to horrific and self-defeating means. Impurity is a part of life, Greene suggests, and to attempt to rid the world of it entirely is, therefore, to become a killer.

Part II: Chapter One

Summary

On a mule, the priest flees from the police, who are rapidly closing in on him. Although he did not intend to head in the direction of his hometown, the police are moving in such a way that he is headed in that direction. When he reaches the town, the priest first encounters a woman named Maria who seems less than thrilled to see him again. The priest, who had been feeling somewhat lighthearted, is saddened by the chilly reception given to him by the villagers, until he learns the reason for it: they have heard that the police are taking hostages from villages in which he is reported to have stayed. Maria leads him to a hut where he is to rest for the night and, after the priest asks after her, calls in a young girl named Brigida. The priest is overwhelmed with feeling, especially with a feeling of responsibility because, we soon discover, Maria is a woman with whom he has had a brief, but significant affair, and Brigida is his illegitimate daughter. Not much is said between father and daughter, but he feels an overwhelming need to protect her.

The priest awakes before dawn to say mass for the villagers and is about halfway through the service when a report comes in that the police are approaching the town. He continues with the ceremony as the authorities close in, and by the time he is finished, they have the town surrounded. In the centre of the village, the lieutenant calls everyone from their houses, and the priest, who is aware that he now faces recognition and capture but who sees no way out, obeys. One by one, the lieutenant calls up the townsfolk and asks them to introduce themselves to him. When the priest approaches, the lieutenant asks him questions, and then asks to see his hands. Calloused and hard from his weeks of evading the police, the priest's hands are no longer the soft and delicate hands of a clergyman, and the lieutenant passes him by. The lieutenant then announces that he will take hostages if no one comes forward to give him information and the priest waits, with eyes cast downward, for someone to turn him in. No one steps forward, however, and the lieutenant selects a hostage. The priest then steps forward and offers to go in the man's place, but the lieutenant refuses him and the police detail moves out of town. The priest says a rather strained goodbye to Maria, who feels ashamed of him, and goes to the town rubbish heap to look for his traveling case, which Maria has thrown away. There he meets his daughter Brigida again. She tells him that the other children mock her because of him, and he is again overwhelmed with the feeling that he wishes to protect her from the decay, the pain, and the cruelty of the world. He sees, however, that it is too late, that she has grown up in a culture of violence and intolerance and that there is nothing he can do to change that. He tells her how deeply he cares for her and takes his leave of her and the town.

The priest moves south and after six hours of travel he reaches the town of La Candelaria. He talks to the mestizo, and asks him how far it is to Carmen. He leaves the man and travels out of the town, fording a river on his mule. Not long after he has reached the other side he hears someone calling for him—it is the mestizo, who catches up with him, claiming that he too wants to go to Carmen. The mestizo is a shifty and seemingly untrustworthy fellow who immediately begins baiting the priest, trying to get him to admit his true identity. Suspicious of each other, the two men get along uneasily and spar verbally. They stop at a hut to sleep, and the mestizo continues to tell the priest that he knows who he is.

The priest realizes that he is in the presence of Judas, the betrayer, and tries to remain awake, on guard against the machinations of his wily sidekick. He sleeps some, dreaming about his life as an indulgent parish priest, and then wakes and meditates on his unworthiness, and the uncertainty of his future. He steps outside the hut, over the mestizo who is lying on the floor in a feverish condition, weeping over the state of his soul. After finding the mule in the dark, the priest attempts to ride off in silence, but the mestizo comes out of the hut and follows him, begging the priest not to abandon him.

Continuing his journey, the priest begins to repent over the way he has treated the mestizo. Despicable as the man might be, the priest thinks, he is still a child of God, and therefore the priest has as much a duty to him as he does to anyone else. He switches places with the ailing man, letting the mestizo ride the mule while he walks beside it.

After some time the mestizo asks him directly whether he is a priest and the priest, unwilling to evade and deny any longer, tells him the truth. When they approach Carmen he sends the mestizo and the mule down one road while he takes another. The mestizo, angered that he will not get his reward money, shouts in protest, but he is too weak from the fever to do anything about it. The priest, unable to go to Carmen and afraid to go to any other town for fear that by doing so he will put its residents at risk, meditates upon what he will do next.

Analysis

Chapter One of Part II is the longest chapter in the book, and it introduces the rest of the novel's significant characters. Brigida will be a continual presence in the priest's thoughts, and the mestizo will appear again at crucial points in his journey. This is also our first extended encounter with the priest's broodings about himself—about his unworthiness, his confused sense of purpose, his inability to forgive himself.

An incredibly important theme that arises in this chapter is the interaction of representation and real life. In his hometown, the priest realizes that he, like Padre Jose, bears the burden of representing the priesthood itself to people who will have no other encounter with clergymen in their lives. Maria says to him, "...suppose you die. You'll be a martyr, won't you? What kind of martyr do you think you'll make? It's enough to make people mock.'" Our protagonist is no longer just "a" priest, he is "the" priest in this area and his actions and example have far more significance as a result. He himself becomes acutely aware of his own significance in this chapter, both because he learns that the lieutenant has begun to take hostages based on his movements and because Maria introduces the term "martyr." The theme of representation in reality thickens with the priest's encounter with the lieutenant. The priest's hands, which should give him away, have become as weather-beaten and calloused as any other person's. This is a very obvious indication that the stereotypical notion of what a priest should be does not always hold true. The priest has been transformed through the persecution he has undergone. Fittingly, another one of the novel's most important themes is the idea that adversity and suffering are necessary to a person's moral and spiritual development.

The contrast between the priest and the lieutenant deepens in this chapter. The priest is unsure of what he is to do next. Unlike the lieutenant, who moves with uncompromising vigour across the landscape, the priest has trouble deciding

Part II: Chapter Two

Summary

In the capital city, the priest sits on a bench watching the people pass. A beggar approaches him and asks for money. The priest tells him that he has very little money, and that he wants to spend what money he has on alcohol. Of course, he is looking for a bottle of wine so that he can say mass, but to the beggar he pretends that he is simply a drunk looking for booze. As they talk, the priest sees the mestizo walk by in the town square. The beggar agrees to show the priest to a place where he can get alcohol. He takes the priest to a hotel down by the river, where they wait in a large, spare bedroom for the beggar's contact, the Governor's cousin, to arrive. The beggar suggests that after he buys the alcohol, the priest should, out of courtesy, offer his host a drink.

Soon the Governor's cousin arrives and, after a somewhat tense conversation, agrees to sell the priest a bottle of brandy and a bottle of wine. The priest offers the governor's cousin a drink of brandy, but the other man wants wine, and drinks a glass. The three men start talking, and the Governor's cousin continues to make toasts and drink glass after glass of the wine. Helpless, the priest watches despondently as the wine that he has especially procured for mass disappears down the governor's cousin's gullet. The jefe arrives and begins to drink the wine as well. The men are surprised when they notice that the priest is quietly crying. But they attribute his emotionality to his being drunk and having the soul of a poet. The jefe talks about the manhunt his officers are on, telling his drinking companions that they are searching for a priest, and that they have a man in custody who says he spent some time with the outlaw and can recognize him. The men continue to talk and, curiously, often use quasi- religious terminology in their speech, such as "mystery", "soul" and "source of life." After more drinking and talking, the wine is gone, and the priest takes his leave of the men, dejected, with the bottle of brandy in his coat pocket. When he leaves the hotel, the priest notices that it is raining, and he quickly ducks into a cantina to avoid getting wet. Inside, he accidentally bumps into a man who is playing billiards. When he collides with the man, the brandy bottle clinks in his pocket. A group of men begin to take an interest in the priest with his hidden contraband liquor, and begin to tease him. The priest suddenly dashes out the door, and he is pursued by a group of men.

They chase him through the city streets, and the priest runs to the house of Padre Jose, hoping the former priest will take pity on him and hide him in his house. But Padre Jose, unwilling to take on the responsibility, refuses to admit the hunted priest. Soon the group of men, which includes policemen, catches him. The police don't recognize him as the famous wanted priest. Instead, they ask him to pay a fine for the alcohol and when he can't, they take him to jail.

Analysis

The narrative voice has shifted slightly from the previous chapter: where chapter one focused on the priest's thoughts, his assessment of himself and his situation, chapter two is more action-based. For the first half of the chapter, we get almost no descriptions of what the priest is thinking at all: the narrative is almost exclusively focused on dialogue, plot and external description. It is only after the priest leaves the hotel that we return to a perspective that lets us see "inside" his mind. On one level, obviously, Greene refrains from giving us too much of the priest's thoughts during the drinking scene. He does not want to interrupt a tension-filled scene, where action and dialogue are of paramount importance, with too many side-glimpses into the world of thought. Greene is a master of suspense, and this is one of the most edgy scenes in the entire novel.

On a thematic level, in the beginning of the chapter the priest finds himself, for the first time in awhile, animated by a sense of immediate purpose: he needs to find a way to procure wine for mass. This part of the chapter is narrated with particular emphasis on the action of the plot because the priest himself is acting and not simply reacting. He has made a bold move into the heart of the state and is driven by a very real goal. The fact that even this relatively modest plan falls through only emphasizes that the priest's destiny is not in his control, that anything he undertakes must be carried out within a matrix of forces that are not subject to his control—in this case, the forces of authority and etiquette.

The narration returns to the priests thoughts after he leaves the hotel. Now completely broke, his mission frustrated, the priest turns inward, unsure of what to do next. The end of the chapter shows him once again forced to react to the actions of others-running, hiding, lying, trying to evade detection and capture for as long as he can. As evidenced by his encounter with Padre Jose, the priest can count on no help from anyone, not even a fellow member of the clergy, and his powers of persuasion do him no good. The only person in town to whom he could look as a friend or ally has denied him, and he can do little else besides wait. Finally, captured and powerless, thinking, repenting, worrying, praying are all that is left to him. The whole chapter is a story of rapid unraveling. As in the previous chapter, the authorities searching for him ironically cannot recognize him as the priest even though they arrest him on another charge.

Part II: Chapter Three

Summary

In the dark jail cell, the priest stumbles around, confused amid the prone bodies of the other prisoners. Voices ask him for cigarettes, money, for something to eat, and he hears the sound of two people making love somewhere in the darkness. He finally finds a place to sit in the crowded cell. Almost immediately, the conversation turns to priests. One of the prisoners blames priests for all of his problems.

Feeling that there is no use in trying to hide his identity any longer, the priest speaks up and announces that he, in fact, is a priest. In response to criticism from one of his cellmates, the priest admits that he is a bad priest, a whisky priest. He admits his fear of death, denies that he is worthy to be considered a martyr, and confesses that he has an illegitimate child. A prisoner tells him that he need not be afraid of being turned in by any of them because they are not interested in taking the state's "blood money."

The priest feels an overwhelming affection for these people, and a sense of companionship he sorely lacked during his time on the run. A pious woman, who is in jail for keeping religious articles in her house, speaks to the priest. A self-righteous person, she is outraged at the other prisoners, and at having to be in the same cell with them. The priest tries to explain that, to a saint, even the most ugly scene of suffering still contains beauty, but the woman is offended that a priest could sympathize with people whom she considers utterly repugnant. "The sooner you are dead the better," she concludes, and then, with idiotic bluster, implies that when she gets out of prison she will inform the higher church authorities of the priest's behaviour. But the priest is not really all that scared of the bishops anymore.

The next morning, the priest awakens, sure that the police will soon identify him. They call all of the prisoners outside, but pull the priest aside, telling him that his job is to empty the buckets of human waste from the jail cells. Entering one, he notices that its occupant is none other than the mestizo, who is staying in a jail cell as a guest of the police. The priest attempts to ignore him, but the mestizo persists in trying to get his attention. After the priest finally replies to him, the mestizo recognizes to whom he is speaking. But the mestizo does not immediately turn the priest in, reasoning that he won't receive the reward money if the priest is already in police custody and besides, he is comfortable living temporarily in the jail cell. The priest continues cleaning the cells, and when he is finished, he is brought before the lieutenant. Although the two men have been face to face once before, the lieutenant does not recognize the priest. He asks the priest where he is headed, to which the priest replies, "God knows." The lieutenant replies that God doesn't know anything, and asks him how he will live without any money or anyplace to go. The priest says, vaguely, that he will find some sort of work and the lieutenant, taking pity on a man who seems too old to be much of a worker, gives him five pesos and sends him on his way. The priest tells the lieutenant that he is a good man, and then leaves.

Analysis

In a cell full of murderers and thieves, it is ironic that it is the pious woman who turns out to be the least admirable figure. Actually, this is a classic Christian story, reminiscent of many stories in the New Testament. Although it is not an exact parallel by any means, this scene resonates thematically with the gospel story in which Christ intervenes between a mob of self-righteous people and a woman whom they are about to stone to death for adultery. Jesus, alarmed at this violent display of self-righteousness, tells the crowd that only those who are without sin are allowed to condemn her. As both the Christian story and this scene in the novel seem to indicate, hypocritical confidence and pride in one's own moral rectitude are in many ways worse than sins of the flesh. As we saw with the lieutenant, this woman's outrage at the sins of others prevents her from seeing the hypocrisy of her own attitude. In many ways, moreover, the pious woman is the least admirable character in the novel, worse even than the mestizo and the lieutenant. Although at first glance, this may seem ridiculous, given the fact that the lieutenant is, for all intents and purposes, a murderer and the mestizo is a conniving betrayer, Greene asks us to think beyond our customary sense of good and evil.

Indeed, being able to think past our customary, ingrained ideas is the overall theme of this chapter. The lieutenant is sure that he knows exactly what kind of person he is searching for, and he lets the priest slip from his fingers. He is once again face-to-face with his target, and he once again fails to recognize him as the man he has been searching for. In these scenes, Greene seems intent on highlighting the lieutenant's blindness. The lieutenant's attitude towards priests is to hate them all indiscriminately and, as a result, he is unable to think of them as anything other than stereotypes. This priest, however, thanks to his long months on the run, no longer resembles or behaves like a stereotypical priest. The lieutenant's single-minded hatred makes him unable to adjust his expectations and, once again, he misses his prey. And, once again, his intense focus on achieving his goal has made him blind to what should be most important.

Lastly, through the scene in the jail cell, Greene asks us to re-examine our conventional notions about where goodness can be found. The priest, as harried, uncomfortable and seemingly doomed as he is, elatedly feels a sense of solidarity with his fellow prisoners. The jail cell is a metaphor of sorts for human society as a whole. Moreover, the jail cell indicates that suffering must reach a certain peak before positive change seems possible. Only when the state tightens its grip most firmly on the people can they find a certain strength in brotherhood and common suffering that allows them to resist the state's coercion.

Part II: Chapter Four

Summary

Having left the capital city, the priest returns to the Fellows' home to seek help from Coral Fellows, but he discovers that she and her parents have abandoned the house. He searches the house and the barn for food, but finds nothing. His situation grows more desperate: he has no food, money and no place to take shelter, and he knows that the rainy season is approaching. The only creature he finds on the Fellows' premises is an old, crippled dog. Like the house, the dog has been abandoned. He searches the house but finds little of interest: empty medicine bottles, old homework papers and textbooks. But when he returns to the kitchen, he finds the dog lying on the floor with a bone beneath its paws. Famished, he uses a piece of wire to strike at the dying dog while he pulls the bone away from her. Promising himself that he will save some of the meat to give back to the dog, he ends up eating the whole thing and tossing the eaten-clean bone back to her.

Leaving the Fellows' homestead, and feeling as if he is in a state of limbo, the priest finds shelter in a hut in a village. Strangely, the village has also been abandoned. Only one woman remains, and the priest spots her lurking outside his hut. When he steps outside, she disappears into the forest; but in a short while, after he goes back inside, she returns and the priest reasons that something valuable must be in the hut in which he is squatting. He begins to search the dark hut with his hands, and eventually discovers a child hidden underneath the maize. The child is wet with blood, riddled with bullet holes, and just moments from death. The woman approaches. An Indian, she speaks little Spanish, but she communicates to the priest that this violence is the work of the gringo, the outlaw "Americano." She understands when he tells her that he is a priest, and, after the child dies, she begs him to go with her to a church to bury her son. Doubtful that they can find one, the priest nevertheless agrees to accompany the woman.

The two travel for miles. On the second day, they come upon a wide plateau that is, to the priest's amazement, covered with Christian crosses. The woman brings her child to the tallest cross, touches the child to it, and lays her child at its foot. She begins to pray, and ignores the priest's entreaties to depart with him before an approaching storm reaches the plateau. Unable to convince her to depart, he leaves her there, and soon begins to chastise himself for abandoning her. He is worried that the gringo, who may still be in the area, may come upon her, and he therefore feels responsible for the woman's safety and the gringo's soul, reasoning that one shouldn't tempt a fellow human being to commit sin.

The priest is beginning to come unglued at this point: he is confused, drifting in and out of feelings of guilt, paranoia, and pervaded with a free-floating ache that at times seems to be coming from without, and at other times seems to be coming from within. He returns to the plateau, but the woman has left. Guiltily, he eats the sugar cube she has left by the mouth of her dead child so that if, by some miracle, he awakens from death he will have some sustenance to go on living. The priest leaves the plateau and thinking that futility and abandonment lay behind him, trudges forward.

Hungry, exhausted, psychologically wasted, he can feel the life ebbing from him. After some time, a man with a gun approaches him. When asked to identify himself, the priest, no longer concerned about getting captured by the police, gives his real name. He stumbles away and falls against a whitewashed building on the edge of the forest. But the man with the gun turns out not to be a police officer at all; instead, he seems happy when he learns that the man he is speaking with is a priest, and he tells him that the whitewashed building is the town church. The priest has crossed the border into a state where religion is not outlawed; he is safe from the authorities.

Analysis

In this chapter, the priest is in limbo, a word that is as appropriate a description of his spiritual condition as it is of his physical surroundings. The chapter itself is more about the evocation of a certain brooding, silent, forsaken atmosphere than anything else. Just as limbo is a state halfway between heaven and hell, the world the priest stumbles into is a world of half-things: the mongrel and the child are half-dead, the hut he finds only half shelters him from the rain, and it is raining about half of the time, he can only half communicate with the woman. Fighting with a dog over a scrap of meat, he feels only half-human, and by the time he leaves the woman, he is only half-alive. More importantly, perhaps, it is also like limbo in that it is a world of abandonment: the abandoned house and the abandoned village are two very obvious and noteworthy examples. The old dog has been abandoned by the family, the priest finds the child abandoned in the maize, the woman has been abandoned by her family and her fellow villagers and he, in turn, abandons her on the plateau. When he returns, he finds only the child's corpse abandoned at the foot of the cross. Moreover, he abandons the dog and the dead child to the force of hunger when he steals the meat off the bone and the sugar cube, respectively.

It is also clear that he has abandoned all hope of escape or survival when he freely confesses to the man with the rifle that he is a priest. All of these details in their consistency and subtly make for a chapter remarkable for its creation of a sense of fading life and desolation. If the priest were in limbo, then crossing the border into a safe haven would seem to indicate a movement out of limbo and into paradise. We will have to wait until the next chapter to find out if this is the case, but we already know enough about Greene to suspect that he is unlikely to let his protagonist find any kind of true paradise on earth. The episode with the murdered boy is significant because it allows us to have a glimpse of the real suffering and sorrow the gringo has caused.

The lieutenant romanticizes the gringo in the early part of the novel. The gunslinger, the cowboy, the outlaw—he is a type we are all familiar with, the subject of many movies and novels. Greene here shows us the bloody and hateful consequences of such a person's lawlessness. Once again, Greene provokes the reader to think beyond conventional types and to confront the ugly reality beneath. But Greene himself walks something of a fine line.

As we have discussed earlier in relation to the pious woman, he seems to argue that sins such as pride and complacency are in some ways worse than sins of passion. And while this still may be Greene's point, he has to be careful not to minimize or trivialize the real suffering inflicted by egregious, violent, extreme actions. Showing the bloody infant and the suffering mother helps to qualify his point somewhat, that negatively motivated passions may indeed be just as reprehensible—if not more so—than apathy and complacency.

Part III: Chapter One

Summary

The priest sits on a veranda with Mr. Lehr and his sister, Miss Lehr, two German-American Protestants living in Mexico. Well-rested and comfortable, the priest has been staying with the Lehr's for a few days, recovering his strength. The Lehr's disapprove of Catholicism, believing it to be too luxurious and mired in "inessentials", such as rituals and ceremonies. Taking a bath in the river, the priest chastises himself for lapsing back into "idleness," a sense of guilt he feels acutely when he compares the ease of his life at the Lehr's house with the misery and hardship of the prisoners, the mestizo, and Brigida.

Later that day the priest walks into the town where he meets villagers who are overjoyed to have him with them. He thinks about how different this welcome is from the chilly receptions he has become used to receiving. There has not been a priest in town for three years, and the townspeople are eager to have someone to baptize their babies and hear their confessions. A woman bargains with the priest over what he will charge for the baptisms, agreeing on one peso fifty per child. He can feel the old ways and his former habits returning to him. After drinking a glass of brandy with a local barkeep the priest thinks that it is appalling that he can so easily go back to his old ways and he wonders whether God, who can forgive cowardice and passion, can also forgive the pious human's bad habits. But he continues drinking. In an act of spontaneous generosity, he tells someone to inform the people that he will charge only one peso for the baptisms. Later, listening to the confessions of the townspeople, the priest is struck at how run-of-the-mill their sins are, and feels unable to be particularly encouraging or interested in them. He makes a few attempts to provoke people out of their sense of complacency, but to no avail. The result is only further feelings of failure and unworthiness on his part.

The next day the priest prepares to ride off to a larger city, Las Casas. First he says mass, and feels particularly contemptible doing so. Even though he has escaped danger, he has not escaped the sin and the shame he carries with him. When he goes to where his mules are waiting, he finds a familiar figure waiting for him as well. It is the mestizo, who has followed him into the state to tell him that the gringo has been badly wounded in a shootout with police and is asking for someone to come to hear his confession before he dies.

The gringo, of course, is on the other side of the border, and for the priest to go see him would be to put himself in harm's way once again. The priest knows he is walking into a trap, but, after some time debating with the mestizo, decides that he will return to absolve the dying man. It is his duty, he reasons, and besides, he does not believe that he can really find peace in Las Casas or anywhere in this state. He will put his neck in the mestizo's noose. On his way out of town, the priest donates the money he has received from the baptisms to the schoolteacher, telling the mestizo that he is well aware that, where he is going, he won't need money.

Analysis

Initially, we may feel surprised at how deep the priest's sense of shame is when, from the very beginning, the priest feels guilty for the complacency that sets in at the Lehr's house. Maybe we feel he is judging himself a little too harshly. After all, he has been through a trying ordeal, and has been resting for only a few short days. Plus, while life in this town is certainly a lot easier than it was in all the other towns he has been in, it is far from luxurious. Does he really need to feel guilty over taking a bath?

Although it is hard to know exactly how harshly Greene means for us to judge the people in this town, it seems that he is less interested in skewering people like the Lehr's than in showing just how much the priest has changed as a result of his months of hardship. Although he is still far from perfect—dipping into his old habits—this priest has become a truly extraordinary man, and the constant lamentations he makes over his own unworthiness are meant to show the mark of true humility. When the mestizo approaches, the choice before him is clear: physical salvation versus spiritual salvation. It takes him some time to decide to turn his mule around, but, in the end, the priest knows what he must do: "The oddest thing of all was that he felt quite cheerful: he had never really believed in this peace."

Throughout the chapter, the issue of money recurs again and again. The priest's changing attitude towards money becomes a barometer of sorts, indicating his changing attitude toward the world itself. He needs money to live, so when he initially sticks firm at one peso fifty, it is understandable, if not particularly admirable. When he suddenly decided to drop his rate to one peso, we can see that it is animated by a true sense of decency and concern for what is fair. But it is still a half-measure, since it indicates that the priest continues to make plans for making a home for himself in this world, charging money for performing what it is his duty to perform. It is only when he gives all the money away that he has given himself over entirely to his faith.

After all, Jesus teaches in the New Testament that to be saved one must be prepared to give up all of one's earthly possessions and give them to the poor. Once again, abandonment is the key term. The priest, in abandoning the money, abandons the world, and, in turn, abandons himself to God. The issue of money and the Catholic Church is obviously an important one for this book and, in this chapter, Greene has his protagonist nearly run the gamut of priestly attitudes towards worldly wealth: from complacency, to qualified generosity, to saintliness. In doing so, he also runs the gamut from the real to the ideal, showing what Christians are called to do, while refraining from too harshly condemning what most of them do instead.

Part III: Chapters Two–Three

Summary

On the journey back, the mestizo continues to argue that he is not leading the priest into a trap, while the priest gently indicates that he is not going to be fooled by the mestizo's transparent lies. Nearing a cluster of huts where the gringo is supposed to be, the priest dismisses the mule driver, to the consternation of the mestizo. The priest is not angry with his treacherous companion. Instead, the priest laments the fact that the mestizo is burdening himself with such a grievous sin by involving himself in his murder. The priest filled with nervous impatience, and with the complaining mestizo in tow, hurries towards the hut. He has a drink of brandy to lend him courage. When they reach the hut, the gringo is, indeed, inside, and in bad shape. He is not the menacing outlaw figure of the wanted posters. Instead, the dying man looks like an ordinary tramp. When the priest draws near, the gringo twice tells him to "beat it." The priest persists, trying to get the gringo to hurry up and confess his sins before it is too late.

The gringo, meanwhile, convinced that he is damned, is not interested in confessing his sins and only exhorts the priest to get out of the hut as soon as he can, before the authorities arrive. He offers the priest his gun, which the priest refuses. The priest continues to urge the gringo to repent and confess, but to no avail. Finally the gringo dies. A voice comes from the doorway asking if he has finished. It is the lieutenant, who has now trapped the priest. The priest faces his enemy with resignation. He thanks the lieutenant for allowing him time to speak with the dying man. The lieutenant replies, "I am not a barbarian." Because it is raining too hard to set out for the capital city where the priest will be tried, the lieutenant pulls up a crate and lights a candle and the two men begin to talk inside the hut. The lieutenant vaguely recognizes the priest, who tells the lieutenant about their two previous meetings, at the village and in the police station.

The lieutenant tells the priest that he despises the church because it exploits the poor and, to his surprise, the priest agrees with him. The priest says that there is much he and the lieutenant agree upon: both seem to believe that the world is a corrupt place, and that it's difficult to be truly happy unless you are some kind of saint. The lieutenant keeps looking to pick an argument, but, to his frustration, the priest always admits that, indeed, he is a flawed, weak person. He tells him why he decided to remain in the state after all the other priests had fled, attributing it not to courage but to vanity. He says that he was, unfortunately, prideful, and that he wanted to stay to show that he was a good man. A man enters the hut to inform the lieutenant that the storm has passed, and the men prepare to embark on the trip. The priest says goodbye to the mestizo, refusing to bless the unrepentant man, but saying that he will pray for the mestizo's soul.

Analysis

This chapter highlights significant differences between the priest and the lieutenant. Although the priest is allowed to visit with the dying man, the gringo refuses to repent and once again, as they have so many times before in this novel, the priest's efforts fail. At the same time, however, the lietenant succeeds in trapping his prey, the priest. But the situation raises an extremely significant point. That is, the priest fails based on one definition of failure, which is to fall short of attaining one's goal. But, in a deeper sense, the priest has succeeded, and succeeded brilliantly. Although he may not have been able to perform the duty he came to perform, he was focused on doing the right thing at all times.

Although in their conversation, the priest and the lieutenant find that they in fact have much in common, one incredibly important difference is highlighted here: throughout the novel, the lieutenant single- mindedly pursues his goal, while the priest has difficulty even deciding what his goals should be. While the priest has been obsessed with his own unworthiness, he has, by and large, ended up making the right choices. In contrast, the lieutenant has been incredibly confident in his righteousness and has committed some rather horrific acts. Here, by the end, it is clear that the priest has learned something that the lieutenant hasn't: one must act always with good intentions, even if one knows that those actions are doomed to failure.

The fact that the world is imperfect and almost impossible to change is not a reason to give up. Rather, the world's inherent imperfection is a reason to adjust one's mindset, to turn one's attention to whether one is a good person, not whether one's actions are necessarily the most effective ones. This is what he means when he tells the lieutenant: "That's another difference between us. It's no good your working for your end unless you're a good man yourself. And there won't always be good men in your party."

Moreover, the lieutenant's words give credence to the priest's criticism. When he informs the priest that he will be taken back to the capital city to be tried, he says, "I am not a barbarian. You will be tried...properly." Of course, everyone knows that there will not be a "proper" trial. The lieutenant's own sense of honour prompts him to tell the priest that he will not be treated unfairly, but the pause in his speech, indicated by an ellipse in the text, hints that he recognizes the fallacious nature of what he is saying. The lieutenant himself may be a good man, but the movement he belongs to is one that will not make good on his promises of fairness and justice.

Part III: Chapter Four

Summary

After dark, the lieutenant travels to Padre Jose's house to ask him to come to the police station. Padre Jose's first reaction is fear. He assumes that the police officer is there to arrest him for some perceived infraction. His wife wakes up and begins to argue for her husband's innocence. The lieutenant informs them that he is wanted at the station to hear the confession of the priest who is to be executed the next day. Although Padre Jose feels pity for the condemned priest, his wife forbids him to go, believing the lieutenant is trying to trick them. She argues that the priest is a drunkard, and not worth the trouble. Padre Jose makes a feeble attempt to argue with his wife about his duty, but she merely mocks him, and he tells the lieutenant that he cannot go with him.

The lieutenant returns to the police station and informs the priest of the bad news. The priest feels utterly abandoned. Showing remarkable and perhaps unexpected compassion, the lieutenant gives the priest a bottle of brandy, hoping that it will help to ease his fears. Returning to his desk, the lieutenant feels depressed, as if his life has now lost its purpose. The priest, taking swigs of brandy on the floor of his cell, tries to make a solitary confession. He finds he cannot repent, however, and prays to God to save his daughter. Once again, he chastises himself for his partiality to the girl, believing that he ought to feel that kind of intense love for every person on earth. He tries to pray for others, but his thoughts return to his daughter. He thinks himself an utter failure.

Reflecting on the eight years he has spent running from the law, he cringes at the thought of how little he accomplished. He begins to think about the pain that is in store for him, and wonders if it isn't too late for him to renounce his priesthood like Padre Jose. He has a dream in which he finds himself eating at a large table in a cathedral, waiting for the best dish to be served and paying no heed to the ceremony that is taking place in front of him. When he awakes, it is morning and the feeling of hope that was instilled in him by his dream disappears when he sees the prison yard. Overwhelmed by a feeling of disappointment, he no longer worries about the state of his soul. He can only feel regret over his missed opportunities in life, and the fact that he is going to meet God "empty-handed."

Analysis

The identities of the characters in the novel begin to shift in this chapter. The lawful lieutenant himself breaks the law twice in this chapter, trying to sneak Padre Jose into the jail cell to hear the priest's confession, and then delivering the condemned man a bottle of contraband brandy. Compassion for a human being and a former enemy has led him to violate the laws he has sworn to uphold. Padre Jose may have renounced the priesthood, but in this chapter it is the lieutenant's decision to betray his own order that is most significant. His actions testify to the effect the priest has had on him, and indicate that even this zealous lieutenant, who was formerly so full of hatred, is capable of change and spiritual regeneration. The hapless Padre Jose is caught between two incompatible identities in this chapter: the priest in him knows it is duty to go to the police station, but his much more forceful wife finally brings her husband to heel, scoffing at the notion that he is still a priest. Although he obviously doesn't admire Padre Jose's spinelessness, Greene depicts him as more of a broken, pathetic person than as an indifferent or cold-hearted one.

The priest's qualms over his impending execution are extremely significant, showing that Greene refuses to turn his protagonist into a simple hero. The priest displayed remarkable courage in returning to the gringo fully aware of what he was facing. Here, however, Greene again depicts the priest's wavering thoughts, his self-doubt and his fear, preferring a flawed, noble hero to an idealized model of perfect courage. The priest continues to berate himself for loving his daughter so much, a response that makes him a much more sympathetic and human character.

Although the priest's waking thoughts are self-critical and mired, as ever, in his past sinfulness, his dream seems to represent his breaking beyond the conventions of his old life. He awaits the final dish, which presumably symbolizes the reward he will receive in heaven. His ignoring the mass in front of him could suggest that he is moving beyond the church, beyond the ceremonies and rituals to a more direct communion with God. Upon seeing the prison yard again after he awakes, his fear returns and we see that he has not yet broken free of the cares and anxieties and imperfections of this world.

But, he is no longer concerned with the state of his soul, however. All he can do is regret the mistakes and missed opportunities of his life, and wish he could go to God a more "successful" human being. This is, of course, true humility, and we sense that he is going to God with quite a lot. Here especially, with the interpolation of the dream, we are aware of the discrepancy between the priest's self-conception and Greene's attitude towards him. This gap has grown wider as the book has progressed and the priest has continued to berate himself while acting nobly and selflessly. He may not consider himself a hero, but he has made the most of the opportunities for heroism that Greene affords him.

Part IV

Summary

Mrs. Fellows lays sick in bed with a handkerchief over her face and Captain Fellows tends to her needs. Notably absent from the scene is Coral Fellows, who has died, and her parents both go to great pains not to mention her. Mrs. Fellows is eager to move back home, but her husband, suddenly defiant, says he refuses to leave. After his wife begins to cry, he relents. They begin to talk about the priest who visited them all those months ago.

Mr. Tench, the dentist, treats his patient, the jefe, whose teeth are in a very bad state of decay. As he works, Tench speaks about his wife, from whom he has unexpectedly received a letter. She writes that she has found religion, and has forgiven him. Looking out the window, Tench sees a firing squad preparing to execute a man in the courtyard. It is, of course, the priest. Tench watches as they swiftly shoot the man. He seems to try to yell something out before he dies, but it comes out garbled and Tench thinks he said something like "excuse." Soon the man is a heap against the wall and the officers drag his corpse away. Tench, overwhelmed by a feeling of loneliness after witnessing the execution, vows that he will leave Mexico for good. A woman finishes the story of Juan the young martyr, who faces death with complete courage, shouting, "Hail Christ the King!" as the squad in the story raises their rifles. The boy asks whether the man the police shot today is a martyr of the Church like Juan, and his mother tells him that he is indeed a great hero. The boy becomes despondent thinking that since the police have killed the last priest, there are no more heroes left in the realm. Looking out the window, he sees the lieutenant pass, and spits at him.

That night, the boy has a dream about the priest. He dreams that the man is laid out stiffly, as at a funeral. While the boy is watching him, the priest winks at him. Waking up, he hears a knock at the door and goes to answer it. He meets a stranger who tells him that he is a priest on the run from the authorities, and the boy opens the door for him.

Analysis

On some level, this chapter is meant to re-establish a sense of perspective, to emphasize that the story is no longer about one man's struggle with himself and with his enemies, but about his impact on those around him. Fittingly, therefore, having followed the priest for so long, his final day is reported to us only indirectly, as it is registered in the minds of others. We watch the execution of the priest from Mr. Tench's perspective. The priest's life is over, but the struggle against the state, and against the forces of persecution, goes on. He does not die with heroic flourish and defiance, and the novel's distant perspective on the scene only emphasizes this fact. We see him only as a very small figure, dying quickly in a heap against the wall.

On some level, therefore, Greene seems to be arguing that the kind of valiant final gesture we associate with heroes is not what is important, and not what truly defines a hero. One obvious question is why does Greene have the priest's last word be "excuse", or, at least, something that sounds like "excuse." Although it is impossible to say for certain what the priest was trying to convey, the word is nevertheless full of possible meanings. First, it is significant because excuses are one thing the priest never allowed himself to make. Or is "excuse" a verb? Is the priest asking for God to excuse him and his unworthy soul? Or is he, in a final act of forgiveness, asking for God to excuse those who have persecuted and executed him. Its very ambiguity provokes us to turn over possible meanings and, therefore, think more about the priest and his story.

It is striking that at the end of the novel we find all the expatriates fleeing the state, and that their flight coincides with the execution of the last remaining priest, but compared with the others, only Mr. Tench seems to have made a significant improvement in his outlook. His flight seems to represent a first, tentative step towards giving his life some sense of direction, and Greene makes it clear that his brief encounter with the priest had some kind of lasting impact upon him. Mr. Tench, appalled by the sight of the priest's execution and obviously stirred in some way by his wife's letter, decides that he will leave Mexico for good. In the previous chapter, the priest despaired about having to return to God "empty-handed", but it is evident from this scene that he made more of an impact on people than he realized.

The priest's positive influence becomes even more obvious in the book's final episode. The priest's execution has made the priest a martyr in the young boy's eyes and, to his mind, the state has taken away the last hero in the land. The priest and the lieutenant unknowingly vied throughout this novel for the boy's soul, and the boy now makes it clear that he has chosen to emulate the priest not the lieutenant when he spits at the lieutenant in disgust. The spirit of defiance, fueled by the priest's sacrifice, lives on. The boy's dream of the dead priest flickering his eyelids is a kind of mini-resurrection scene. Indeed, the dream itself is an indication that the priest's example and his influence have transcended his death. And in the book's final scene, a man known simply as "the stranger" knocks at the boy's door. The book has come full circle: another unnamed priest has emerged from the shadows to defy the state by remaining among the people. The lieutenant, by attempting to stamp out religion, has only helped it to take root more firmly in the land.

Chapter 10

Important Quotations Explained

That was another mystery: it sometimes seemed to him that venial sins—impatience, an unimportant lie, pride, a neglected opportunity—cut off from grace more completely than the worst sins of all. Then, in his innocence, he had felt no love for anyone: now in his corruption he had learnt.

This quotation, from Chapter Three of Part II, is striking because of the way it sets up familiar contrasts only to rethink and rework them. 'Venial' sins, what we normally think of as very minor wrongs, are here suggested to be the very worst kinds of failing. Greene suggests that venial sins can pass unnoticed in people's day-to-day lives, and can add up—if unrepented for and unacknowledged—causing a kind of slow deadening of one's spirit.

Greene then indicates that even though venial sins are worse, the people who commit them are actually more "innocent", presumably because they are unaware of how far they have really drifted from goodness. Interestingly it is actually in his "corruption" that the priest learns how to feel love. Greene's attitudes towards matters such as sin, innocence and grace are extremely important and also extremely complicated.

Heat stood in the room like an enemy. But he believed against the evidence of his senses in the cold empty ether spaces. A radio was playing somewhere: music from Mexico City, or perhaps even from London or New York filtered into this obscure neglected state. It seemed to him like a weakness: this was his own land, and he would have walled it in with steel if he could, until he had eradicated from it everything which reminded him of how it had once appeared to a miserable child. He wanted to destroy everything: to be alone without any n:emories at all.

This is a compelling portrait of the lieutenant from the second chapter of Part I, emphasizing his belief in emptiness. Interestingly, the narrator says that he believed "against the evidence of his senses", implying that the lieutenant, on some level, has to have faith, even if it is faith in purposelessness. Belief in nothing, like any belief, requires one to accept something that cannot necessarily be proven. Furthermore, it is significant that his enemies in this scene are warmth and music—things that sustain life and lend it beauty. As seen by the end of the quotation, where the key words are "steel", "eradicated," and "destroy," the lieutenant's wishes and beliefs, although springing from noble sentiments, are filled with violence and the denial of life.

One mustn't have human affections—or rather one must love every soul as if it were one's own child. The passion to protect must extend itself over a world—but he felt it tethered and aching like a hobbling animal to the tree trunk. He turned his mule south.

This quote, from Chapter One of Part II, very nicely illustrates the fine line that exists between the desire for spiritual perfection and the possibility that the attainment of that perfection is inhuman. The priest feels guilt about how much love he has for his daughter, wishing that he had the selflessness to love all members of the human race without partiality. Even if he doesn't recognize it, however, we realise that the priest's love for his daughter—while perhaps not the all-embracing love he seeks—is one of the most admirable, praiseworthy and human responses he has to almost anything in the novel. This is an implicit question throughout the novel and one that Greene himself perhaps doesn't have the answer to: to what extent are humans obliged to break free from ordinary, habitual responses and seek something loftier, and when is it better to accept one's fallible human nature as it is? The quote is also interesting for the "hobbling animal" metaphor it employs.

The metaphor evinces despair over the local, limited nature of his love by comparing it to a creature that cannot move at all, but the priest then "turned his mule south." That is, he moves much more slowly across the landscape than he imagines he should, but he is still moving. Greene subtly shows us the slight, but important, discrepancy between the priest's self-conception and what he really does.

He dreamed that the priest whom they had shot that morning was back in the house dressed in the clothes his father had lent him and laid out stiffly for burial. The boy sat beside the bed and his mother read out of a very long book all about how the priest had acted in front of the bishop the part of Julius Caesar: there was a fish basket at her feet, and the fish were bleeding, wrapped in her handkerchief. He was very bored and very tired and somebody was hammering nails into a coffin in the passage. Suddenly the dead priest winked at him—an unmistakable flicker of the eyelid, just like that.

In the novel's final chapter, Greene depicts the reactions of various people to the priest's execution. Fittingly, he ends with the young boy. Extremely significant here is the way Greene weaves imagery of Jesus Christ into the boy's dream. "Julius Caesar" of course, besides being another victim of betrayal and murder, has the same initials "J.C." Notice also the mention of baskets of fish, feet and bleeding, references to both the wedding feast of Cana, the multiplication of the loaves and fishes, and the crucifixion. The "resurrection" here is much less dramatic, but still significant: the priest flickers his eyelids, implying that he has returned to life after his execution. In fact, the priest has attained a kind of resurrection primarily because his image and his example remain in the boy's mind after the priest dies.

The lieutenant said in a tone of fury: "Well, you're going to be a martyr—you've got that satisfaction." "Oh, no. Martyrs are not like me. They don't think all the time—if I had drunk more brandy I shouldn't be so afraid."

In this interchange between the lieutenant and the priest in Chapter Three of Part III, the priest's retort voices an idea that has been implicit throughout the novel—that thinking and true holiness are somehow opposed to each other. As a kind of snare, thought is something we have seen in many places in this book. While most stories of saints and martyrs are stories of action, defiance, heroism, and conviction, the priest's story is one of introspection, self-doubt, self-abuse, anxiety, and uncertainty. Considered from a different perspective, however, the priest's thoughts do not prevent him from doing good—in fact, in many ways, it is his tendency toward second-thoughts that lead him to make the right decisions. Although his relentless introspection may keep him from being a purely spontaneous agent of goodness, thought ultimately helps him to overcome many of his selfish instincts, including the instinct for self-preservation. His self-sacrificing actions combined with his constant soul-searching ultimately make him seem a martyr to everyone but himself.

Chapter 11

Key Facts

Full title: The Power and the Glory
Author: Graham Greene
Type of work: Novel
Genre: Realist novel; novel of spiritual development; saint's life
Language: English
Time and place written: 1938–9, Mexico and London
Date of first publication: 1939
Publisher: The Viking Press
Narrator: Anonymous

Point of view: The narrator speaks in the third person and reports the characters' thoughts and self-analysis but only rarely offers his own opinions. He primarily gives us an account of the priest's actions and thoughts.

Tone: The narrator is earnest and although he usually withholds his explicit opinion about the priest, the arrangement of the plot implies a sense of respect and admiration for him.

Tense: Past tense
Setting (time): Mexico during the 1930's
Setting: Chiapas, Mexico

Protagonist: The last priest in the state, on the run from the authorities

Major conflict: The priest is trying to evade capture by the police and struggling internally with his own sense of sinfulness and unworthiness.

Rising action: The priest moves from village to village trying to escape from the lieutenant and his men. An untrustworthy man, known as the mestizo, learns his true identity and begins working with the police to capture him. After a few very close calls with the police including being arrested for smuggling, the priest finally escapes danger and makes his way across the border and out of the reach of the authorities.

Climax: The priest, knowing he is walking into a trap set by the mestizo, decides to return to the state to hear the confession of a dying man and is captured by the lieutenant.

Falling action: The priest and the lieutenant finally face one another and discuss their differences; the priest is brought back to the capital city where he is executed;

Themes: The dangers of excessive idealism; the disparity between representation and reality; the interrelated nature of so-called opposites; the paradox of Christian humility

Motifs: Animals; half-things; abandonment

Symbols: Alcohol; Christian symbolism; children

Foreshadowing: Almost immediately upon meeting him, the priest calls the mestizo "Judas", anticipating the role he will in fact play in the priest's story; the girl singing on the boat at the conclusion of the first chapter does not know why she is so happy, foreshadowing the uneasy nature of happiness and the fact that most of the characters in the novel will be riddled with troubles.

Chapter 12

Analysis

Metaphor Analysis

Greene uses metaphors, symbols and similes to convey his idea of the bleakness of human life.

In the very first chapter, Mr. Tench waits for an ether cylinder that never arrives. Since he is a dentist, the purpose of the cylinder is to anaesthetize his patients from the pain of surgery. The fact that the cylinder does not arrive (and we later see Mr. Tench performing dental work on the Chief of Police without anaesthetic), suggests that the pain of life cannot be avoided. The absent ether cylinder is thus a symbol for a nonexistent balm for human misery, whether mental or physical.

The scene in which the priest spends a night in jail is also symbolic. The jail is a metaphor for the entire world. It is a place of darkness and misery. Life goes on but humans must stumble on through it without any light or guidance. It is a grim vision of human life reduced to its essential nature. The priest makes the point explicit when he realizes that "this place was very like the world elsewhere: people snatched at causes of pleasure and pride in cramped and disagreeable surroundings: there was no time to do anything worth doing, and always one dreamed of escape."

The novel contains many striking similes that also point to the inherent corruption in human life. The priest believes that "evil ran like malaria in his veins" ; of his daughter he believes that "The knowledge of the world lay in her like the dark explicable spot in an X-ray photograph" ; and again he observes of his daughter, "The world was in her heart already, like the small spot of decay in a fruit".Other similes are equally striking, each in their own way, as when the priest reflects on his faith: "He was on the defensive all the time about his faith, as if he was perpetually conscious of some friction, like that of an ill-fitting shoe". When the priest hears the mestizo's story that the dying American asked for him, he disbelieves most of it, but the note from the American convinces him: "But what remained was this note, like a memorial stone you couldn't overlook". The image contained in that simile is especially appropriate, since a memorial stone records someone's life and death, like a tombstone. By going back to attend to the American, the priest is effectively ensuring his own death.

Theme Analysis

Politics and Religion: Like a number of Graham Greene novels, The Power and the Glory deals with the interaction of politics and religion. In this case, there is utter hostility between the two. Politics, as represented by the socialism of the lieutenant, concerns itself with improving social conditions, especially for the poor. Religion, as represented by the priest, concerns itself with the salvation of souls. The novel suggests that both ways of approaching life are flawed.

The lieutenant cannot see that his zealous idealism may well create as much harm as it does good (a danger to which the history of political revolutions in the twentieth century gives ample testimony.) In trying to stamp out religion, the lieutenant's approach ignores the deep longing people have for a transcendental reality. But on the other hand, there are plenty of hints about the hypocrisy of the church, which is always ready to take people's money while ignoring the miserable social conditions in which they live. And the priest as a representative of the church is of course a badly flawed figure.

But the fact that he constantly indulges in an orgy of self-reproach about his own sins may raise questions for the reader about the value of a religion that leads its representatives into such an overwhelming, soul-destroying sense of guilt. After all, the priest does his best in extremely difficult circumstances.

The Meaningless of Life

Although the priest never wavers in his belief that as a priest he has the power to save souls, and to communicate, through the Mass, the essence of God, the novel is so bleak that it raises questions about whether God is active in the world at all, or even if He exists.

The question is posed through imagery of insects, which are mentioned frequently in the novel. In one incident, the lieutenant sees a tiny insect racing across the page of a book in front of him. He crushes it with his finger. Another insect appears on the book, "scurrying for refuge: in this heat there was no end to life".

In another passage, beetles rush around aimlessly and get crushed or injured; insects seem to be everywhere. The imagery seems to raise the possibility that human life has no more purpose or value than that of an insect, and is easily crushed by a superior power. At least in part, this is what the lieutenant believes. He looks on the earth as a "dying, cooling world, of human beings who had evolved from animals for no purpose at all" . The episode with the dog abandoned by the Fellows, in which the dog and the priest struggle over a bone, shows life reduced to its essentials, the struggle for survival. This is not a pretty world—everything in it is in pain or want of some kind. Seen against this bleak background, the priest's attempt to cling on to some higher meaning and purpose to human life may seem either heroic or a contradiction of the facts, according to one's point of view.

Top Ten Quotes

- "There is always one moment in childhood when the door opens and lets the future in."
  Mr. Tench's reflections on why his life turned out the way it did.
- "He had tried to escape, but he was like the King of a West African tribe, the slave of his people, who may not even lie down in case the winds should fail."

The narrator's comments about the situation of the persecuted priest.

- "He walked slowly: happiness drained out of him more quickly and completely than out of an unhappy man: an unhappy man is always prepared."
  A description of Captain Fellows when he finds out that the priest is hiding in his barn.
- "He would eliminate from their childhood everything which had made him miserable, all that was poor, superstitious, and corrupt."
  The lieutenant's ideals.
- "The men and women had the air already of people condemned by authority—authority was never wrong." The villagers as they assemble for inspection by the police.
- "Suppose you die. You'll be a martyr, won't you? What kind of a martyr do you think you'll make? It's enough to make people mock." Maria speaking to the priest.
- "The knowledge of the world lay in her like the dark explicable spot in an X-ray photograph." The priest's realization about his daughter, Brigida.
- "You've killed a lot of people—that's about all. Anybody can do that for a while, and then he is killed too. Just as you are killed. Nothing left except pain." The priest speaking to the dying American.
- "I don't know a thing about the mercy of God: I don't know how awful the human heart looks to Him."
  The priest speaking to the lieutenant.
- "He knew now that at the end there was only one thing that counted—to be a saint." The priest on the morning of his death.

About the Author

Graham Greene was born on October 2, 1904, to Charles Henry and Marion Raymond Greene. He was the fourth of six children. Greene attended the Berkhamstead School, where his father was the headmaster, and then Balliol College, Oxford. After graduation, he became a journalist, and in 1926 he was appointed Sub Editor for The Times. In that same year he became a Catholic.

Greene's first novel, The Man Within, was published in 1929. It was a success with critics and readers. The Name of Action and Rumour at Nightfall, his next two novels, did not fare so well, but Stamboul Train (1932), his fourth novel, established his literary reputation.

During the 1930s, Greene became book and later film reviewer for the magazine The Spectator. He became a renowned film critic. His books during this period included It's a Battlefield, England Made Me, A Gun for Sale and Brighton Rock.

Greene also traveled extensively, in Europe and Mexico. In Mexico during the winter of 1937-38, he investigated the persecution of the Catholic church. This resulted in two books, The Lawless Roads in March 1939, and The Power And The Glory, in September 1939. The latter is regarded as one of Greene's finest novels, and it was awarded a major literary prize, The Hawthornden.

Greene first conceived the idea for The Power and the Glory when a Mexican man told him about a priest who had been so drunk at the baptism of the man's son that he had given the baby a girl's name. The priest had then disappeared into the mountains. Possibly he had been killed by soldiers or he might have escaped.

During World War II, Greene worked for the Ministry of Information In 1941 he joined the British secret service and was assigned first to Sierra Leone and then to counter-intelligence in London. Greene left the service in May 1944. After the war, Greene collaborated with Carol Reed in writing a film, The Third Man, which won First Prize at Cannes in 1949. In 1955, he wrote The Quiet American, about American involvement in Indochina. More novels followed, including Our Man In Havanna , The Honorary Consul (1973), and The Human Factor (1978). The latter stayed on the New York Times bestseller list for six months.

Greene married Vivienne Dayrell-Browning in 1927, with whom he had two children. The couple separated in 1948 but never divorced. In the last years of his life, Greene lived in Vevey, Switzerland, with his companion Yvonne Cloetta. He died there on April 3, 1991.

Chapter 13

Analysis of Graham Greene

Graham Greene on The Power and the Glory:

Now, of course, when I reread The Lawless Roads, I can easily detect many of the characters in The Power and the Glory. The old Scotsman, Dr. Roberto Fitzpatrick, whom I met in Villahermosa, with his cherished scorpion in a little glass bottle, was the kind of treasure trove that falls to the lucky traveller. In recounting the story of his own life he told me of the kindly disreputable Padre Rey of Panama with his wife and daughter and the mice – not a scorpion – which he kept in a glass lamp. So it was that the doctor put me on the track of Father Jose in my novel... "I asked about the priest in Chiapas who had fled. 'Oh,' he said, 'he was just what we call a whisky priest.' He had taken one of his sons to be baptized, but the priest was drunk and would insist on naming the child Brigitta. 'He was little loss, poor man.'"

But long before the drunken priest another character had come on board my awful boat in Frontera,where my story was to open – the dentist I called Mr. Tench, who made his living with gold fillings even in that abandoned little port...His character needed no "touching up."

The novel draws parallels with T.S. Elliot's poem "The Hollow Men". The hollow men wander in a barren landscape, trying to remember the line after "For Thine is the Kingdom" in the Lord's Prayer. The phrase happens to be "the Power and the Glory". He was as complete in The Lawless Roads as he was in The Power and the Glory, and as I read on I encounter more and more characters whom I have forgotten, who beckon to me from the pages and say ironically, "And did you really believe you had invented me?"

Here is the amiable corrupt Chief of Police in Villahermosa,and in the village of Yajalon I encountered "a mestizo with curly sideburns and two yellow fangs at either end of his mouth. He had an awful hilarity and an inane laugh which showed the empty gums. He wore a white tennis shirt open at the front and he scratched himself underneath it." After a week of his company I would find it impossible to abandon him forever, and so he became the Judas of my story. And the Lehrs – the kindly Lutheran couple – they didn't belong to my imagination, for here they are giving shelter to a tired traveller in the same fashion as they did to the whisky priest. Of invented characters how very few seem to remain apart from the two protagonists, the priest and the Lieutenant of Police; when I came to write I was handing out alternative destinies to real people whom I had encountered on my journey.

The Power and the Glory was published in 1940 and won the Hawthornden Prize. The Vatican did not condemn it until 1953, leading Evelyn Waugh to advise Greene that "they have taken fourteen years to write their first letter. You should take fourteen years to answer it." Greene did not directly refuse the Church's demands for revisions but rather replied that the copyright was in his publishers' hands.

The matter was dropped. I think The Power and the Glory is the only novel I have written to a these: in The Heart of the Matter Wilson sat on a balcony in Freetown watching Scobie pass by in the street long before I was aware of Scobie's problem – his corruption by pity. But I had always, even when I was a schoolboy, listened with impatience to the scandalous stories of tourists concerning the priests they had encountered in remote Latin villages (this priest had a mistress, another was constantly drunk), for I had been adequately taught in my Protestant history books what Catholics believed; I could distinguish even then between the man and his office.Now, many years later, as a Catholic in Mexico, I read and listened to stories of corruption which were said to have justified the persecution of the Church under Calles and under his successor and rival Cardenas, but I had also observed for myself how courage and the sense of responsibility had revived with persecution – I had seen the devotion of peasants praying in the priestless churches and I had attended Masses in upper rooms where the sanctus bell could not sound for fear of the police.

I had not found the idealism or integrity of the lieutenant of The Power and the Glory among the police and pisteleros I had actually encountered – I had to invent him as a counter to the failed priest: the idealistic police officer who stifled life from the best possible motives: the drunken priest who continued to pass life on.

Critics on Graham Greene:

Mr. Greene is a story-teller of genius. Born in another age, he would still be spinning yarns...His technical mastery has never been better manifested than in his statement of the scene — the sweat and infection, the ill-built town which is beautiful for a few minutes at sundown, the brothel where all men are equal, the vultures...the snobbery of the second-class public schools, the law which all can evade, the ever-present haunting underworld of gossip, spying, bribery, violence and betrayal...the affinity to the film is everywhere apparent. It is the camera's eye which moves from the hotel balcony to the street below, picks out the policeman, follows him to his office, moves about the room from the handcuffs on the wall to the broken rosary in the drawer, recording significant detail. It is the modern way of telling a story.

Evelyn Waugh

Graham Greene was in a class by himself...He will be read and remembered as the ultimate twentieth-century chronicler of consciousness and anxiety.

William Golding

Greene appears to share the idea, which has been floating around ever since Baudelaire, that there is something rather distingué in being damned; Hell is a sort of high-class nightclub, entry to which is reserved for Catholics only.

George Orwell

Catholicism as a public system of laws and dogmas is far from being an adequate key to Greene's fiction. There is a good deal of evidence, internal and external, that in Greene's fiction Catholicism is not a body of belief requiring exposition and demanding categorical assent or dissent, but a system of concepts, a source of situations, and a reservoir of symbols with which he can order and dramatize certain intuitions about the nature of human experience — intuitions which were gained prior to and independently of his formal adoption of the Catholic faith. Regarded in this light, Greene's Catholicism may be seen not as a crippling burden on his artistic freedom, but as a positive artistic asset.

David Lodge

It is, in fact, the ultimate strength of Greene's books that he shows us the hazards of compassion. We all know, from works like Hamlet, how analysis is paralysis and the ability to see every side of every issue prevents us from taking any side at all. The tragic import of Greene's work is that understanding can do the same: he could so easily see the pain of the people he was supposed to punish that he could not bear to come down hard on them. He became hostage to his own sympathies and railed at pity with the fury of one who was its captive. The most sobering lesson of Greene's fiction is that sleeping with the enemy is most with us when we're sleeping alone; and that even God, faced with a wounded murderer, might sometimes feel himself agnostic.

Pico Iyer

In one book at least, The Power and the Glory, he transcends his perverse and morbid tendencies and presents a whole and memorable human being; this wholeness is exceptional, for Greene is generally an impressionist, or rather a cutter of mosaics. We expect from incisive talents some kind of diagnosis, some instinctive knowledge of the human situation which we have not attended to; this Greene has had. His subjects are the contemporary loneliness, ugliness, and transience.

V. S. Pritchett

The three novels...Brighton Rock, The Heart of the Matter, and The End of the Affair...all have claims to greatness; they are as intense and penetrating and disturbing as an inquisitor's gaze. After his modest start as a novelist under the influence of Joseph Conrad and John Buchan, Greene's masterly facility at concocting thriller plots and his rather blithely morbid sensibility had come together, at a high level of intelligence and passion, with the strict terms of an inner religious debate that had not yet wearied him.

Graham Greene on Writing

In most of my novels I can remember passages, even chapters, which gave me at the time I wrote them a sense of satisfaction—'this at least has come off.' So I felt, however mistakenly, with the trial scene in The Man Within, and later with Querry's voyage in a Burnt-Out Case, with the three-cornered love scene in The Quiet American, the chess game in Our Man in Havana, the prison dialogue in The Power and the Glory, the intrusion of Miss Paterson in the Boulogne chapters of Travels with My Aunt — I don't think a single book of mine failed to give me at least once a momentary illusion of success except The Name of the Action.

From A Sort of Life

In most of my books, however well I might know the scene, there is one lay figure who obstinately refuses to live, who is there only for the sake of the story — Krogh in England Made Me, Smythe in The End of the Affair, Wilson in The Heart of the Matter, the journalist Parkinson in A Burnt-Out Case. The sad truth is that a story hasn't got room for more than a limited number of created characters. One more successful creation and like an overloaded boat the story lists.

From Ways of Escape

Excitement is simple: excitement is a situation, a single event. It mustn't be wrapped up in thoughts, similes, metaphors. A simile is a form of reflection, but excitement is of the moment when there is no time to reflect. Action can only be expressed by a subject, a verb and an object, perhaps a rhythm—little else. Even an adjective slows the pace or tranquilizes the nerve.

From A Sort of Life

The main character in a novel must necessarily have some kinship to the author, they come out of his body as a child comes from the womb, then the umbilical cord is cut, and they grow into independence. The more the author knows of his own character the more he can distance himself from his invented characters and the more room they have to grow in.

From Ways of Escape

There are, I think, a few points of academic interest in Stamboul Train. The young dancer Coral Musker had surely appeared at the Theatre Royal in Nottwich, like Anne, a character in a later book, A Gun for Sale, and I can detect in both books the influence of my early passion for playwrighting which has never quite died. In those days I thought in terms of a key scene—I would even chart its position on a sheet of paper before I began to write. "Chapter 3. So-and-so comes alive." Often these scenes consisted of isolating two characters —hiding in a railway shed in Stamboul Train, in an empty house in A Gun for Sale. It was as though I wanted to escape from the vast liquidity of the novel and to play out the most important situation on a narrow stage where I could direct every movement of my characters. A scene like that halts the progress of the novel with dramatic empahsis just as in a film a close-up makes the moving picture momentarily pause. I can watch myself following this method even in so late a book as The Comedians. I had long abandoned that sheet of paper — otherwise perhaps I would have written on it, "Scene: Cemetery. Jones and Brown come alive." It might even be said that I reached the logical climax of the method in The Honorary Consul where almost the whole story is contained in the hut in which the kidnappers have hidden their victim.

From Ways of Escape

T.S. Eliot and Herbert Read were the two great figures of my young manhood (they meant more to me than Joyce, and as for Pound he was somehow always a very long way off – an explorer of whose survival at any particular moment one could never be quite certain.) I had not the courage to approach Eliot or Read myself. What interest could they feel for a young and unsuccessful novelist? So it must have been chance which led to my first encounter with Read, and I was proud, surprised and a little daunted when I received a letter from him inviting me to dinner. "Eliot is coming, but no one else, and everything very informal." To me it was a little like receiving an invitation from Coleridge — "Wordsworth is coming, but no one else."...(At that dinner with Eliot we had talked of Arsene Lupin — a subject which always helped Eliot to unbutton — perhaps for a moment it made him feel safe from ladies going to and fro talking of Michelangelo.)

Chapter 14

Study Questions and Answers

Q. Write an essay on the Graham Greene and the Art of the Novel.

Bernard Bergonzi is a longstanding doyen of English literary studies, particularly those concerning the Catholic literary revival. Now in the twilight of a heroic career, Bergonzi has distilled a lifetime of reflection on one crucial member of that renascence, Graham Greene, into a slim volume that seeks to validate Greene's achievement and to encourage further examination of his oeuvre. Although it contains some piquant arguments and striking discrete insights, A Study in Greene is beset with an analytical lassitude and an untenable methodological bifurcation between Greene's art and his life and thought. It is thus of limited value to Greene scholarship, and a disappointing valediction from an eminent critic.

Bergonzi contends that Greene's best work was his early fiction, from The Man Within (1929) through The End of the Affair (1951). This preference is shared more widely among Greene scholars than Bergonzi postulates, but his grounds for it are nonetheless thought-provoking. Bergonzi believes that these early tales had compelling poetic and mythopoeic qualities, which gave them a memorable imaginative energy and vision. In his view, Greene's turn to a sparer realism in the late 1940s divested most of his subsequent works of that dynamism, and hence yielded less potent, if still professional, stories (although Bergonzi does exempt The End of the Affair and, to a lesser extent, The Heart of the Matter from this censure). He detects a brief return by Greene to a more fabular vein in his 1980s novels, Dr. Fischer of Geneva or The Bomb

Party and Monsignor Quixote, and therefore has greater regard for them than for the bulk of Greene's later fiction, which he considers comparatively derivative and diluted. Bergonzi's paradigm prompts him to deem Brighton Rock (1938) Greene's masterpiece, a judgment one can welcome without embracing fully Bergonzi's broader thesis. Similarly, scholars who have a higher opinion of Greene's later texts will still profit from Bergonzi's musings about the earlier titles, especially his conclusion that those first writings were a distinctive blend of Greene's interests in early modern drama, Victorian adventure stories and historical romances, and early twentieth-century popular culture, such as the cinema and Mass Observation.

Bergonzi's taste for the younger Greene further helps spotlight hitherto underrated books such as It's a Battlefield (1934). But it also hinders meaningful critical engagement with several late novels, even when pregnant analytical possibilities arise, as in Bergonzi's jejune treatment of characters and symbolism in The Human Factor and his patronizing dismissal of The Comedians as "an accomplished adventure story".

Yet his discussion of the later work does propound some seminal notions, most notably his clever coinage of the "Greene Man" to brand numerous protagonists who are marked by "world-weariness, cynicism, experience with women, and sexual jealousy". Likewise, amid a largely pedestrian understanding of Greene's politics, Bergonzi highlights well how his interwar novels were part of the "literature of preparation" that anticipated World War II; moreover, he argues insightfully that Greene's hostility to American culture was less that of a self-described social democrat and more that of a "traditional European conservative, in contrast to the later attitudes of the global Left, which excoriated American political behaviour whilst accepting American popular culture". In short, Bergonzi's general hypotheses and close readings should spur fresh and productive considerations of the Greene corpus, even when those appraisals are impelled by "creative disagreement" with his specific models and interpretations.

Such benefits to Greene studies, however, are limited by more serious, structural shortfalls in A Study in Greene. Bergonzi describes his tome as "an essay rather than a thesis", and there is a corresponding lack of analytical rigor. Bergonzi frequently raises weighty topics but does not then explore them with commensurate concentration and depth; some of these elisions have direct bearing on key arguments of his book. For instance, Bergonzi objects to customary acceptances of Greene's distinction in Brighton Rock between those with "the religious sense" who believe in Good and Evil, and those naturalists who believe in Right and Wrong.

Yet this differentiation underpins Greene's distaste for the disenchanted realism of literary modernism, which he thought was missing the essential supernatural dimension of life. His contrary conviction that fictional characters must have "the solidity and importance of men with souls to save or lose" therefore helps explain the more transcendent and mythic tone that Bergonzi lauds in works like Brighton Rock. Had Bergonzi grappled more carefully and thoroughly with these kinds of issues, his inquiries would have been more suitably textured.

Even more disabling is Bergonzi's effort to segregate his literary analysis from other relevant discourses. Out of Bergonzi's justified dismay with procrustean reductions of Greene's art to his life comes an overreaction that tends to hermetically seal off criticism from biography and aesthetics from themes. This endeavor proves unsuitable, as Bergonzi often cites elements of Greene's life and thought to illuminate passages in his literature, be they his manic-depressive temperament, his friendship with Father Leopoldo Duran, his debt to the philosopher Miguel de Unamuno, or the "easily deciphered personal signals" present in "A Visit to Morin" and A Burnt-Out Case.

But Bergonzi's continued insistence on these separations creates contradictions that undercut otherwise sound critiques. For example, he declares that "the quality of Brighton Rock as a literary work does not depend on its theological dimension." Yet he simultaneously asserts that that quality rests "above all" on the "literally inhuman force" of its protagonist, Pinkie, a force that Bergonzi has already rightly demonstrated depends on thinking of Pinkie in theological terms: "Pinkie is far more than a juvenile delinquent; he is presented as a demonic figure of extraordinary power and cruelty.... He is a dark angel, not subject to time and human limitations... who has enough religious sense to feel despair and to be concerned with damnation".

Bergonzi's attempt to isolate Greene's art from his experiences and intellectual and spiritual concerns is not only unworkable; it is also unwarranted. Greene's life and thought were crucial formative factors in his fiction, even as he transmuted them imaginatively into characters and tales that make a general statement about the human condition and can therefore withstand independent aesthetic scrutiny. To sequester Greene's history and ideas when assessing his subcreation is hence to present an unrounded portrait of the art. The pertinence of these extra-literary sources is especially true of his Roman Catholicism.

Greene's religion was central to his aesthetic, both in helping him to select subject matter and to govern its treatment, and in supplying his imagination with the religious sense that he felt was required for substantial, lasting literature. Bergonzi thus errs when he opts to not pursue the nature of Greene's later Catholicism, regarding it as immaterial to his literary evaluations of the later novels and stories. In discussing The Honorary Consul (1973), for instance, Bergonzi asserts that whether or not the lapsed priest Rivas hold heretical views and whether or not Greene intended him to are "irrelevant to the reader's response to the novel".

On the contrary, these theological opinions and Greene's stance toward them shape how readers understand Rivas's character, motives, and fate, and thereby mold reactions to him and the plot, particularly when he reverts at its climax to his traditional sacerdotal duties at the cost of his life. What Bergonzi's more truncated methodology fails to comprehend is that, when employed skillfully, biography, intellectual history and theology enrich literary criticism rather than impoverish it.

A Study in Greene consequently provides only a hint of an explanation of Greene's significance or Bergonzi's stature. Scholars stimulated by its keen New Critical commentary on specific passages and texts will need to draw on a wider range of disciplines and conceptual tools to convey the nature and scope of Greene's accomplishment ac urately.

Critics disheartened by Bergonzi's laxity and unwillingness to keep the giddy line midway between aesthetic insularity and crude reductionism will need to review his more acute, nuanced studies of Great War poetry and 1930s literature to be reminded of his just claim to intellectual renown. A Study in Greene may be Bernard Bergonzi's last word on Graham Greene; it should not be a reader's last reading of either.

Q. Write a short note on Graham Greene, travel and the primitive.

Or

Q. Greene was bitten by the travel bug that swarmed among the British literati in the 1930s. Discuss

IN 1962, Evelyn Waugh reflected that "one of the many sharp differences" between his generation of British authors and writers of other eras was that "we got about the world, noting that the likes of himself, Robert Byron, Peter Fleming and "Mr. Graham Greene" "spent much of their youth in enterprising and arduous journeys... For some—Mr. Greene in particular—the habit has proved ineradicable" .

Waugh's remarks suggest two important truths about some of the British intellectuals who came of age between the two world wars: first, they traveled outside of the United Kingdom more extensively than their predecessors had and brought a distinct vision to the places they observed; second, Graham Greene was especially and enduringly affected by the experience of travel abroad.

Greene was bitten by the travel bug that swarmed among the British literati in the 1930s, and he remained restless for the remainder of his days, as he eventually traversed distant lands as diverse as the Congo, Kenya, Vietnam, Malaysia, Israel, Haiti, Cuba, Argentina, Panama, and Nicaragua. Greene frequently filed newspaper and magazine dispatches on the political situation in such countries and often set his fiction in these locales; indeed, eighteen of his twenty-six novels have a non-English setting.

But Greene's most sustained and extensive reflections on remote places were inspired by two sojourns of the 1930s: a three-month excursion through Sierra Leone, French Guinea and Liberia in 1935, chronicled chiefly in Journey Without Maps (1936); and a two-month trip to Mexico in 1938 to observe the effects of the revolutionary regime's religious persecution of Catholics there that had commenced in 1925, which he reported on primarily in The Lawless Roads (1939).

Greene's reactions to what he saw on these voyages, especially the contrasts he drew between the "primitive" abroad and "civilized" Britain and Europe, became crucial components of the religious and cultural framework with which he critiqued both foreign nations and his homeland thenceforth.

Greene recognized the pivotal nature of these two trips, a judgment that several scholars have seconded. Yet critics have not adequately realized that Greene's travel writings are a microcosm of his distinctly Roman Catholic protest against modern Western secularism and materialism. Greene echoed many of his peers in asserting that the primitive had a superior cultural ethos to that of European industrial civilization. But his version of this general judgment was highly individualized, being shaped crucially by formative personal experiences and by Catholicism, to which he had converted in 1926. To Greene, the primitive was more aware of and respectful of the sempiternal significance of human life, evil's persistence, the supernatural, tradition, and elemental faith, while also being more able to integrate life's various activities and stages.

He also found it a repository of virtues like a sense of community and social justice that he associated with Europe's pre-industrial places and past. Greene concluded that all these beliefs, institutions and values that he thought the primitive upheld were threatened by modern civilizing forces and were best conserved by Roman Catholicism. But the tragic view of life that he derived from early personal suffering and found confirmed by Catholicism kept him from idealizing primitive people and places. Analyzing the motives for Greene's trips, the components of the differences between the primitive and civilization that he adduced from them, and the role of Catholicism in shaping this outlook will thus reveal both Greene's participation in the travel literature of protest that his generation pioneered, and the particular stamp of his religious faith on his rebeilion against modernity.

It will hence complement discussions of his travel writings that are less detailed, less comprehensive or more focused on the aesthetic implications of these journeys ; and it will help correct unnuanced treatments that dismiss the centrality and gravity of Greene's religious concerns.

Paul Fussell has defined well the sort of travel and travel writing that Greene's generation undertook. Fussell notes that the travel book is a distinct genre, one characterized by an "active, organic, and, if you will, `creative' mediation between fact and fiction", as "the autobiographical narrative arises from the speaker's encounter with distant or unfamiliar data, and in which the narrative—unlike that in a novel or a romance—claims literal validity by constant reference to actuality". Although this form was not invented by Greene's generation of thinkers, Fussell explains that it was given a special shape by them.

In broad terms, growing disillusionment with liberal values and industrial capitalism occasioned by the Great War and the Hungry Thirties made discontent with all things English both a dominant motive for travel during this period and a rhetorical feature of books about these excursions; an almost obligatory "I Hate It Here" section became a unique feature of interwar travel writing: "literary travel between the wars constitutes an implicit rejection of industrialism and everything implied by the concept `modern northern Europe'". In addition, the increased sensitivity to international issues stimulated by the war and Fascism's rise allowed epistles from abroad to perform a function exercised by sages and men of letters in less cosmopolitan days, becoming "a subtle instrument of ethics, replacing such former vehicles as sermons and essays". A further moral feature of these accounts is their use of spatial voyages as vehicles for internal examinations of consciousness and conscience, making them both "a record of an inquiry and a report of the effect of the inquiry on the mind and imagination of the traveller". In short, travel books act out "the basic trope of the generation... journey itself, the most insistent of `thirties metaphors'".

Although Greene's travels continued long after the thirties ended, the kinds of places he visited and the concerns he expressed in his writings about them varied little. In a sense, then, all his travel books are thirties travel books, for his travelogues and fiction based on trips, both in the thirties and later, fulfill this model's general terms, as well as other more specific elements of it, while also being molded distinctively by his religious considerations and convictions. Greene often attributed his wanderlust to boredom , but he also admitted to being influenced by adventure stories he read as a youngster , and to having been fascinated by some of the places he visited, such as Africa and Panama, from boyhood ; and even before he went abroad, he made experience of foreign lands crucial to a character in It's a Battlefield. Other aspects of his childhood and his reactions to it also shaped his reasons for traveling, and these impinged on his religious and cultural interests directly.

Initially, Greene sought in travel A.E.'s "ancient shadows and twilights / Where childhood had strayed" that he invoked in discussing his own lost childhood. The seminal event of Greene's life was an adolescent breakdown that occurred in 1919-1920. Greene at this time was a boarding student at Berkhamsted public school, where his father was headmaster, a situation that permanently divided Graham's loyalties between his schoolmates and his family. Other pupils preyed on the isolated boy, tormenting him physically (with dividers) and manipulating his craving for affection emotionally. When one of his few friends conspired with his worst foe to betray his friendship, Greene became desperate and even attempted suicide. His alarmed family soon sent him to London for psychoanalysis. Greene derived from this episode a vivid sense of evil's reality, a corresponding deep skepticism of innocence, and a scorn for his parents' liberal Christianity and humanitarian progressivism, which now seemed fatally insensitive to human malevolence.

These incidents and attitudes helped spur his eventual conversion to Catholicism and became a permanent subtext of his adult writing. In his travel works, Greene frequently juxtaposed memories of his youth and school years with his accounts of occurrences abroad; but he was particularly straightforward about this personal motive for travel in his rendering of his journey without maps to Liberia. In 1935, he associated Africa with "death and forest and maps and school and dust and darkness, unhappiness... the face of an unpleasant boy and evensong and a pair of dividers" . He further compared his trek directly to the kind of psychoanalysis he had undergone as a teen:

The method of psychoanalysis is to bring the patient back to the idea which he is repressing: a long journey backwards without maps, catching a clue here and a clue there, as I caught the names of villages from this man and that, until one has the face, the general idea, the pain or memory. This is what you have feared, Africa may be imagined as saying, you can't avoid it, there it is creeping round the wall, flying in at the door, rustling the grass.

Greene makes the twin meaning of his book's title obvious here, but a similar dynamic is at work in all his travel writings, which is unsurprising given his fixation on his painful memory of his school experiences of evil: "As the vision of evil becomes crusted over with characteristically deadening maturity, the need becomes urgent to seek it out again by returning to the youthful terror". Although governed by such particular concerns, then, Greene's travel books are like his fellow travel authors' in being reports of both external and internal inquiry, something Greene acknowledged in fact and fiction (Search 19, Burnt 131, Short Stories 212, Allain 98). Yet Greene's chosen destinations reveal that he was pursuing not only his own lost childhood, but his race's as well. He sought out what he deemed primitive locations because—as Auden's words used as an epigraph for Journey Without Maps indicate—when Greene's footsteps felt from granite to grass, he was diligently looking to discover what was lacking in modern industrial society.

Greene tried to uncover the stage of social development at which Britain and cultures like it began to decline, as though he could isolate original sin anthropologically: "when one sees to what unhappiness, to what peril of extinction centuries of cerebration have brought us, one sometimes has a curiosity to discover if one can from what we have come, to recall at which point we went astray". In attempting to suggest a sense of what Britain's past may have been like through descriptions of other nations' presents, with this purpose of moral instruction, Greene is acting as both sage and prophet; and his accounts often read like extended sermons and essays, making them again typical of the travel genre.

They also demonstrate Greene's tendency to think in polarities, for "the primitive" and "civilization" are clear antitheses in his reports. In this respect, his work belonged to a Western literary tradition dating from at least the late eighteenth century that posits the particular virtue of primitive people and places ; but his use of this paradigm was shaped by his more personal perception of industrial modernity's religious and cultural effects.

Greene distinguished between two attitudes to reality, belief in Good and Evil and belief in Right and Wrong: the former, epitomized by Catholicism, is teleologically-oriented, stressing ends, theology and metaphysics, and the transcendent; while the latter, reaching its quintessence in modern secularism, is deontologically inclined, accenting means, ethics, and the solely natural and human. Greene thought that only believers in the absolutes of Good and Evil are fully human, for their moral imaginations alone are attuned to the eternal dimension of existence; believers in the mediated reality of Right and Wrong have had their sensibilities attenuated by exclusive focus on ephemerals, making them a kind of sub-humanity. He began to formulate this distinction between "the ethical mind and the religious" (Greene to Nancy Pearn, 9 April 1937; quoted in Sherry 1: 639) in the mid-1930s, arguing that modern secularists have a "much thinner reality, they are not concerned with eternal damnation" or salvation, and thus cannot comprehend those, like Catholics, who assert the importance of "eternal issues, of the struggle between good and evil, between vice that really demands to be called satanic and virtue of a kind which can only be called heavenly" .

He elaborated this dichotomy and its implications most fully in Brighton Rock (1938) through the clash of the Roman Catholics, Pinkie and Rose, and archetypal secularist Ida Arnold: "the idea is that Pinkie and Rose belong to the real world in which good & evil exist, but that the interfering Ida belongs to a kind of artificial surface world in which there is no such thing as good & evil but only right & wrong". Ida's ethic of adherence to social conventions and pursuit of material success and pleasure is hence painted as radically incompatible with, and deficient in comparison with, the two "Romans'" belief in eternal verities and in the supernatural dimension and destiny of human life. Ida's mantra that "I know the difference between Right and Wrong" can thus not persuade Rose to leave the murderous, manipulative Pinkie:

Rose didn't answer; the woman was quite right; the two words meant nothing to her.

Their taste was extinguished by stronger foods—Good and Evil... she knew by tests as clear as mathematics that Pinkie was evil—what did it matter in that case whether he was right or wrong?... "Right and wrong. That's what she talks about... As if she knew... Oh she wouldn't burn. She couldn't burn if she tried." Greene applied this taxonomy to societies that he observed, asserting, in general terms, that primitive societies uphold Good and Evil but civilized ones profess Right and Wrong. He claimed that "there is no peace anywhere where there is human life... the horror may be the same, it is an intrinsic part of human life in every place: it attacks you in the Strand or the tropics" (Lawless 33-4). Yet he argued further that places like the tropics or Mexico are more sensitive to that aboriginal horror than are the Strand or the United States because they have been less narcotized by consumerist civilization:

So many years have passed in England since the war began between faith and anarchy: we live in ugly indifference. Over here lay the grave of Pro, Tabasco with every Church destroyed, and Chiapas, where the Mass was forbidden. The advertisements for aerated waters and patent medicines line the modern highway which leads to the front line and the tourists go back and forth, their cars laden with serapes and big hats, and their minds sprightly with the legend of a happy and picturesque Mexico... life among the dark groves of leaning crosses in Chiapas was at any rate concerned with eternal values.

Greene put this contention in explicitly theological terms in 1939, appropriate to his views at that time, when reflecting on his stay in "civilized" San Antonio: "Original sin under the spell of elegance had lost its meaning... The horror and beauty of human life were both absent". Greene believed that he had discovered human life and nature stripped of their elegant veneer in primitive areas, and hence exposed in their more genuine horror and beauty. Even before he first went abroad, Greene asserted that the British cloaked disreputable occupations with an elaborate air of respectability . Such euphemism was part of why he hated it here and wanted to "get out of this bloody country". He claimed that abroad, people—British and otherwise—were more transparent, as Scobie's ruminations on Sierra Leone (where Greene was also stationed for part of World War II) reveal:

Why, he wondered... do I love this place so much? Is it because here human nature hasn't had time to disguise itself?. Here flourished the injustices, the cruelties, the meanness that elsewhere people so cleverly hushed up. Here you could love human beings nearly as God loved them, knowing the worst: you didn't love a pose, a pretty dress, a sentiment artfully assumed. It was because Greene, like his character Arthur Rowe, "preferred human nature plain" that he sought out areas as unlike civilization-encrusted Britain as he could envision. NOT surprisingly, given his tragic view of life, Greene focused more on the horror, the injustices, cruelties, and meannesses, of the areas he visited. He maintained that Liberia attracted him because "there seemed to be a seediness about the place you couldn't get to the same extent elsewhere;" and seediness satisfied a core need that drove his excursions, "the sense of nostalgia for something lost; it seems to represent a stage further back."

Because it is closer to human origins, Greene argued, primitive seediness is "not, after all, so far from the central darkness," making it "deeper and purer" than its civilized counterparts: "it hasn't reached so far away as the smart, the new, the chic, the cerebral." He argued that civilization teaches people to forget this primitive "finer terror," and thus replaces a sense of "supernatural evil" with Right and Wrong's "small human viciousness": "There was cruelty enough in the interior, but had we done wisely exchanging the supernatural cruelty for our own?" He thus concluded that his African sojourn had only "reinforced a sense of disappointment with what man had made of the primitive, what he had made out of his childhood," and hence had strengthened his distaste for Progressive ideologies, "a distrust of any future based on what we are".

The primitive, then, substantiated Greene's tragic view of life by providing an entire culture as an objective correlative for the intuitions about evil's presence and power, and about civilized modernity's ignorance of its force and perdurance, that he had possessed since Berkhamsted. Although Greene was in many ways seeing what he wanted to see abroad, possible factual inaccuracies should not obscure this tactical importance of primitive areas to his rebellion against modernity. Greene was not blind to what he considered the beauty of life in its primitive forms, though. Just as he felt that the primitive had a sharper sense of evil, so he deemed its discoveries and displays of goodness sweeter than civilization's corruptions. He held that among African natives he met "gentleness, kindness, an honesty which one would not have found, or at least dared to assume, was there in Europe" because "Love... existed here without the trappings of civilization". Greene extolled specific virtues of primitive societies, such as a more authentic art; a greater acceptance of the unknown; increased sensitivity to natural rhythms; more just treatment of racial minorities; and enhanced recognition of public charity's value, all of which made them superior in his mind to modern civilization. To him, the primitive social order as a whole was rooted in "a greater simplicity, an older, more natural culture, and traditions of honesty and hospitality".

Because the primitive's apprehension of Evil is more acute, Greene implied, its comprehension of Good is equally astute. Only with civilization's corroding effects, he thought, are these perceptions diluted into the confused perversions of Right and Wrong. Despite his paeans to primitive culture's charms, though, Greene was finally more fascinated by its abominations, regarding these as life's more vivid portion in a fallen world: to him, "failure, ugliness, the primitive are in some sense truer than success, beauty and civilization with their deceptive gloss" .

In addition to his broad use of trips as an opportunity for Eliot's backward half-look over the shoulder towards the primitive terror, Greene also isolated more specific differences between primitive and civilized societies. Initially, he judged the primitive to be more religious. In 1939, Greene claimed that Africa's fascination for him was "a religious fascination: the country offers the European an opportunity of living continuously in the presence of the supernatural," something he no longer deemed possible in post-Christian Europe ; and he repeated this conviction over forty years later. This disparity between primitive native and secular European attitudes to religion was a persistent theme of Greene's factual and fictional presentations of remote places. For instance, he felt that civilized, modern ideas, even religious ones, were so saturated with Right and Wrong that they failed to comprehend the horror and beauty of primitive religions based on Good and Evil. Evaluating the liberal Christian missionaries of his youth retrospectively, Greene commented that they were "not only innocent beside our own masters, they were innocent among the blacks they taught." He contended that they were more concerned with raising money to support "the hideous tin church" than with the "sense of sin," and he thus doubted that they could have had much influence among men "whose secret ritual it is to sacrifice a child once a year to the great python".

Greene reiterated this perceived incompatibility between civilized and primitive approaches to religion often, as in confidential agent D's contrast between "the civilized" ethic of "no religious faith, but a lot of Gregorian chants and picturesque ceremonies" and his preference for "the distrust, the barbarity, the betrayals... even the chaos" that accompanied eras of authentic faith, like the Dark Ages . Even in the mid-1960s, Greene portrayed an exemplar of modern civilization as incredulous that a Sorbonne-educated poet could be attracted to Haitian voodoo ceremonies (Comedians 180). As well as asserting this general contrast, Greene posited further that primitive religion was closer to the essentials of faith, enriched other aspects of culture, and was better equipped to deal with matters shunned by civilized moderns. His Mexican whiskey priest reflects that "life without books, without contact with educated men, had peeled away from his memory everything but the simplest outline of the mystery" ; and Dr. Colin judges the Congolese leper colony's less intellectualized Catholicism to be closer to the Apostles' than Europe's civilized scholasticism is.

It was this focus on the elementary, suprarational elements of Catholicism that led Greene to state expressly, "I like the so-called `primitive' manifestations of the faith". Not only is Christianity reduced to its basic components in primitive settings, Greene thought, but native religions share this uncomplicated character: "One felt that the two religions here were appealing on the simplest terms". He held that this emphasis on fundamentals keeps such religions closer to actual religious experiences, and hence avoids the ratiocinated "abstractions of the Methodists and Anglicans" and Catholic scholastics, which he found less convincing and lasting than the "magical heart of the faith" that he took note of among

Mexican Indians and chided civilized Europeans for neglecting: "we are too apt to minimize the magic elements in Christianity—the man raised from the dead, the devils cast out, the water turned into wine". Put another way, primitive religion corresponds to fulfilling, enduring, mystical "faith" in Greene's schema and civiliza-tion's to arid, ephemeral, rationalistic "belief".

Beyond exemplifying Greene's dictum that "religion is simple, dogma is simple" primitive religion also illustrated for him the correct relationship between religion and the rest of life . In the case of art, for example, whereas D's civilized nemeses find religion of only cultural interest, Greene argued that primitive societies consider artistic expression valuable only because of its religious significance. His description of the Liberian bush devil's dance exemplifies this perceived contrast: "it was a carnival, but it wasn't a carnival in the vulgar sense of Nice and the Battle of Flowers: it wasn't secular and skittish; like the dancing in the Spanish cathedral at Easter, it had its religious value."

More generally, Greene praised one African tribe for making "a work of conscious art in the service of a belief," while criticizing another for their "lack of religious enthusiasm," which "diminishes their artistic talent" , a view anticipating his 1945 assessment of literary modernism as a failure due to its lack of a religious sense . Besides providing proper focus for life's creativity, Greene also postulated, the primitive deals better with its conclusion.

South African expatriate Sarah Castle tells her English husband, Maurice, that "we used to have better funerals in Africa" than civilization's cremations; and she chides the English boast of being a venerable civilization, to which Maurice responds, "old civilizations are not always famous for feeling deeply about death", especially when their modern avatars have embraced Ida Arnold's fear of it: Death shocked her, life was so important. She wasn't religious. She didn't believe in heaven or hell, only in ghosts, ouija boards, tables that rapped and little inept voices speaking plaintively of flowers. Let Papists treat death with flippancy: life wasn't so important perhaps to them as what came after; but to her death was the end of everything.

Such juxtapositions between the primitive and civilization and between Catholicism and secular modernity function throughout Greene's travelogues and fiction both as a "no" to modernity and a simultaneous "yes" to an alternate path for Britain and the civilized world to follow. As Carolyn Scott explains, "Greene sees in primitive ritual and myth making something which can potentially revitalize our own civilized institutions, most of which have their origins in ancient rites... the hope that a supernatural power can permeate all things. In this realization Greene hopes for a coherent ritual not incompatible with modern institutions".

Greene sought to fill this modern form with the traditional content of his own faith, for he felt that "in the civilized world Catholicism held something of the mystery the primitive offered... religious experience offered unspoken understanding. It was, in its literal, root meaning, a bond, something by which people might be linked together" (Adamson 35-6). In addition to replicating the primitive's mystical coherence in civilization, Greene contended further, "the Catholic attitude gave a unity and a purpose, and thus a permanence" to those primitive societies that had accepted it. It hence created a "solid block of culture" that he considered superior to the "polo, Sunday school teachers and ministers" that typified modern British Protestantism and its cultural concomitants to him, and that he thought was its evanescent legacy abroad and at home.

Because Greene believed that Catholicism and the primitive share a teleological bent; a tragic view of life; an emphasis on mystery, simplicity, and experience (at least when "faith" is prioritized over "belief"); and a sacramental perspective on life's activities and its termination, he considered Roman Catholicism the best vehicle for subverting "civilized" norms, and for protecting these "primitive" values and inculcating them into Western cultures too long starved of their finer taste and terror." Primitive beliefs and practices not only resonated with Greene's specifically religious concerns about culture, but also with his respect for tradition. He asserted that traditions are both more enduring and more venerated in primitive areas than in industrial civilization.

The Human Factor's John Hargreaves rebukes the idea advanced by a representative of modern civilization that the "old Africa" is gone forever by drawing on his experiences in that continent: "if we destroy the world, the roads will become overgrown and all the new luxury hotels will crumble, the forests will come back, the chiefs, the witch doctors—there's still a rain queen in the northeast Transvaal". The Quiet American's Fowler had expressed the same idea in discussing Vietnam's ancient peasant culture, and Greene had even asserted the persistence of Mexican traditions of which he disapproved . In the main, though, he considered this primitive sense of continuity beneficial, especially given the alternative he saw of accepting civilization's rootlessness. Thus he described favorably a leper who shuns a modern clinic's amenities when death approaches because "he was prepared to die only where his ancestors had died, in the darkness surrounded by the smell of dry mud and leaves", rather than in the antiseptic anonymity in which It's a Battlefield's Conrad Drover had breathed his last in a London hospital.

As admirable as Greene judged these sorts of religious and cultural attitudes, he was also convinced of the constant peril posed to them by industrial civilization. He opined in 1936 that in Africa , "Civilization here remained exploitation; we had hardly, it seemed to me, improved the natives' lot at all" either physically or spiritually, for to "have been touched by civilization" was to "have learnt to steal and lie and kill" . Subsequent history only strengthened these sentiments, as twenty-five years later he challenged the notion that natives who fear the consequences of introducing modern technology are simple-minded Luddites: "in our century you could hardly call them fools. Hola Camp, Sharpeville, and Algiers had justified all possible belief in European cruelty". Nor did Greene consider this cruelty confined to Europeans. He perceived in Mexico the extent to which an indigenous government could exercise it against citizens' religion when corrupted by "dusty rationalist" ideologies like naturalism and Marxism imported from civilized lands.

Yet he also asserted the existence of a more insidious attack on traditional religion by modern civilized values. For instance, Greene contrasted a Mexican cathedral, where "the mortification goes on. This is the atmosphere of the stigmata," with a "squalid" tourist market and its firewalker who practices "mortification for money, the stigmata of the pleasure fair." It is in places like Mexico City or Puebla, which Greene found most dominated by commercial values, that he thought religion becomes superstition, esteemed for the price its quaintness can fetch among visitors from post-Christian lands. He contended that this sort of environment contaminates even those attempting to adhere to authentic faiths.

Among his co-religionists in Puebla, for example, he detected degeneration into "a kind of social Catholicism" that seemed worlds away from the "wild region of great crooked crosses, of the cave dweller faces bowed before the crucified Christ, of the talking saint," that was more rustic Chiapas, where life was palpably concerned with eternal values . In short, Greene worried that primitive societies, perhaps without realizing it, were in danger of succumbing to the secularizing and fetishizing pressures he associated with civilization, ones that he considered it essential to rebel against both at home and abroad. Modern civilization must also be resisted, in Greene's mind, to prevent the primitive from losing the traditional way of life already smashed in metropolitan areas. In particular, he feared that the machine that had blighted the shire now threatened to blemish the savanna and pampa, warning in 1940 that "heartless industrialization" imperiled "the wide rapid river, the dense tangled forest and the volcanic mountains" of primitive lands. Greene was encouraged by Liberian areas in which "the forest stayed forest, it was hardly pitted at all by the little holes white prospectors had dug.

The minerals remained where they were in the soil of the country, and the images had certainly not been pulled down out of the temples." Yet he saw ominous signs elsewhere in Africa, such as the advent of cars in Sierra Leone, which frightened natives "as civilization went terrifyingly by them in a fume of evil smoke" . In many ways, he deemed Mexico even more degraded, often complaining that there was little difference between it and the "bloody country" he had left behind, but finding the growing hegemony of an ethic rooted in "the petty social fulfillment, the tiny pension and the machine-made furniture" to be "peculiarly unnatural" where it had taken root in Mexico .

GREENE felt that a more genuine way of life was available in pastoralism, especially the kind mythologized in his own green and pleasant land. Although he reproved the Romantics' view of nature as sentimental throughout his travel books (see, e.g., Journey 158; Lawless 61-2), he was at one with them in using rural England as a standard for judging social orders. Greene was charmed by a Liberian village because there was something "peculiarly English" about it ; and this cross-cultural comparison was even more overt in Mexico, as he admitted evaluating the country according to the works of Trollope and Cobbett he had brought with him.

Mexico's inability to provide tangible equivalents to the society described in those "English books" made Greene homesick, for "there was nothing in this country so beautiful as an English village" . His use of this template indicates, as Mafia Cuoto explains, that his concerns about the course of African and Mexican development were prompted by "an agonizing recall of the loss of the innocent beauty of undespoiled, rural England," and the contrast between that arcadia and the "soulless brashness of the urban bourgeoisie" in modern Britain, one that led him to warn against and lament industrial civilization's expansion. In doing so, Greene's travel writing not only fits within a tradition of British religious and romantic anti-industrialist protest writing dating to the eighteenth century ; but it also meets a convention of its own genre, as "the pastoral is a powerful element in most travel books" of this period, serving as a salutary counterpoint for their authors to the industrial world they hated there.

One pre-industrial value Greene deemed especially besieged was the sense of community. Again revealing his debt to the myth of meerie England, Greene described his brief residence in a Chipping Camden thatched cottage as living out "that pastoral Georgian dream of the industrial twenties" and maintained that "the life of a village is intimate and dramatic. There is a sense of community.

People talk. In a city there may be a suicide in the next street and you will never hear of it". Even before he went abroad, Greene considered civilization afflicted with "Metroland loneliness", for the sense that "loneliness was only too easily attained" in urban modernity pervades It's a Battlefield. Greene argued consistently that societies under industrial civilization's sway discover community only in such ersatz venues as partnership in crime, madness, prison, refuge from political oppression, and television.

He blamed public schools in part for weakening what he deemed a student's natural loyalties to the society of his birthplace and producing class-conscious prigs instead ; but he regarded schools as only agents oi the urban, industrial, consumerist culture underlying this erosion of solidarity.

As Cuoto concludes, the sense of a rich and close community life replaced by an urban desert is very strong in all Greene's fiction and an important element of the dream England that died with "growing up"... the fiction is underpinned by disgust with the endless gratification of consumer tastes, of a civílization that panders to human acquisitiveness. Greene held that less acquisitive societies existed in primitive areas. For example, he described his Liberian trip as a deliberate exodus from "the depraved individualists to the old, the unfamiliar, the communal life" of Africa.

Additionally, he maintained that Europeans who live in primitive areas soon unlearn their snobbery and develop a sense of social solidarity because "a common danger, purpose or way of life can very nearly destroy differences of intellect and class" (Journey 23-4). Yet Greene also feared that these victories might be hollow.

He regarded the Europeans' new-found communitarian sensibility as based more on the circumstances of their relative isolation than on commitment to a less individualistic culture;

in fact, he considered Europeans incapable of comprehending fully the African taste for the other: "they seemed to like to touch each other, as if it made them feel good to know the other man was there. It wasn't love; it didn't mean anything we could understand".

This ignorance made Greene anxious that the primitive sense of community could not survive industrial capitalist civilization's steady encroachment. In the areas of Africa that had accepted its influence by 1935, for instance, he discerned a change even in the rationale for forced labour from one that "at least pretends to be for the good of the community" to one that stresses "the good of shareholders". Given his sense of communitarian values' existential frailty, Greene sought some institution to ground them in. As with other virtues he associated with the primitive, he seems to have concluded that Catholicism was their best repository.

Maurice Castle is driven into a Roman Catholic church by an "emotion of loneliness," and this search for fellowship also appears to have motivated his creator. Even after excommunicating himself in the 1950s due to an inability to repent his sexual sins, Greene claimed that he still went to Mass for, amongst other things, exactly what he had found in village life, "a sense of community". Because it rebels against modernity and its atomizing tendencies, Greene believed, Catholicism's centripetal bond of common convictions and practices gives its adherents the sense of place and purpose that It's a Battlefield's Jules Briton found salvific: "He wanted to be saved from the counter and the tea urn, the `Weights,' and the heartless flippancy of the cafe.... Always in the badly lit church, surrounded by the hideous statues of an uncompromising faith, listening to the certainty of that pronouncement—peche, peche, peche he was given confidence, an immense pride, a purpose. However lost in the cafe... here he was at home". The Church is hence a positive and distinct alternative to both acquisitive anomie and the impersonal, degraded substitutes that Greene thought civilization offers for pre-industrial fellowship, even as its sense of purpose gives primitive areas a permanent source of cultural unity. To

Greene, then, Catholicism was the best contemporary upholder—for himself, civilization, and the primitive alike—of the ideal of social fraternity that he had derived from a myth of rural "Englishness," and that primitive locales had exemplified to him.

IF the English village and its contemporary primitive counterparts were Greene's spatial referents for anti-modern values, his temporal one was often the Middle Ages. Greene had a youthful interest in things medieval, as "the first stories I tried to write were of the Middle Ages".

Yet even in these early tales, Greene depicted medieval ideals as precarious, having a knight declare, "I and my kind are dead" (The Berkhamstedian, March, 1921; quoted in Sherry 1: 81). In his adult trips abroad, medievalism was one of Greene's standards for assessing primitive places and practices.

In Africa, he dubbed villages that gave him the sense of being "a small courageous community" as "like medieval towns". He deemed a mined Mexican palace and chapel "as beautiful as anything out of the Middle Ages" ; and one of his initial impressions of the Indo-China that he would grow to love was of its being "a very strange medieval place". Additionally, Greene affirmed medieval mores and beliefs. He defended a corporatist economic model that he uncovered in Mexico, differentiating the moral economy he thought practiced by General Saturnino Cedillo and the peasants who worked for him from the wage-labour system adopted by other Mexicans:

The General gave them no pay, but food and clothes and shelter and half of everything the farm produced, and ready cash too if they asked for it and he had it... And they gave him labour and love. It was not a progressive relationship; it was feudal; you may say it was one-sided and he had everything... but they possessed at any rate more than did their fellow-peasants in other states, living at best on the minimum wage of thirty five cents a day, with no one caring if they lived or died. Greene did not consider this paternalism a form of despotism, but rather an example of a governor who did not abdicate his responsibilities. Yet, as laudable as he judged medieval principles and social orders based on them to be, he also continued to think them tenuous.

In 1935, for instance, he labeled pre-invasion Abyssinia "the last medieval State" and warned that it is "more worth preserving than the bright slick streamlined civilization which threatens it", one that had already reduced Britain from a place where people "lived here once and died with their feet crossed to show they had been on a crusade" to a "Metroland" dominated by "the estate agents, the cafes and the two super-cinemas" . As this passage implies, Greene ascribed such cultural decline to a fundamentally religious cause, feeling that modern secularism could not sustain the cultural integrity that the primitive derived from faith in the supernatural's pervasive presence, a spiritual coherence he thought medieval Christendom had shared and that the industrial, individualistic West had lost. As D puts it, extending his comparison of the primitive, pious Dark Ages and the civilized, disenchanted Modern Age, "Roland had companions at Roncesvalles—Oliver and Turpin: the whole chivalry of Europe was riding up to help him. Men were united by a common belief...

Now there were so many varieties of economic materialism, so many initial letters" . It was thus in that common belief uniting the actual medievals that Greene thought their norms were best preserved in modern times. A Mexican bishop symbolized to him how Catholic, medieval Good and Evil survives in the midst of secular, modern Right and Wrong: "In the modern city—among the American tea shops, the advertisements for safety razors, the dapper night clubs—there existed, besides medieval violence, this medieval sanctity". Greene also praised the Papal social encyclicals for their condemnation of both capitalist and communist economic materialism in his Mexican travelogue, suggesting further that he regarded Catholicism as a philosophical ally of the medievalist, anti-modern economic system he found more just in practice.

Unlike fellow Catholics like G.K. Chesterton or

Christopher Dawson, Greene did not detail how Catholicism should give such medieval notions currency in contemporary cultures; but he did share their sense of an essential link between the two outlooks, making medievalism yet another ideal associated with the primitive that Greene thought his church guarded best, and could embody most credibly in the post-Christian world.

As these mores are ultimately rooted in the timeless truths of Catholicism, they are equally timely for all cultures and ages: "if one believes in Christianity at all, one must believe in its universal validity.

A Christian cannot believe in one God for Europe and another God for Africa," nor in one for the medieval era and another for the modern epoch. To Greene, then, Catholicism was both a source of internal cultural unity and a transcendent tie across cultures and generations.

Although Greene clearly preferred his perception of the primitive to his conception of civilization, his view was not uncritical. His travelogues and letters from abroad contain a frequent tension between approval of more primitive conditions and yearning for modern amenities. Greene admitted that some of his more outrageous outbursts were largely a result of trying to do too much in an unfamiliar climate, but other criticisms of primitive life were more substantive.

For example, he charged that there was "a virtual enslavement of women" in Africa. Moreover, Greene satirized the kind of primitivist who refuses to recognize native people's vices in The Comedians's Mr. and Mrs. Smith.

These absurdly well-intentioned American vegetarians try to excuse the corruption and persecution practiced by Papa Doc Duvalier's Haitian regime by asserting, amongst other things, that "we must not judge a colored dictatorship as we judge a white one". If the primitive's cruelty is supernatural, Greene thought, it is still cruel; and he distanced himself explicitly from a Rousseauean rendering of remote peoples: "The `noble savage' no longer exists; perhaps he never existed".

The reason for that possibility, in Greene's mind, is the most salient motive for his only partial embrace of the primitive, his tragic view of life. He concluded that, whatever its considerable virtues, the primitive can only approximate prelapsarian perfection: although people "can never quite forget" such a paradise, it is "a way of life we have hopelessly lost". He held that, despite its many advantages, the primitive is essentially similar to civilization ontologically: "what had astonished me about Africa was that it had never really been strange... The `heart of darkness' was common" to both Africans and Europeans ; and he reiterated this sentiment about Mexico: "Did I really expect to find there what I hadn't found here?... The world is all of a piece, of course; it is engaged everywhere in the same subterranean struggle" (Lawless 17, 33). At the conclusion of both his Thirties travelogues, Greene juxtaposes the civilization he has returned to with the primitive just departed to stress this likeness . This rhetorical strategy reinforces his belief that all people are implicated in the aboriginal calamity; and it also subverts a norm of the travel genre by having an "I Hate It Here" section conclude as well as originate the book, leaving the inference that in coming home "one is not fleeing to something nicer, one is returning to something which travel has exposed as equally loathsome".

This perception of his own culture's loathsomeness was widely echoed by Greene's generation of travel writers, but its cause and cure took a distinctive shape in his mind. Greene shared his fellow authors' motive in going abroad, as he wished to discover social orders less touched by industrialism; and, like many of them, he used his accounts as jeremiads about the condition of England and of modern civilization generally. Greene also followed the common pattern of using these journeys as internal explorations, particularly of outlooks stemming from his school sufferings. Yet his travelogues were also molded by his distinct, Roman Catholic rebellion against modernity. Whether it was in choice of location (as in Mexico), topics discussed, or criteria used to evaluate what he witnessed, Greene's religion was an indispensable lens through which he viewed remote places.

His conviction that Catholicism could best preserve for the primitive and transmit to the civilized West traditional beliefs and virtues that he found more vivid and vital in primitive areas exemplifies how much this element of his cultural criticism depended at times on his religion. In positing that industrial, post-Christian Britain also was one of the dark places of the earth, Greene discerned that its enlightenment would arise from renewal of its pre-industrial patrimony and the ever-ancient, ever-new faith that had infused it: the modern "Dark Age of... civilization" would be redeemed by recovery of the permanently pertinent principles of the creed and culture that dawned in the original Dark Ages. He descried hints of this explanation in various primitive places; but he felt that these diverse avenues of cultural deliverance must converge along a wider concourse, one that the crooked timber of humanity could never make straight by itself. Like J.R.R. Tolkien, Greene believed that the road goes ever on and on, until it joins some larger Way where many paths and errands meet.

Q. Compare G.K. Chesterton, Graham Greene, Christopher Dawson, and David Jones

Or

Q. In 1852, John Henry Newman preached a sermon at the first Provincial Synod of Westminster in which he spoke of the restoration of the Catholic hierarchy in Britain as the coming of a "Second Spring. Discuss

In 1852, John Henry Newman preached a sermon at the first Provincial Synod of Westminster in which he spoke of the restoration of the Catholic hierarchy in Britain as the coming of a "Second Spring... a restoration in the moral world, such as that which yearly takes place in the physical" (Sermons Preached on Various Occasions).

Accompanying the more juridical aspects involved in this budding season of British Catholicism was the fact that a good number of British intellectuals had also turned to Rome, among whom were notables such as Coventry Patmore, Alice Meynell, Oscar Wilde, and, of course, Newman himself. For Newman in particular, the decision for Roman Catholicism meant more than simply his acknowledgment that only Rome had preserved the historical link to the apostolic church and to Jesus himself. Rome alone, he had decided, was the church's only hope for standing strong against 19th-century liberalism's disregard of dogma, authority, and tradition, and its naive belief in inevitable human and historical progress. Ironically, Newman, with his theories of the authority of the laity and his notions of doctrinal development, was often suspect within his new church. However, his conviction that liberalism's path led ultimately to the betrayal of Christianity never wavered.

In this scholarly yet readable book, Schwartz builds on Newman's image of a "Second Spring," naming an early 20th-century movement in British Catholicism a "Third Spring." In this new springtime, what most attracted the "considerable number of intellectuals" who joined the Catholic Church was its strong opposition to modernity, liberalism in doctrine, and secularism. "Thinkers drawn to the church," S. says, "were... almost exclusively those enticed by its own increasingly radical rebuttal of prevalent norms". Christianity's task, they were convinced, was not to reconcile itself with contemporary culture, but to take a countercultural, prophetic stance that preserved the truth of Christian tradition.

The book focuses on four thinkers—all men—who illustrate in a particularly vivid way this early 20th-century, general countercultural pattern of women and men attracted to Catholicism. They are the journalist, poet, and novelist G. K. Chesterton, the novelist Graham Greene, the historian Christopher Dawson, and the poet David Jones. While each is unique, all shared a distaste for what they considered a doctrinally weak Anglicanism, a suspicion of modern relativism, and a love for Catholicism's strong authority and rich tradition.

Chesterton is described as a seeker who found wonder and joy in life, and found these deepened by his Catholic faith, wherein lay true safety and sanity in an age of "Progress, industrialism and imperialism". Despite the fact that he had difficulty with a number of the Church's dogmatic teachings, Greene felt deeply that the Church's greatest strength was its "contrarian ethic". Dawson saw Catholicism as "the sole avatar of faith that had retained its subversive legacy", and Jones was convinced that only Rome's doctrine and authority could effectively rebel "against dehumanizing modern technocracy".

The three who lived into the Second Vatican Council felt betrayed and disillusioned by some aspects of the Church's commitment to aggiornamento, especially regarding liturgical reform. "I thought the Church and I wanted the same thing," a frustrated Greene cried out. However, some rethinking of Vatican II during the pontificate of John Paul II, as well as contemporary movements such as Pentecostalism, S. suggests, might be proving his subjects' conviction to be correct. In any case, he says, their prophetic stance still poses a challenge that is constantly proving relevant in today's rootless world.

Some years ago in America magazine, Avery (now Cardinal) Dulles wrote that Christianity is always in some sense countercultural. Christianity also, however, signifies much more than a prophetic stance against this age. There exists a specifically "Catholic imagination" that embraces the world, its goodness, and its cultures, as sacraments of God's presence in a creation that is nevertheless shot through with imperfection and evil. S. does not totally deny this Catholic imagination to his subjects, but it is clear that his interest in their lives and witness lies elsewhere.

Q. Themes in the novels of Graham Greene

Or

Q. One moral theme in The Tenth Man was the willingness to give up your life for another and the motives for doing so. Discuss.

Moral themes are prevalent in the novel The Tenth Man by Graham Greene. One moral theme in this book was the willingness to give up your life for another and the motives for doing so. People sometimes sacrifice their life for another. Perhaps the author put this in the book because in today's society very few people are willing to give up their life to save another, and if they are willing they usually would do it for the wrong reasons. For example in the book Janvier gave up his life for another but his motive was unclear. He could have done it for his own personal glory because he would have died a rich man what should not be important to you. He could have also done it for his family so they didn't have to live the rest of their life in a struggle to survive. He could have also done it to save Chavel life because he thought it was the right thing to do.

Also in the end of the book Chavel gave up his life so Therese would have no problems with land arguments and because he loved her. In present day life I believe that most people would hesitate to save someone else if they could end up dying or getting seriously injured. For example if someone was going to get hit by a car and another person had a chance to push the other person out of the way but they may injure or kill themselves in the process, I don't think they will try to save them. People today have the attitude that someone else will do it or I am not going to do it because I don't like that person. If people are willing to try and save the person they will do it for the the wrong reason. People today are looking for some way to become the great hero so they can have their picture on the news and everybody will remember who they were. Another reason people would try and save someone else would be because of money or some other form of reward.

There are some people who would do it for what I think are the right reasons. I believe if you do it because you care for some else or for that other persons well-being you are doing it for the right reasons. If you do it because you are trying to get into heaven you are also doing it for the right reason, because after all our goal in life is to go to heaven because we are promised a better life once we get there. I don't know if would try and save some one if I know I would die trying. I am unsure because at the time I would probably not have chance to way the situation and would the consequences of my actions would be. I can not also speak about what I would do in this situation because I was never in one, I presume that instinct would take over and probably do what would be needed to be done to help that person in their time of need.

Another moral value in the book was giving up your

values to save your own live not thinking of others in any way what so ever. People who believe in something, when faced with problem or difficulty take the values of the people imposing the problem on them. I think the author included this issue in the book because In today's world people sell out what ever they believe in just so they can get a little ahead in life. In the book they talk of collaborates who sold out o the Germans and agreed to follow their rules just so they would not be killed. What they didn't think about is the many people who died trying to fight for what they believed in and what the many people who were now forced to live under these rules would have to go through because they were scared and wouldn't stand up for what they believed in.

In today's society, especially in the business world people disregard what they value because they want that better job or that raise or just to get on the bosses good side. This is not excluded to the business world though, many people lie about what they believe just to belong to a group are to impress someone. This is a real problem among children they give up in what they believe in because they friends ridicule or mock them because of that. I am not immune to this problem I have changed some of my values because my friends made fun of me because I believed in what I did Through the years I have done this less and less because I learned to hold fast to what I believe in and not change because I am jeered.

One more moral value in The Tenth Man was not to take advantage of some one who is depressed, hurt, injured, etc. in any way. Alot of people use someone who has just gone through a loss to take advantage of them. Once again the author put this in the book because it is a pre prevalent problem in the world throughout it's history. He also include this issue because it can lead to more serious problems because these people were already hurt and now they are hurt worse. In the book after Therese's mother died she was very upset as any child would be, and Chavel felt an attraction towards here. He was warned by the priest not to take advantage of her. He made the right decision in the book by not mentioning it and taking it to his grave.

In society today many people prey on people who have been hurt or depressed for one reason or another and take advantage of them. These people win these weak people's love and then take them for everything they have. The right thing to do in these situations would be to care for the person who is hurt or down and get them through their problem. Once they are stable you can tell them how you feel towards them or anything else. I have never to my knowledge taken advantage of someone who was in no shape to be told any thing that could make their condition worse then it already was. Deceiving someone else about who you truly are is another moral issue in the book. People deliberately lie about their identity or other information to take advantage of another person and to hide information from that person that they don't want them to find out about.

The author included this in the story to teach that deception is wrong in any way you look at. In the story Chavel pretended that he was Charlot. He did so so that Therese would not find out that he was responsible for her brother' demise. In the end it back fired and caused more problems then it solved. Many people do not tell important information of themselves to other people so it does not cause friction between them or others. One main example of this is when applying for a job you are asked if you were ever arrested. Many people lie and say no so they get the job but lying causes them to not get the job because the employer will find out one way or another.

One moral that was not given right out in the open but could be received indirectly was about war. I think the author was for war if the cause was a fair one as was World War 2. This is still an area of controversy today. In all the wars we have fought since WW2 we have questioned if it was really necessary. I believe that you should not be forced to fight in any war that you do not believe that we should be fighting in as a nation

The book portrayed many morals that society of today needs to learn. If society learns these morals this place will be a very better place to live of everyone and everything.

Q. Write a Passage on the most skillful and complex novels of Graham Greene.

Or

Q. Diemert sees much of the complexity of this novel as stemming from Greene's attempt.Discuss.

In his timely study of Greene's early "entertainments" and their use of the thriller format, Diemert argues convincingly for the seriousness of these works and of The Ministry of Fear, "one of Greene's most skillful and complex novels", in particular. Further, as my first epigraph testifies, Diemert sees much of the complexity of this novel as stemming from Greene's attempt, through his adoption of such a popular narrative form, to repudiate the aesthetic elitism and dubious politics of that generation of high modernist writers that preceded his own.

Indeed, in so situating Greene's early works, Diemert concurs with the standard critical wisdom on British writers of the 1930s and their relationship to the modernists who went before them. 2 Yet it is my contention that Greene's work, and The Ministry of Fear especially, cannot be so neatly disentangled from the project of Anglo-American modernism. Indeed, Greene's sole novel written during the war years 3 remains an essentially moderni st one, in that the Second World War is made comprehensible here by taking its place in that history of repetition that was the touchstone of those modernists whom Orwell saw as "temperamentally hostile to the notion of 'progress"'. That is to say, the war, as Greene figures it, is both understandable and inevitable precisely as it is mandated by a Western history conceived, in modernist terms, as the ceaseless rehearsal of past atrocity. Greene, in The Ministry of Fear's "attempt to find a discourse to make a sense of the world of the blitz" (R. Smith 115), thus extends the modernists' own repudiation of the meliorist historiography of liberal thought, presenting instead a history that inexorably reenacts past rituals of violence.

This bloody repetition, moreover, perpetuates itself, for Greene, through a process of forgetting akin to that which Lyotard decries in my second epigraph. Central to the story of Arthur Rowe is not only the shellshock amnesia that disrupts the narrative but also his persistent forgetting, not, significantly, of the past but of the present real condition of self and others. Greene's novel, in its treatment of Rowe's steady adherence to the adventure-tale ethics learned in childhood and of his resulting susceptibility to pity as a destructive emotion, shows both Rowe and his war-torn world more generally to be repeating their respective pasts in the form of deadly force. While the engine of such dire repetition is thus revealed as a kind of remembering, this memory acts also as a forgetting in Lyotard's sense, a holding for certain of an inherited ethos that is oblivious both to the actual character of the self and to the very selfhood of others.

In this way, Greene's text, in its presentation of the war as r ehearsal, repeats, in its turn, the modernists' antiliberal sense of history, but does so by diagnosing Western history as the necessary, if slaughterous, result of a refusal to grant the other particularity and autonomy, to grant her, in other words, selfhood in liberal terms. Yet before proceeding to examine Greene's explication of the war as an instance of modernist thinking on history, I want first to proffer some defence for my claim that Anglo-American modernism centers on this sense of history as tragic repetition. To be sure, current formulations of modernism tend to paint a rather different picture, with many critics, indeed, reading modernism as nothing other than a retreat from questions of history. 4 Thus Marianne DeKoven sees modernist fiction as deliberately suppressing the historical referent, seeking instead "to save the world through an art purified of history", 5 though, on her account, this suppression is doomed to the happiest of failures, such strategies only serving "to render those historical facts with greater power than direct representation would give". When, moreover, critics do acknowledge how "the problematic of time occupies a central place" in modernist thought (Nicholls 165), they tend to cast this problematic in terms of rupture ra ther than repetition.

Thus, for Paul Fussell, modernist literature adheres to "the image of strict division which dominates the Great War conception of Time Before and Time After". As this claim would suggest, the notion of history thus ascribed to modernism is one not only of discontinuity but of decline as well, and perhaps the most prevalent understanding of modernism in recent scholarship is one that sees it as essentially nostalgic or elegiac, driven, in Frank Lentricchia's words, by a "need to turn back the clock".

Thus many critics agree with Surette that modernism is an articulation of "the antique view of history as a decline from some pure origin". Art Berman, for example, proclaims this elegiac sense of history's course the very sine qua non of Anglo-American modernism: "this decline is modernism's subject: there would be no modernism without it". Likewise, Meisel argues that what he deems the Eliotic assumption of "a lost golden age in the Renaissance" constitutes a "cruci al myth of the modern". Even Levenson, while he insists that Anglo-American modernism was "anti-traditional before it was traditional", nonetheless claims that the very seeds of modernism in Conrad are already moving "toward the undermining of the sovereign individual and toward nostalgia for more traditional, precapitalist values"

Modernism, as depicted in recent scholarship at any rate, is thus a project that, when it deigns to consider history at all, does so in the mode of nostalgic lament, calling for the resuscitation "of values which are explicitly anti-modern" (Nicholls 167). Yet I contend that such an account largely mistranslates what modernism has to say about the nature and value of Western history. If, as Nicholls noted above, the problematic of time is central here, it is so because history, for the modernists, represents not a process of decline but rather a persistent repetition of the past, figured not as some forfeit Golden Age but as the site of senseless violence. The masterworks of high modernism, in other words, convey a dread of the historical present, not as it fails to sustain past grandeur but as it tiresomely reenacts past enormity. Indeed, if we examine two signal texts from 1922, British modernism's annus mirabilis, what we find is not, in Eysteinsson's phrase, "the music played to the imminent decline of Western culture", but rather an anatomy of the history of that culture which identifies it as horribly consistent in its rehearsal of past bloodshed.

Thus despite Batchelor's claim, consonant with so much modernist criticism, that all of Woolf's major novels are written in the elegiac mode, Woolf's modernism, as reflected in the watershed of Jacob's Room at any rate, is obsessed with history, not as a counterpoint to, but as the prime determinant of, a martial present. This sense that the world of the doomed Jacob Flanders is a legacy bequeathed by a still vital cultural past is captured early on, in Woolf's portrait of Cambridge before the Great War: The stroke of the clock even was muffled;...as if generations of learned men heard the last hour go rolling through their ranks and issued it, already smooth and timeworn, with their blessing, for the use of the living.

While the undergraduate Jacob basks in the favour of this gift, pleased to think "himself the inheritor" and fulfillment of this seamless history, it soon becomes clear that this inheritance is not quite the boon he thinks it is. To be sure, this sense of himself as beneficiary of the treasures of a glorious occidental past ironically engenders in him a sense of a ruptured history and a nostalgia for a classical Golden Age: "Ages lapped at their feet like waves for sailing. And surveying all this, looming through the fog, the shades of London, the two young men decided in favour of Greece". Yet Woolf's narrator refuses to let us endorse this lapsarian view of history, or that sense of history as cultural treasure trove from which it springs. If, musing on the press's treatment of Europe's march to war, this narrator must note, "when a child begins to read history one marvels, sorrowfully, to hear him spell out in his new voice the ancient words", it is because present history is figured here a s repetition, and this is itself worthy of lament, not Jacob's celebration. Indeed, the war that finally claims his life must, for Woolf, be seen not as a break in, but as a bloody extension of, Western history as a martial continuum. Thus the war's onset is cast here in terms binding it to those very "glories" of Greece that Jacob saw as incommensurate with a peculiarly modern squalor:

But the red light was on the columns of the Parthenon, and the Greek women who were knitting their stockings and sometimes crying to a child...were as jolly as sand-martins in the heat, quarreling, scolding, suckling babies, until the ships in the Piraeus fired their guns.

Thus the Woolf who, in 1938, would lament that "it seems as if there were no progress in the human race, but only repetition" mounts this same case 16 years earlier, and it is, I suggest, this argument that is central to her literary modernism, as indeed it is integral to that even more formidable literary monument of 1922, Joyce's Ulysses. If Stephen's history lesson in "Nestor" centers, significantly, on the exemplary story of Pyrrhus, of "progress" revealed as bloodiest failure, it is clear that this history, "a tale like any other too often heard", is still very much an operative and oppressive presence: "As it was in the beginning, is now". Indeed, in the "old wisdom" kept alive and transmitted by Mr. Deasy, this persistence of the past is the persistence, too, of violence, as Stephen sees in Deasy's "glorious, pious and immortal memory" visions of "the lodge of Diamond in Armagh the splendid behung with corpses of papishes". Further, the lesson, accordi ng to this custodian of the living past, to be gleaned from its bloody course is one that, in its anti-Semitic fervor, can serve only to reproduce historical violence—thus Stephen's conclusion that "istory... is a nightmare" from which he must strive to awake. While Stephen is hardly reliable as the conscience of Ulysses, he seems, in his sense of history both as continuous and as cruel, to be borne out by the text, for we shall indeed see Mr. Deasy's lesson taken to heart and acted upon by the Citizen in "Cyclops", an attempt at unholy repetition—"By Jesus, I'll crucify him Bloom so I will" which, by means of this chapter's mock-epic recourse to past idioms of heroism, is placed firmly in a still vital occidental tradition. Likewise, that this history persists in the present specifically as nightmare is amply demonstrated by the passion play of "Circe," where history, both personal and cultural, explodes as a sinister phantasmal force still scourging the living.

For these seminal works of British modernism, then,

history is indeed a depressing, and murderous, form of repetition, and.not some squandered estate we must work to reclaim. Yet Quinones, noting the early modernist sense of history as "a kind of repetitive sameness", nonetheless sees modernism as moving, by the 1930s, toward a new embrace of the cultural past, now "humanized and regarded as necessary to the comforts and continuities of civilized life". I contend, however, that that sense of history traced above is reiterated by certain writers of this period, and that modernism, so understood, persists as the primary schema for understanding the Second World War in Greene's Ministry of Fear. To be sure, as Diemert, Sharrock, and others have stressed, Greene does at times take issue with the modernist project as he sees it, and particularly with its Bloomsbury variant.Thus, in his literary criticism, we see him attacking the fiction of Woolf and Forster for a lack of religious dimension that renders their characters mere "cardboard symbols wandering through a world which is paper-thin". Likewise, in a 1938 essay on Dorothy Richardson, Greene suggests that the hyper-subjectivism of Richardson's stream-of-consciousness technique can only make us pine for "the old dictatorship" of plot.

Yet, such barbs notwithstanding,Greene consistently traces for his own work a decidedly modernist pedigree. In a 1949 interview, for example, Greene, when asked to name his own literary staples, mentions not only Conrad, James, and Ford but also such "high" modernists as Eliot and Pound. Such a modernist personal canon is proffered in Ways of Escape, as well, with Greene there declaring Eliot and Herbert Read "the two great figures of my young manhood", and still noting with fondness "a kind phrase from Ezra Pound, and some words of praise from Ford Madox Ford" for It's a Battlefield, published in 1934. This high estimation of modernist writers persists, indee d, even in the posthumously published dream diary, A World of My Own, in which Greene's dream meetings with writers are almost wholly devoted to such figures as Ford, James, and Eliot.

This affinity for much of the modernist movement in

English is, further, matched in Greene by that modernist sense of history as tragic rehearsal outlined above. If the modernists do hold a certain allure for him, it is because they share with him a common conception of, and moral judgment on, Western history. Certainly, Greene himself proclaims his own fascination with history; as he tells us in Ways of Escape, what the 1930s gave him above all was a passion, not for politics or religion but for history, "a desire to be a spectator of history, history in which I found I was concerned myself'. Yet as such a witness to history, Greene, like the modernists generally, has been commonly read as chronicling a history of rupture and decline. Grahame Smith's claim that "Greene's melody is elegiac" is representative of much critical consideration of Greene's treatment of history, and such scholarship thus figures him as fundamentally nostalgic in his outlook.

But if Greene is, as Evans notes, in revol t against "that liberal, optimistic view of the world nurtured by the Enlightenment and brought to fruition in the nineteenth century", his revolt consists, I argue, not in reversing the trajectory of this linear history, so that progress becomes degeneration, but by, in modernist fashion, replacing this line altogether with a sense of history as something both cyclical and terrible. Thus when pressed, in a 1949 interview, to comment on the apparently unprecedented horrors of the present century, Greene dismisses the notion that such violence can be seen as any great departure from past history. Rather, the crises and bloodshed of the first half of the century are, for him, "humanity's normal state. Certain epochs create the illusion of being calmer, but they are rare". The horrors of the present, then, are, in Greene's view, continuous with a past figured in rather grisly terms, a point made again in Ways of Escape, in Greene's reflections on postwar conflicts. Here, present violence is un derstood explicitly as a rehearsal of more ancient barbarity, such that war in Vietnam constitutes "the return of the watchtower and the border castle in Saigon" , and the Kenya of the Mau-Mau uprisings has "gone back to the bamboo tower, the wall of pointed thorns, the stakes slanting in the ditch".

Thus for Greene, as Friedman notes, life is cast "as accretion, endless repetition, rather than as expansion or repletion". 10 In other words, history for him wears the same wearisome face it presented to the modernists who went before him. And this specifically modernist understanding of history is precisely the medium through which the Second World War becomes comprehensible in his work. If, as McEwen argues, Greene understands war generally as continuous with putative "peace," as only "bringing into the open conditions which peacetime disguises", it is also clear that modern war is, in his mind, congruous not only with the prewar condition but also with more ancient history, with indeed the whole cultural heritage of the West.

Thus D. of The Confidential Agent is, in his own participation in a war narrative, presented as existing thereby as a kind of cultural avatar and fulfillment: "Five hundred years of inbreeding had produced him, set him against an exact background, made him at home, a nd at the same time haunted—by the vices of ancestors and the tastes of the past". D., then, has been made for war, precisely insofar as he has been fashioned in the image of a remote cultural past, and that the war he has been so readied to participate in is itself likewise a repetition is underscored by the novel's use of The Song of Roland, its tale of medieval warfare stressing both the present's status as repetition and history's bloody nature. This sense of history, here applied to the Spanish Civil War, is also deployed as the means for coming to terms with that more global conflict that followed. Writing during the London blitz, Greene, in a 1940 essay, marvels at the ease with which the British have accommodated themselves to the war, yet deems this, given his understanding of European history, as perhaps not so marvelous after all: "Violence comes to us more easily because it was so long expected—not only by the political sense but by the moral sense. The world we lived in could not have ende d any other way". Again, the war here is predictable, indeed inescapable, because it is the very culmination of our cultural traditions, the latest conflagration for which Western history, in its insatiable restaging of old conflicts, has served to prepare us, just as D. has been prepared. This view of European history as of a piece with, rather than distinct from or superior to, the present's destructive course is central, too, to Greene's fictional exploration of World War II in The Ministry of Fear. Here, both the carnage of the blitz and the fascism of Greene's fifth columnists are presented, not as in opposition to, but rather as rehearsals of, the more or less remote prewar past. Both the nihilistic Willi Hilfe and the more apparently compassionate Dr. Forester, for example, share more than just their Nazi sympathies, in that these sentiments themselves are revealed, in both, as being tied to the past. Thus Willi and sister Anna seem, to Rowe, to form "a Victorian family group", and Willi speaks always in "antiquated slang," more at home in the last century . Likewise Forester presents to Rowe a face "hawk-like and noble and a little histrionic, like the portrait of a Victorian". Those characters, then, who by their struggles for the Nazi enemy, may be seen as engines of the present war are conspicuous in their being palpably of another, earlier time. So, too, is the destruction they and their allies visit upon England. London bombarded, here, represents not novelty but repetition of an age-old suffering, such that Rowe remarks "the strange, torn landscape where London shops were reduced to a stone ground-plan like those of Pompeii".

If such an echo of past violence would thus liken the war to natural disasters, it is clear elsewhere that the present war must be seen, even more, as a rehearsal of a human perversity of some long historical standing. Thus Rowe, in a book auction, comes upon an antique Roman Catholic missal that serves to underscore the present's implication in a history of violence seemingly as old as history itself: "oddly enough, it was the only thing that spoke of war in the old quiet room. Open it where you would, you came on prayers for deliverance, the angry nations, the unjust, the wicked". In this passage, Greene situates the pr esent war in a very human past, one which, in its most ancient occidental documents, already chronicles repeated war, oppression, and lament.

Yet this is not, to be sure, the way Rowe himself views

the war and its place in history. Rather, his understanding of history is one that accords instead with those critics who take both Greene, and modernism more generally, to write a literature of nostalgia; indeed, many have taken Rowe's elegiac yearning for the pastas proof of Greene's own nostalgic outlook. 1 As we first meet Arthur Rowe, mercy killer and self-styled pariah, we see him drawn to the fete that will embroil him in the novel's thriller plot precisely as it seems to offer access to a personal and national past he deems both edenic and irrevocably lost: "The fete called him like innocence: it was entangled in childhood, with vicarage gardens and girls in white summer frocks". The past for which Rowe, from the very outset, is desperately searching is both the ostensibly innocent age of his own childhood and the utopia of a pastoral British prewar existence.

What is conveyed on this very opening page, then, is that Rowe experiences hist ory, both biographical and cultural, in terms not only of rupture but also of decline. Despite the fact that Greene, even here, undermines such sentiments—the fete band, after all, plays "a faded song of the last war", thus signaling the present conflict as very much in line with the past—Rowe remains, like the Little Duke of the novel's many epigraphs, a quester, and what he seeks is the retrieval of a past he sees as lamentably divorced from the present. Thus he experiences the fete as instructional, as demonstrating for him just this rupture and the consequently dire necessity of his quest: "it was as if Providence had led him to exactly this point to indicate the difference between then and now. These people might have been playing a part in an expensive morality play for his sole benefit"

Rowe certainly takes the moral of this perceived performance very much to heart, clinging throughout the novel to a belief in the past's superiority and thus to an acute longing for its resuscitation. Indeed, as outlined in Book One, his character is that almost of an acolyte before the altar of past history, striving through a private liturgy to keep it alive; thus he ritually reads his two Dickens novels "as people used to read the Bible, over and over again till he could have quoted chapter and verse, not so much because he liked them as because he had read them as a child".

In other respects, too, his wartime home remains a kind of temple to the cult of childhood, with his radio dial producing "a homely effect like a nightlight in a child's nursery", and his "last remaining treasure—a big schoolboy's knife" holding talismanic significance for him. This brand of piety, which we will see again in Rowe's devotion to the heroic virtues of his childhood adventure-tale reading, draws its rigor from Rowe's firm belief that history is a process of decline and fall, a downward-tending line catastrophically broken by war, on the one hand, and his killing of his wife, on the other. Thus as he dreams of his mother who "had died before the first great war", Rowe insists that the enormity of his present could only have been as inaccessible to her understanding as the past world she represents for him is to his grasp: "She could no more have imagined this than that her small son in his brown corduroy knickers...should grow up to be a murderer". If, then, the prewar past of which Rowe dreams here "isn't real life any more", this is tragic because Rowe remains convinced that it was once real and undeniably more human than the present world he suffers.

Yet holding certain, as he does, the chasm that exists between then and now, Rowe, all his devotions notwithstanding, cannot reconstruct Eden; his private theology admits no New Jerusalem. As he is told by the policeman in the above dream, this war-tom world "is home. There isn't anywhere else at all". This being the case, Rowe's quest for the past becomes a longing not so much for memory as for oblivion. That is, if the past he defines in polar opposition to a degraded present is truly inaccessible to all but memory, then what is required, in lieu of its recapture, is forgetting, a forgetting specifically of this postlapsarian present. This wish will find its fulfillment in the amnesia of Book Two, whose title, "The Happy Man," underscores that equation between ignorance and bliss Rowe has made throughout the novel's first 100 pages. From the very outset, Rowe's desire for the past has been tied to a concomitant longing for the obliteration of present historical reality, the fete serving to hei ghten his need "to mislay the events of twenty years".

And in ways Rowe himself never seems to become aware of, the text highlights how this nostalgic longing for the erasure of the present dovetails with the wholesale destruction of modern war itself. Thus Rowe, eager to forget, welcomes the violence of the blitz, as it quite forcibly eradicates that present life he, burdened with dreams of an idyllic past, cannot abide: "After a raid he used to sally out and note with a kind of hope that this restaurant or that shop existed no longer—it was like loosening the bars of a prison cell one by one". In a paradoxical way, then, the war he seeks to escape through forgetting garners his blessing precisely because in violence, in death—and, of course suicide, too, remains a persistent temptation for him —his beloved oblivion beckons.

If Rowe's nostalgia, through its transformation into an ethics of forgetting, is thus presented as implicated in, rather than at odds with, the war from which it ostensibly recoils, this same forgetting is cast by Greene as indeed definitive of the war. The project of forgetting thus not only sanctions massacre but also generates a history at odds with its own nostalgic underpinnings, that is, one not of rupture but of repetition. The war symbolizes—but also, through the bomb that induces Rowe's amnesia, enables—forgetting, and does so by making his life history mirror the war's own status as historical rehearsal. For through his amnesia, Rowe wins not only that oblivion for which he has ached but also something more, namely, a return to that childhood he has idealized. In Forester's "shell-shock clinic," Rowe still retains some memories, but only those that will make of his present condition a reenactment of his own past: "You see, I remember things quite clearly until, say, eighteen". What Rowe, th rough the agency of the war, has forgotten, then, is his adult identity, and this forgetting permits a joyous repetition of his own age of innocence. Thus his regular visits with Dr. Forester are, now, "like visiting a benign headmaster out of school hours", and his stirring affection for Anna Hilfe is experienced as an "adolescent love". Even in his ultimate rebellion against

Forester's strictures, his clandestine foray into the clinic's "sick bay," Rowe, as Greene's narrator underlines for us, is repeating the antics of youth: "He was back in his own childhood, breaking out of dormitory, daring more than he really wanted to dare, proving himself'. In Rowe's forgetting, then, personal history, at least, is shown to follow patterns, not of decline and fall but of continuity and recurrence.

And as the last citation demonstrates, what recurs here is a particular kind of childhood past, one suffused with the conventions of romantic adventure as delineated by boyhood reading. As Diemert has noted, in The Ministry of Fear "the war...is fought not only with bombs and guns but with texts as well". Indeed, Greene is famous for believing in the great power over us of those texts, in particular, which we read as children. For him, only this reading has any lasting influence on the adults we become: "In later life we admire, we are entertained, we may modify some views we already hold, but we are more likely to find in books a confirmation of what is in our minds already".

For Rowe, at least, this is certainly true, and he returns to his past in large part by returning to a system of belief nurtured by childhood reading of such adventure tales as Yonge's The Little Duke. As longingly recalled in Book One, such reading involved for Rowe an education in a stable and optimistic worldview, one in which "our heroes are simple: they are brave, they tell the truth, they are good swordsmen and they are never in the long run really defeated". Indeed, it was as just such a hero that the young Rowe understood himself, a dashing figure "capable of extraordinary heroisms and endurances which would make the girl he loved forget the awkward hands and the spotty chin of adolescence".

If this passage indicates how such aggrandizing self-definition is at odds with, is a kind of forgetting of, the self's actuality, such adventuretale dreams nonetheless became, in his youth, as much an article of faith as his nostalgia would become in later life: "It was like the religious discipline: words however emptily repeated can in time form a habit...until one day to your own surprise you find yourself acting on the belief you thought you didn't believe in". That such an ethos of romantic heroism has indeed persisted in him is underscored by Rowe's actions as the amnesiac Digby. In speculating on the true nature of his forgotten adult identity, Rowe wonders, for instance, whether he became an explorer, a la Burton and Stanley, as he had dreamed of being in childhood. Indeed, his sole complaint about his apparently idyllic existence at the clinic is that it does not afford him the properly heroic narrative he believes should be his. As the fortune-telling Mrs. Bellairs astutely observed at the fete, Rowe "sometimes feels he has not been allowed a proper scope for his gifts. He wants to do great deeds, not dream them all day long".

This same self-estimation and frustration surface even in Rowe's return to the Eden of childhood, as he laments, "there was no satisfaction in shining before assistant Johns....He dreamed wildly between the box hedges". When, finally, he embarks upon his great adventure, his search for the dreaded "sick bay, " it is at least in part because this will satisfy his thirst for adventure, his desire to be the romantic hero of childhood storybooks: "He was afraid of undefined punishments and for that reason he felt his action was heroic and worthy of someone in love". Such attempts at casting himself in the role of the extraordinary, heroic protagonist of adventure tales continue, even after his expulsion from Forester's garden. In his reimmersion in the novel's thriller plot of wartime espionage, Rowe stays true to this same heroic ethos, so "happily drunk with danger and action" that even "the ruins from which he and investigator Prentice emerged were only a heroic back-cloth to his personal adventure".

This last point is significant, for what it highlights is that the rehearsal of childhood Rowe's amnesia permits does not, as O'Prey argues, leave him "detached from the chaos and violence" of the war. In returning, through forgetting, to the past and its notions of heroism, Rowe is repeating not only his own personal history but also the characteristic actions of the war to which he sees his past as opposed. For despite Diemert's claim that the novel "discredits the ethos of the romantic adventure tale by contrasting it with the thriller world of war-ravaged London" , The Ministry of Fear effects its debunking of this ethos precisely as it identifies it with the horrors of war. Rowe's persistent desire to be the hero of children's literature does not, as he thinks, distinguish him from that "History of Contemporary Society" he deems rightly written in the thriller mode.

Rather, his need to be the extraordinary man, living out a life of derring-do, allies him with those very fifth columnists who drive the novel's thriller plot. It finds an echo, for instance, in Poole's solicitous talk of "the sheep" to whom both he and Rowe are, naturally, superior, and this spy's use of the first-person plural here is both telling and astute. Likewise the spy-ring's chief, Willi Hilfe, admits that he, too, is "a romantic", and that "a story of intrigue like Rowe's excites him. It seems to give an opportunity, well, to take a more violent line". No wonder, then, that Rowe himself is convinced, on first meeting the Hilfes, that "these were the allies he needed".

And such an alliance, or affinity, continues throughout the novel, as the amnesiac Rowe's lust for romantic adventure keeps him at the centre of this very contemporary tale of war and espionage. Not only is the clinic in which his wholesale return to this ostensibly dated worldview takes place run by the very spies and traitors who populate the modern thriller world, but also it is his childish need to be the her o in the spotlight that prompts him to withhold from police the telephone number that will lead to the spies and the stolen film. Thus does the hero of his boyish imaginings find himself at home in the war-torn present that itself endorses such a heroic ethos.

Rowe's forgetting does not, then, release him from the present but rather highlights the continuities between his idealized childhood world and the treacherous world of the war. Thus the "Arcady" in which his amnesia lands him in Book Two is revealed to be a myth, the past being, in its vision of valor and heroism, at one with the carnage of the present.

Indeed, it is this shared ethos, and the sense of self and others on which it rests, that Greene proffers as the very principle of a forgetting that constitutes Western history as modernism's nightmarish process of repetition. For in dreaming oneself the noble hero, one does not only, in Greene's view, elide one's own "spotty" imperfections but further justifies actions that deny, and even destroy, the selfhood of other human beings. The deadly force of this heroic self-conception Rowe shares with his Nazi foes, and the present shares with the past, is made clearest in the novel's dissection of Rowe's defining quality, namely, pity. For despite Watts's claim that the morality of Greene's fiction centers on "the value of the charitable action—the altruistic deed motivated by pity", 13 Greene's treatment of this "virtue" puts it at the heart of the psychology of the war and of his explanation of history's repetitive and murderous course. It is, after all, this trait that is the source of Rowe's own status as wife murderer, and thus of his ties to such wartime villains as Willi and Poole. Like these characters, Rowe too is a killer, and what has driven him to emulate their war ethos is nothing other than the quality of mercy—" mercy to his wife or mercy to me," remaining, as Rowe himself notes, unclear.

Pity for his ill wife, his inability to stand her pain, has made him a killer, and the text underscores how this, too, figures as a repetition of, rather than fall from, the past by relating a cognate, if lesser, "murder" from his childhood: "Suddenly he couldn't bear the sight of the wounded rat's pain any more; he picked up a cricket-bat and struck the rat on the head over and over again". Thus, for Greene, this mercy is and was indeed "dangerous pity", for what it sanctions are actions akin even to those of murderer Willi Hilfe, whose suggestive last name signals such kinship between Rowe's "virtue" and the workings of war. Indeed, Greene makes this connection even more explicit in his narrator's gloss on the meaning of the Catholic missal: "It wasn't only evil men who did these things. Courage smashes a cathedral, endurance lets a city starve, pity kills"

But in order to clarify how pity, for Greene, can exemplify the ostensibly pitiless violence of war and the West's war-tom history, we must follow the hints this passage gives us and trace the links between pity and that adventure-tale ethic already seen to be definitive of the prewar past, as much as the World War II present. For despite Rowe's own belief that pity stands in opposition to this ethos as maturity to immaturity, pity counts, as the passage from page 74 quoted above indicates, as one of the cardinal virtues of the hero of the adventure tale. If the heroic faith of the past that Rowe has learned so well centers on such concepts as "sacrifice, courage, virtue", so does their restatement as sources of destruction on the very next page situate Rowe's pity as part of the hero's constitution, and part of the danger he represents for others. Pity may be so embraced by the romantic values of past and present, of war and prewar, because at its heart, for Greene, lies the conviction he deems d efinitive of heroic self-conception, namely, that one is extraordinary and uniquely equipped to serve more, presumably, ordinary others.

If Rowe's dreams of himself as hero, both in adolescence and amnesiac adulthood, focus, as we have seen, on service to, trials endured for, a beloved other, so, too, is pity revealed as validating action in the best interests of others, even to the point of their annihilation. Thus the amnesiac Rowe, caught up in adventure-filled plans for his illicit trip to the "sick bay," is appalled by the pacifism he reads in Forester's copy of Tolstoy's What I Believe. Such a worldview jars with Rowe's heroic persona and its need for Willi's "more violent line," but the way he articulates this to himself stresses the connections between the proper virtues of the hero and pity's own capacity to sanction any action: "why does he write as if the worst thing we can do to our fellow-man is to kill him? Everybody has to die and everybody fears death, but when we kill a man we save him from h is fear".

This line of reasoning thus defends the murder of others as, indeed, for their own good, and thus consonant with heroism. So long as we act heroically, so long that is, as we act in the interests of another, any act, for Rowe, may be justified: "there was the point—not to kill for one's own sake. But for the sake of people you loved,... it was right to risk damnation". Such thinking, that of the "immature," romantic Rowe, seems, then, very much in accord with that of the "mature," pitying

Rowe who would serve his wife the poisoned milk, for her own good, to end her pain, even though "he could never know whether her fear of his act had been worse than the pain". Though he cannot, as he himself admits, ever know whether she might well have preferred "any sort of life to death", he has been able, with pity and romantic heroism both to guide him, to decide what her preference should be, and act on her behalf, to the point even of her own destruction.

As the threads of historical continuity, then, both heroism and pity serve to make of history a continuum of violence, through a shared paternalism that underwrites any action at all that can be argued to serve or to spare another. Such paternalism is also, for Greene, the very pith of the forgetting that is the very essence of the war and of the history of which it constitutes an emblematic part. As the above passages make clear, what it entails is the forgetting or repression of the other, of her actual preferences, of her capacity to decide and act upon her own "best interests." Likewise are the actual interests and weaknesses of the heroic/pitying self elided and in their place erected a form of heroic infallibility, a certain knowledge of what is best for the other that can cloud both what the other might desire and what the heroic agent might truly be seeking through such "other-centered" action—hence Rowe's post facto fears that he might well have acted to end his own pain, not his wife's. This is, then, forgetting in Lyotard's mode, a forgetting of the other as agent that substitutes instead a certain belief in the rightness of one's own actions, as well as of one's right to undertake them.

And it is such forgetting that, in its erasure of the other as a self capable of self-determination and its dictation of certain goods for all, Greene sees at the root of the twentieth-century's own genocidal reenactment of the historical nightmare. Thus, as McEwen notes, for Greene "it is dreadful to be sure of oneself", for what such certainty, in its heroic or pitying justifications, permits is an imposition of will, a quashing of the other, very much at home with the violence of war: Do you know what happens...when you wish the world to be neat and orderly and precise, a closed, untroubled place? You try to make it that way. And when people don't respond (and they don't), you end up with Belsen.

Certainly, The Ministry of Fear attempts to provide plenty of evidence that this is so. Not only does Rowe's pity drive him to murder, just as his desire for adventure implicates him in the murderous plot of Hilfe and his confederates, but also such certainty as to one's right to decide for others is the common foundation for what will become the novel's "massacre on an Elizabethan scale". Like Rowe, the Nazi spy Poole also believes that "even murder can sometimes be excused," a truth he relates, tellingly, with "an intolerable confidence," as he appeals to Rowe as another man of intelligence, a cut above the sheep who may or may not have to be excusably murdered. So, too, the idealist Dr. Forester, a man of sufficient pity that he does "not approve...of taking animal life", is nonetheless in league with Poole, Hilfe, and the others, and is "quite unmoved by the story of the Nazi elimination of old people and incurables". Indeed, he will be party to the murder of muddled Major Stone, a crime he defends in advance as "the greatest mercy we can ask for him". Forester's own death is, in apt and illuminating fashion, brought about for his own good, with "respectable, hero-worshipping Johns" killing his idol, the fulfillment of his own romantic dreams of heroism, to protect him he was saving him from the interminable proceedings of the law courts, from the crudities of prosecuting counsel, the unfathomable ignorances of the judge, and the indignity of depending on the shallow opinion of twelve men picked at random.

Even Anna Hilfe, with whom a loving Rowe ends up in the novel's conclusion, is, as herself part of her brother's ring, presented as a character of suspect, even oppressive, pity. Thus, visiting an amnesiac Rowe freed from the memory of his wife's murder, Anna refuses to tell him the truth and admits she prefers him so protected from the truth, even if it consigns him to Forester's clinic-cum-prison: "This is how you should be. This is how I like you".

If in all these characters the alchemy of pity and self-certainty yields a precipitate of murder and confinement, Willi

Hilfe reveals the violence of such an imposition of will shorn even of pity's respectability. While the above instances serve to demonstrate, in Webster's words, how suffering in Greene's fiction "is made by idealists who fancy themselves God", Willi, who makes no pretense to ideals of any sort, still starkly illustrates the essence of their idealism and the ends to which it tends. For as Silverstein argues, Willi's nihilism, like Nazism itself, "only carries Rowe's sense of pity to its logical and terrifying extreme". While Anna posits her brother's service to the Nazis as the antithesis of Rowe's pity—"they can bear pain—other people's pain—endlessly" —the narrative rather reveals Willi's mercilessness to be the obverse, not the inverse, of Rowe's quality of mercy.

We have, for example, already seen how Willi's own brand of romanticism, and his surn ame, work to establish a tie between the pitying Rowe and the amoral spy. Such connections are made here because Willi's amorality involves, albeit in a more nihilistic mode, the same kind of erasure of others as does the apparent compassion shared by Rowe, Anna, and Johns. If Willi, for Greene, embodies "the grace and attraction of nihilism—of not caring for anything", what this involves is the use of other people as pawns to further his own ends, a manipulation that can easily lead, as in his attempted murder of Rowe and Anna at the end of Book One, to their destruction. This is, indeed, a matter of course for Willi, simply how the game is played, such that he is offended and amused by Rowe's throwing the attempted murder in his face: "He seemed to accuse them of a lack of humour; it was not the kind of thing they ought to have taken to heart".

What is important, however, is that Willi's own brand of indifferent disregard for the lives of others sheds light on that ethics of care shared by the novel's other characters. They, too, as we have seen, are ready to judge for, manipulate, and kill other people to serve what they take to be the right, and thus the novel argues that their "caring" tends, by its forgetfulness of others, to the same deadly presumption that is the essence of Nazism and the war; in this sense, they are indeed Nazi sympathizers.

Chapter 15

Critical Analysis

Graham Greene on The Power and the Glory

Now, of course, when I reread The Lawless Roads, I can easily detect many of the characters in The Power and the Glory. The old Scotsman, Dr. Roberto Fitzpatrick, whom I met in Villahermosa, with his cherished scorpion in a little glass bottle, was the kind of treasure trove that falls to the lucky traveller. In recounting the story of his own life he told me of the kindly disreputable Padre Rey of Panama with his wife and daughter and the mice - not a scorpion - which he kept in a glass lamp.

So it was that the doctor put me on the track of Father Jose in my novel... "I asked about the priest in Chiapas who had fled. 'Oh,' he said, 'he was just what we call a whisky priest.' He had taken one of his sons to be baptized, but the priest was drunk and would insist on naming the child Brigitta. 'He was little loss, poor man.'"

But long before the drunken priest another character had come on board my awful boat in Frontera,where my story was to open - the dentist I called Mr. Tench, who made his living with gold fillings even in that abandoned little port...His character needed no "touching up."

The novel draws parallels with T.S. Elliot's poem "The Hollow Men". The hollow men wander in a barren landscape, trying to remember the line after "For Thine is the Kingdom" in the Lord's Prayer. The phrase happens to be "the Power and the Glory".

He was as complete in The Lawless Roads as he was in

The Power and the Glory, and as I read on I encounter more and more characters whom I have forgotten, who beckon to me from the pages and say ironically, "And did you really believe you had invented me?"

Here is the amiable corrupt Chief of Police in Villahermosa,and in the village of Yajalon I encountered "a mestizo with curly sideburns and two yellow fangs at either end of his mouth.

He had an awful hilarity and an inane laugh which showed the empty gums. He wore a white tennis shirt open at the front and he scratched himself underneath it." After a week of his company I would find it impossible to abandon him forever, and so he became the Judas of my story. And the Lehrs-the kindly Lutheran couple - they didn't belong to my imagination, for here they are giving shelter to a tired traveller in the same fashion as they did to the whisky priest.

Of invented characters how very few seem to remain apart from the two protagonists, the priest and the Lieutenant of Police; when I came to write I was handing out alternative destinies to real people whom I had encountered on my journey. The Power and the Glory was published in 1940 and won the Hawthornden Prize.

The Vatican did not condemn it until 1953, leading Evelyn Waugh to advise Greene that "they have taken fourteen years to write their first letter.

You should take fourteen years to answer it." Greene did not directly refuse the Church's demands for revisions but rather replied that the copyright was in his publishers' hands. The matter was dropped.

I think The Power and the Glory is the only novel I have written to a these: in The Heart of the Matter Wilson sat on a balcony in Freetown watching Scobie pass by in the street long before I was aware of Scobie's problem - his corruption by pity.

But I had always, even when I was a schoolboy, listened with impatience to the scandalous stories of tourists concerning the priests they had encountered in remote Latin villages (this priest had a mistress, another was constantly drunk), for I had been adequately taught in my Protestant history books what

Catholics believed; I could distinguish even then between the man and his office.Now, many years later, as a Catholic in Mexico, I read and listened to stories of corruption which were said to have justified the persecution of the Church under Calles and under his successor and rival Cardenas, but I had also observed for myself how courage and the sense of responsibility had revived with persecution- I had seen the devotion of peasants praying in the priestless churches and I had attended Masses in upper rooms where the sanctus bell could not sound for fear of the police.

I had not found the idealism or integrity of the lieutenant of The Power and the Glory among the police and pisteleros I had actually encountered - I had to invent him as a counter to the failed priest: the idealistic police officer who stifled life from the best possible motives: the drunken priest who continued to pass life on.

Critics on Graham Greene

Mr. Greene is a story-teller of genius. Born in another age, he would still be spinning yarns...His technical mastery has never been better manifested than in his statement of the scene the sweat and infection, the ill-built town which is beautiful for a few minutes at sundown, the brothel where all men are equal, the vultures...the snobbery of the second-class public schools, the law which all can evade, the ever-present haunting underworld of gossip, spying, bribery, violence and betrayal...the affinity to the film is everywhere apparent.

It is the camera's eye which moves from the hotel balcony to the street below, picks out the policeman, follows him to his office, moves about the room from the handcuffs on the wall to the broken rosary in the drawer, recording significant detail. It is the modern way of telling a story...

Evelyn Waugh

Graham Greene was in a class by himself...He will be read and remembered as the ultimate twentieth-century chronicler of consciousness and anxiety.

William Golding

Greene appears to share the idea, which has been floating around ever since Baudelaire, that there is something rather distingué in being damned; Hell is a sort of high-class nightclub, entry to which is reserved for Catholics only.

George Orwell

Catholicism as a public system of laws and dogmas is far from being an adequate key to Greene's fiction.

There is a good deal of evidence, internal and external, that in Greene's fiction Catholicism is not a body of belief requiring exposition and demanding categorical assent or dissent, but a system of concepts, a source of situations, and a reservoir of symbols with which he can order and dramatize certain intuitions about the nature of human experience-intuitions which were gained prior to and independently of his formal adoption of the Catholic faith. Regarded in this light, Greene's Catholicism may be seen not as a crippling burden on his artistic freedom, but as a positive artistic asset.

David Lodge

Modernism's Shell-Shocked History: Amnesia, Repetition, and the War in Graham Greene's The Ministry of Fear

To fight against forgetting means to fight to remember that one forgets as soon as one believes, draws conclusions, and holds for certain. In his timely study of Greene's early "entertainments" and their use of the thriller format, Diemert argues convincingly for the seriousness of these works and of The Ministry of Fear, "one of Greene's most skillful and complex novels", in particular. Further, as my first epigraph testifies, Diemert sees much of the complexity of this novel as stemming from Greene's attempt, through his adoption of such a popular narrative form, to repudiate the aesthetic elitism and dubious politics of that generation of high modernist writers that preceded his own.

Indeed, in so situating Greene's early works, Diemert concurs with the standard critical wisdom on British writers of the 1930s and their relationship to the modernists who went before them. Yet it is my contention that Greene's work, and

The Ministry of Fear especially, cannot be so neatly disentangled from the project of Anglo-American modernism. Indeed, Greene's sole novel written during the war years remains an essentially moderni st one, in that the Second World War is made comprehensible here by taking its place in that history of repetition that was the touchstone of those modernists whom Orwell saw as "temperamentally hostile to the notion of 'progress"'. That is to say, the war, as Greene figures it, is both understandable and inevitable precisely as it is mandated by a Western history conceived, in modernist terms, as the ceaseless rehearsal of past atrocity. Greene, in The Ministry of Fear's "attempt to find a discourse to make a sense of the world of the blitz", thus extends the modernists' own repudiation of the meliorist historio-graphy of liberal thought, presenting instead a history that inexorably reenacts past rituals of violence.

This bloody repetition, moreover, perpetuates itself, for Greene, through a process of forgetting akin to that which Lyotard decries in my second epigraph. Central to the story of Arthur Rowe is not only the shellshock amnesia that disrupts the narrative but also his persistent forgetting, not, significantly, of the past but of the present real condition of self and others. Greene's novel, in its treatment of Rowe's steady adherence to the adventure-tale ethics learned in childhood and of his resulting susceptibility to pity as a destructive emotion, shows both Rowe and his war-torn world more generally to be repeating their respective pasts in the form of deadly force. While the engine of such dire repetition is thus revealed as a kind of remembering, this memory acts also as a forgetting in Lyotard's sense, a holding for certain of an inherited ethos that is oblivious both to the actual character of the self and to the very selfhood of others.

In this way, Greene's text, in its presentation of the war as r ehearsal, repeats, in its turn, the modernists' antiliberal sense of history, but does so by diagnosing Western history as the necessary, if slaughterous, result of a refusal to grant the other particularity and autonomy, to grant her, in other words, selfhood in liberal terms.

Yet before proceeding to examine Greene's explication of the war as an instance of modernist thinking on history, I want first to proffer some defence for my claim that Anglo-American modernism centers on this sense of history as tragic repetition. To be sure, current formulations of modernism tend to paint a rather different picture, with many critics, indeed, reading modernism as nothing other than a retreat from questions of history. Thus Marianne DeKoven sees modernist fiction as deliberately suppressing the historical referent, seeking instead "to save the world through an art purified of history", though, on her account, this suppression is doomed to the happiest of failures, such strategies only serving "to render those historical facts with greater power than direct represen-tation would give".

When, moreover, critics do acknowledge how "the problematic of time occupies a central place" in modernist thought, they tend to cast this problematic in terms of rupture ra ther than repetition.

Thus, for Paul Fussell, modernist literature adheres to "the image of strict division which dominates the Great War conception of Time Before and Time After". As this claim would suggest, the notion of history thus ascribed to modernism is one not only of discontinuity but of decline as well, and perhaps the most prevalent understanding of modernism in recent scholarship is one that sees it as essentially nostalgic or elegiac, driven, in Frank Lentricchia's words, by a "need to turn back the clock". Thus many critics agree with Surette that modernism is an articulation of "the antique view of history as a decline from some pure origin".

Art Berman, for example, proclaims this elegiac sense of history's course the very sine qua non of Anglo-American modernism: "this decline is modernism's subject: there would be no modernism without it". Likewise, Meisel argues that what he deems the Eliotic assumption of "a lost golden age in the Renaissance" constitutes a "cruci al myth of the modern". Even Levenson, while he insists that Anglo-American modernism was "anti-traditional before it was traditional", nonetheless claims that the very seeds of modernism in Conrad are already moving "toward the undermining of the sovereign individual and toward nostalgia for more traditional, precapitalist values"

Modernism, as depicted in recent scholarship at any rate, is thus a project that, when it deigns to consider history at all, does so in the mode of nostalgic lament, calling for the resuscitation "of values which are explicitly anti-modern" (Nicholls 167). Yet I contend that such an account largely mistranslates what modernism has to say about the nature and value of Western history. If, as Nicholls noted above, the problematic of time is central here, it is so because history, for the modernists, represents not a process of decline but rather a persistent repetition of the past, figured not as some forfeit Golden Age but as the site of senseless violence. The masterworks of high modernism, in other words, convey a dread of the historical present, not as it fails to sustain past grandeur but as it tiresomely reenacts past enormity. Indeed, if we examine two signal texts from 1922, British modernism's annus mirabilis, what we find is not, in Eysteinsson's phrase, "the music played to the imminent decline of Western culture", but rather an anatomy of the history of that culture which identifies it as horribly consistent in its rehearsal of past bloodshed.

Thus despite Batchelor's claim, consonant with so much modernist criticism, that all of Woolf's major novels are written in the elegiac mode, Woolf's modernism, as reflected in the watershed of Jacob's Room at any rate, is obsessed with history, not as a counterpoint to, but as the prime determinant of, a martial present. This sense that the world of the doomed Jacob Flanders is a legacy bequeathed by a still vital cultural past is captured early on, in Woolf's portrait of Cambridge before the Great War: The stroke of the clock even was muffled;...as if generations of learned men heard the last hour go rolling through their ranks and issued it, already smooth and timeworn, with their blessing, for the use of the living.

While the undergraduate Jacob basks in the favour of this gift, pleased to think "himself the inheritor" and fulfillment of this seamless history, it soon becomes clear that this inheritance is not quite the boon he thinks it is. To be sure, this sense of himself as beneficiary of the treasures of a glorious occidental past ironically engenders in him a sense of a ruptured history and a nostalgia for a classical Golden Age: "Ages lapped at their feet like waves for sailing. And surveying all this, looming through the fog, the shades of London, the two young men decided in favour of Greece".

Yet Woolf's narrator refuses to let us endorse this lapsarian view of history, or that sense of history as cultural treasure trove from which it springs. If, musing on the press's treatment of Europe's march to war, this narrator must note, "when a child begins to read history one marvels, sorrowfully, to hear him spell out in his new voice the ancient words", it is because present history is figured here a s repetition, and this is itself worthy of lament, not Jacob's celebration. Indeed, the war that finally claims his life must, for Woolf, be seen not as a break in, but as a bloody extension of, Western history as a martial continuum. Thus the war's onset is cast here in terms binding it to those very "glories" of Greece that Jacob saw as incommensurate with a peculiarly modern squalor:

> But the red light was on the columns of the Parthenon, and the Greek women who were knitting their stockings and sometimes crying to a child...were as jolly as sand-martins in the heat, quarreling, scolding, suckling babies, until the ships in the Piraeus fired their guns.

Thus the Woolf who, in 1938, would lament that "it seems as if there were no progress in the human race, but only repetition" mounts this same case 16 years earlier, and it is, I suggest, this argument that is central to her literary modernism, as indeed it is integral to that even more formidable literary monument of 1922, Joyce's Ulysses. If Stephen's history lesson in "Nestor" centers, significantly, on the exemplary story of Pyrrhus, of "progress" revealed as bloodiest failure, it is clear that this history, "a tale like any other too often heard", is still very much an operative and oppressive presence: "As it was in the beginning, is now". Indeed, in the "old wisdom" kept alive and transmitted by Mr. Deasy, this persistence of the past is the persistence, too, of violence, as

Stephen sees in Deasy's "glorious, pious and immortal memory" visions of "the lodge of Diamond in Armagh the splendid behung with corpses of papishes". Further, the lesson, accordi ng to this custodian of the living past, to be gleaned from its bloody course is one that, in its anti-Semitic fervor, can serve only to reproduce historical violence—thus Stephen's conclusion that "history... is a nightmare" from which he must strive to awake.

While Stephen is hardly reliable as the conscience of Ulysses, he seems, in his sense of history both as continuous and as cruel, to be borne out by the text, for we shall indeed see Mr. Deasy's lesson taken to heart and acted upon by the Citizen in "Cyclops", an attempt at unholy repetition—"By Jesus, I'll crucify him Bloom so I will" —which, by means of this chapter's mock-epic recourse to past idioms of heroism, is placed firmly in a still vital occidental tradition. Likewise, that this history persists in the present specifically as nightmare is amply demonstrated by the passion play of "Circe," where history, both personal and cultural, explodes as a sinister phantasmal force still scourging the living.

For these seminal works of British modernism, then, history is indeed a depressing, and murderous, form of repetition, and not some squandered estate we must work to reclaim. Yet Quinones, noting the early modernist sense of history as "a kind of repetitive sameness", nonetheless sees modernism as moving, by the 1930s, toward a new embrace of the cultural past, now "humanized and regarded as necessary to the comforts and continuities of civilized life".

I contend, however, that that sense of history traced above is reiterated by certain writers of this period, and that modernism, so understood, persists as the primary schema for understanding the Second World War in Greene's Ministry of Fear. To be sure, as Diemert, Sharrock, and others have stressed, Greene does at times take issue with the modernist project as he sees it, and particularly with its Bloomsbury variant. 6 Thus, in his literary criticism, we see him attacking the fiction of Woolf and Forster for a lack of religious dimension that renders their characters mere "cardboard symbols wandering through a world which is paper-thin". Likewise, in a 1938 essay on Dorothy Richardson, Greene suggests that the hyper-subjectivism of Richardson's stream-of-consciousness technique can only make us pine for "the old dictatorship" of plot. Yet, such barbs notwithstanding, Greene consistently traces for his own work a decidedly modernist pedigree. In a 1949 interview, for example, Greene, when asked to name his own literary staples, mentions not only Conrad, James, and Ford but also such "high" modernists as Eliot and Pound.

Such a modernist personal canon is proffered in Ways of Escape, as well, with Greene there declaring Eliot and Herbert Read "the two great figures of my young manhood", and still noting with fondness "a kind phrase from Ezra Pound, and some words of praise from Ford Madox Ford" for It's a Battlefield, published in 1934. This high estimation of modernist writers persists, indee d, even in the posthumously published dream diary, A World of My Own, in which Greene's dream meetings with writers are almost wholly devoted to such figures as Ford, James, and Eliot (8-10).

This affinity for much of the modernist movement in English is, further, matched in Greene by that modernist sense of history as tragic rehearsal outlined above. If the modernists do hold a certain allure for him, it is because they share with him a common conception of, and moral judgment on, Western history. Certainly, Greene himself proclaims his own fascination with history; as he tells us in Ways of Escape, what the 1930s gave him above all was a passion, not for politics or religion but for history, "a desire to be a spectator of history, history in which I found I was concerned myself'. Yet as such a witness to history, Greene, like the modernists generally, has been commonly read as chronicling a history of rupture and decline. Grahame Smith's claim that "Greene's melody is elegiac" is representative of much critical consideration of Greene's treatment of history and such scholarship thus figures him as fundamentally nostalgic in his outlook. But if Greene is, as Evans notes, in revol t against "that liberal, optimistic view of the world nurtured by the Enlightenment and brought to fruition in the nineteenth century", his revolt consists, I argue, not in reversing the trajectory of this linear history, so that progress becomes degeneration, but by, in modernist fashion, replacing this line altogether with a sense of history as something both cyclical and terrible.

Thus when pressed, in a 1949 interview, to comment on the apparently unprecedented horrors of the present century, Greene dismisses the notion that such violence can be seen as any great departure from past history. Rather, the crises and bloodshed of the first half of the century are, for him, "humanity's normal state. Certain epochs create the illusion of being calmer, but they are rare".

The horrors of the present, then, are, in Greene's view, continuous with a past figured in rather grisly terms, a point made again in Ways of Escape, in Greene's reflections on postwar conflicts. Here, present violence is un derstood explicitly as a rehearsal of more ancient barbarity, such that war in Vietnam constitutes "the return of the watchtower and the border castle in Saigon" , and the Kenya of the Mau-Mau uprisings has "gone back to the bamboo tower, the wall of pointed thorns, the stakes slanting in the ditch". Thus for Greene, as Friedman notes, life is cast "as accretion, endless repetition, rather than as expansion or repletion". 10 In other words, history for him wears the same wearisome face it presented to the modernists who went before him. And this specifically modernist understanding of history is precisely the medium through which the Second World War becomes comprehensible in his work.

If, as McEwen argues, Greene understands war generally as continuous with putative "peace," as only "bringing into the open conditions which peacetime disguises", it is also clear that modern war is, in his mind, congruous not only with the prewar condition but also with more ancient history, with indeed the whole cultural heritage of the West. Thus D. of The Confidential Agent is, in his own participation in a war narrative, presented as existing thereby as a kind of cultural avatar and fulfillment: "Five hundred years of inbreeding had produced him, set him against an exact background, made him at home, a nd at the same time haunted—by the vices of ancestors and the tastes of the past". D., then, has been made for war, precisely insofar as he has been fashioned in the image of a remote cultural past, and that the war he has been so readied to participate in is itself likewise a repetition is underscored by the novel's use of The Song of Roland, its tale of medieval warfare stressing both the present's status as repetition and history's bloody nature.

This sense of history, here applied to the Spanish Civil War, is also deployed as the means for coming to terms with that more global conflict that followed. Writing during the London blitz, Greene, in a 1940 essay, marvels at the ease with which the British have accommodated themselves to the war, yet deems this, given his understanding of European history, as perhaps not so marvelous after all: "Violence comes to us more easily because it was so long expected—not only by the political sense but by the moral sense. The world we lived in could not have ende d any other way". Again, the war here is predictable, indeed inescapable, because it is the very culmination of our cultural traditions, the latest conflagration for which Western history, in its insatiable restaging of old conflicts, has served to prepare us, just as D. has been prepared.

This view of European history as of a piece with, rather than distinct from or superior to, the present's destructive course is central, too, to Greene's fictional exploration of World War II in The Ministry of Fear. Here, both the carnage of the blitz and the fascism of Greene's fifth columnists are presented, not as in opposition to, but rather as rehearsals of, the more or less remote prewar past. Both the nihilistic Willi Hilfe and the more apparently compassionate Dr. Forester, for example, share more than just their Nazi sympathies, in that these sentiments themselves are revealed, in both, as being tied to the past. Thus Willi and sister Anna seem, to Rowe, to form "a Victorian family group", and Willi speaks always in "antiquated slang," more at home in the last century . Likewise Forester presents to Rowe a face "hawk-like and noble and a little histrionic, like the portrait of a Victorian". Those characters, then, who by their struggles for the Nazi enemy, may be seen as engines of the present war are conspicuous in their being palpably of another, earlier time. So, too, is the destruction they and their allies visit upon England. London bombarded, here, represents not novelty but repetition of an age-old suffering, such that Rowe remarks "the strange, torn landscape where London shops were reduced to a stone ground-plan like those of Pompeii".

If such an echo of past violence would thus liken the war to natural disasters, it is clear elsewhere that the present war must be seen, even more, as a rehearsal of a human perversity of some long historical standing. Thus Rowe, in a book auction, comes upon an antique Roman Catholic missal that serves to underscore the present's implication in a history of violence seemingly as old as history itself: "oddly enough, it was the only thing that spoke of war in the old quiet room. Open it where you would, you came on prayers for deliverance, the angry nations, the unjust, the wicked". In this passage, Greene situates the pr esent war in a very human past, one which, in its most ancient occidental documents, already chronicles repeated war, oppression, and lament.

Yet this is not, to be sure, the way Rowe himself views the war and its place in history. Rather, his understanding of history is one that accords instead with those critics who take both Greene, and modernism more generally, to write a literature of nostalgia; indeed, many have taken Rowe's elegiac yearning for the pastas proof of Greene's own nostalgic outlook. 1 As we first meet Arthur Rowe, mercy killer and self-styled pariah, we see him drawn to the fete that will embroil him in the novel's thriller plot precisely as it seems to offer access to a personal and national past he deems both edenic and irrevocably lost: "The fete called him like innocence: it was entangled in childhood, with vicarage gardens and girls in white summer frocks".

The past for which Rowe, from the very outset, is desperately searching is both the ostensibly innocent age of his own childhood and the utopia of a pastoral British prewar existence. What is conveyed on this very opening page, then, is that Rowe experiences hist ory, both biographical and cultural, in terms not only of rupture but also of decline. Despite the fact that Greene, even here, undermines such sentiments—the fete band, after all, plays "a faded song of the last war", thus signaling the present conflict as very much in line with the past—Rowe remains, like the Little Duke of the novel's many epigraphs, a quester, and what he seeks is the retrieval of a past he sees as lamentably divorced from the present. Thus he experiences the fete as instructional, as demonstrating for him just this rupture and the consequently dire necessity of his quest: "it was as if Providence had led him to exactly this point to indicate the difference between then and now. These people might have been playing a part in an expensive morality play for his sole benefit"

Rowe certainly takes the moral of this perceived performance very much to heart, clinging throughout the novel to a belief in the past's superiority and thus to an acute longing for its resuscitation. Indeed, as outlined in Book One, his character is that almost of an acolyte before the altar of past history, striving through a private liturgy to keep it alive; thus he ritually reads his two Dickens novels "as people used to read the Bible, over and over again till he could have quoted chapter and verse, not so much because he liked them as because he had read them as a child". In other respects, too, his wartime home remains a kind of temple to the cult of childhood, with his radio dial producing "a homely effect like a nightlight in a child's nursery", and his "last remaining treasure—a big schoolboy's knife" holding talismanic significance for him.

This brand of piety, which we will see again in Rowe's devotion to the heroic virtues of his childhood adventure-tale reading, draws its rigor from Rowe's firm belief that history is a process of decline and fall, a downward-tending line catastrophically broken by war, on the one hand, and his killing of his wife, on the other. Thus as he dreams of his mother who "had died before the first great war", Rowe insists that the enormity of his present could only have been as inaccessible to her understanding as the past world she represents for him is to his grasp: "She could no more have imagined this than that her small son in his brown corduroy knickers...should grow up to be a murderer". If, then, the prewar past of which Rowe dreams here "isn't real life any more", this is tragic because Rowe remains convinced that it was once real and undeniably more human than the present world he suffers.

Yet holding certain, as he does, the chasm that exists between then and now, Rowe, all his devotions notwithstanding, cannot reconstruct Eden; his private theology admits no New Jerusalem. As he is told by the policeman in the above dream, this war-tom world "is home. There isn't anywhere else at all". This being the case, Rowe's quest for the past becomes a longing not so much for memory as for oblivion. That is, if the past he defines in polar opposition to a degraded present is truly inaccessible to all but memory, then what is required, in lieu of its recapture, is forgetting, a forgetting specifically of this postlapsarian present. This wish will find its fulfillment in the amnesia of Book Two, whose title, "The Happy Man," underscores that equation between ignorance and bliss Rowe has made throughout the novel's first 100 pages.

From the very outset, Rowe's desire for the past has been tied to a concomitant longing for the obliteration of present historical reality, the fete serving to hei ghten his need "to mislay the events of twenty years". And in ways Rowe himself never seems to become aware of, the text highlights how this nostalgic longing for the erasure of the present dovetails with the wholesale destruction of modern war itself.

Thus Rowe, eager to forget, welcomes the violence of the blitz, as it quite forcibly eradicates that present life he, burdened with dreams of an idyllic past, cannot abide: "After a raid he used to sally out and note with a kind of hope that this restaurant or that shop existed no longer—it was like loosening the bars of a prison cell one by one". In a paradoxical way, then, the war he seeks to escape through forgetting garners his blessing precisely because in violence, in death—and, of course suicide, too, remains a persistent temptation for him —his beloved oblivion beckons.

If Rowe's nostalgia, through its transformation into an ethics of forgetting, is thus presented as implicated in, rather than at odds with, the war from which it ostensibly recoils, this same forgetting is cast by Greene as indeed definitive of the war. The project of forgetting thus not only sanctions massacre but also generates a history at odds with its own nostalgic underpinnings, that is, one not of rupture but of repetition. The war symbolizes—but also, through the bomb that induces Rowe's amnesia, enables—forgetting, and does so by making his life history mirror the war's own status as historical rehearsal. For through his amnesia, Rowe wins not only that oblivion for which he has ached but also something more, namely, a return to that childhood he has idealized.

In Forester's "shell-shock clinic," Rowe still retains some memories, but only those that will make of his present condition a reenactment of his own past: "You see, I remember things quite clearly until, say, eighteen". What Rowe, th rough the agency of the war, has forgotten, then, is his adult identity, and this forgetting permits a joyous repetition of his own age of innocence. Thus his regular visits with Dr. Forester are, now, "like visiting a benign headmaster out of school hours", and his stirring affection for Anna Hilfe is experienced as an "adolescent love". Even in his ultimate rebellion against Forester's strictures, his clandestine foray into the clinic's "sick bay," Rowe, as Greene's narrator underlines for us, is repeating the antics of youth: "He was back in his own childhood, breaking out of dormitory, daring more than he really wanted to dare, proving himself'. In Rowe's forgetting, then, personal history, at least, is shown to follow patterns, not of decline and fall but of continuity and recurrence.

And as the last citation demonstrates, what recurs here is a particular kind of childhood past, one suffused with the conventions of romantic adventure as delineated by boyhood reading. As Diemert has noted, in The Ministry of Fear "the war...is fought not only with bombs and guns but with texts as well". Indeed, Greene is famous for believing in the great power over us of those texts, in particular, which we read as children. For him, only this reading has any lasting influence on the adults we become: "In later life we admire, we are entertained, we may modify some views we already hold, but we are more likely to find in books a confirmation of what is in our minds already". For Rowe, at least, this is certainly true, and he returns to his past in large part by returning to a system of belief nurtured by childhood reading of such adventure tales as Yonge's The Little Duke. As longingly recalled in Book One, such reading involved for Rowe an education in a stable and optimistic worldview, one in which "our heroes are simple: they are brave, they tell the truth, they are good swordsmen and they are never in the long run really defeated".

Indeed, it was as just such a hero that the young Rowe understood himself, a dashing figure "capable of extraordinary heroisms and endurances which would make the girl he loved forget the awkward hands and the spotty chin of adolescence". If this passage indicates how such aggrandizing self-definition is at odds with, is a kind of forgetting of, the self's actuality, such adventuretale dreams nonetheless became, in his youth, as much an article of faith as his nostalgia would become in later life: "It was like the religious discipline: words however emptily repeated can in time form a habit...until one day to your own surprise you find yourself acting on the belief you thought you didn't believe in".

That such an ethos of romantic heroism has indeed persisted in him is underscored by Rowe's actions as the amnesiac Digby. In speculating on the true nature of his forgotten adult identity, Rowe wonders, for instance, whether he became an explorer, a la Burton and Stanley, as he had dreamed of being in childhood. Indeed, his sole complaint about his apparently idyllic existence at the clinic is that it does not afford him the properly heroic narrative he believes should be his. As the fortune-telling Mrs. Bellairs astutely observed at the fete, Rowe "sometimes feels he has not been allowed a proper scope for his gifts. He wants to do great deeds, not dream them all day long". This same self-estimation and frustration surface even in Rowe's return to the Eden of childhood, as he laments, "there was no satisfaction in shining before assistant Johns....He dreamed wildly between the box hedges". When, finally, he embarks upon his great adventure, his search for the dreaded "sick bay, " it is at least in part because this will satisfy his thirst for adventure, his desire to be the romantic hero of childhood storybooks: "He was afraid of undefined punishments and for that reason he felt his action was heroic and worthy of someone in love". Such attempts at casting himself in the role of the extraordinary, heroic protagonist of adventure tales continue, even after his expulsion from Forester's garden. In his reimmersion in the novel's thriller plot of wartime espionage, Rowe stays true to this same heroic ethos, so "happily drunk with danger and action" that even "the ruins from which he and investigator Prentice emerged were only a heroic back-cloth to his personal adventure".

This last point is significant, for what it highlights is that the rehearsal of childhood Rowe's amnesia permits does not, as O'Prey argues, leave him "detached from the chaos and violence" of the war. In returning, through forgetting, to the past and its notions of heroism, Rowe is repeating not only his own personal history but also the characteristic actions of the war to which he sees his past as opposed. For despite Diemert's claim that the novel "discredits the ethos of the romantic adventure tale by contrasting it with the thriller world of war-ravaged London" , The Ministry of Fear effects its debunking of this ethos precisely as it identifies it with the horrors of war. Rowe's persistent desire to be the hero of children's literature does not, as he thinks, distinguish him from that "History of Contemporary Society" he deems rightly written in the thriller mode.

Rather, his need to be the extraordinary man, living out a life of derring-do, allies him with those very fifth columnists who drive the novel's thriller plot. It finds an echo, for instance, in Poole's solicitous talk of "the sheep" to whom both he and Rowe are, naturally, superior, and this spy's use of the first-person plural here is both telling and astute. Likewise the spy-ring's chief, Willi Hilfe, admits that he, too, is "a romantic", and that "a story of intrigue like Rowe's excites him. It seems to give an opportunity, well, to take a more violent line". No wonder, then, that Rowe himself is convinced, on first meeting the Hilfes, that "these were the allies he needed". And such an alliance, or affinity, continues throughout the novel, as the amnesiac Rowe's lust for romantic adventure keeps him at the centre of this very contemporary tale of war and espionage. Not only is the clinic in which his wholesale return to this ostensibly dated worldview takes place run by the very spies and traitors who populate the modern thriller world, but also it is his childish need to be the her o in the spotlight that prompts him to withhold from police the telephone number that will lead to the spies and the stolen film. Thus does the hero of his boyish imaginings find himself at home in the war-torn present that itself endorses such a heroic ethos.

Rowe's forgetting does not, then, release him from the present but rather highlights the continuities between his idealized childhood world and the treacherous world of the war. Thus the "Arcady" in which his amnesia lands him in Book Two is revealed to be a myth, the past being, in its vision of valor and heroism, at one with the carnage of the present.

Indeed, it is this shared ethos, and the sense of self and others on which it rests, that Greene proffers as the very principle of a forgetting that constitutes Western history as modernism's nightmarish process of repetition. For in dreaming oneself the noble hero, one does not only, in Greene's view, elide one's own "spotty" imperfections but further justifies actions that deny, and even destroy, the selfhood of other human beings. The deadly force of this heroic self-conception Rowe shares with his Nazi foes, and the present shares with the past, is made clearest in the novel's dissection of Rowe's defining quality, namely, pity.

For despite Watts's claim that the morality of Greene's fiction centers on "the value of the charitable action—the altruistic deed motivated by pity", Greene's treatment of this "virtue" puts it at the heart of the psychology of the war and of his explanation of history's repetitive and murderous course. It is, after all, this trait that is the source of Rowe's own status as wife murderer, and thus of his ties to such wartime villains as Willi and Poole. Like these characters, Rowe too is a killer, and what has driven him to emulate their war ethos is nothing other than the quality of mercy—" mercy to his wife or mercy to me," remaining, as Rowe himself notes, unclear. Pity for his ill wife, his inability to stand her pain, has made him a killer, and the text underscores how this, too, figures as a repetition of, rather than fall from, the past by relating a cognate, if lesser, "murder" from his childhood: "Suddenly he couldn't bear the sight of the wounded rat's pain any more; he picked up a cricket-bat and struck the rat on the head over and over again". Thus, for Greene, this mercy is and was indeed "dangerous pity", for what it sanctions are actions akin even to those of murderer Willi Hilfe, whose suggestive last name signals such kinship between Rowe's "virtue" and the workings of war. Indeed, Greene makes this connection even more explicit in his narrator's gloss on the meaning of the Catholic missal: "It wasn't only evil men who did these things. Courage smashes a cathedral, endurance lets a city starve, pity kills"

But in order to clarify how pity, for Greene, can exemplify the ostensibly pitiless violence of war and the West's war-tom history, we must follow the hints this passage gives us and trace the links between pity and that adventure-tale ethic already seen to be definitive of the prewar past, as much as the World War II present.

For despite Rowe's own belief that pity stands in opposition to this ethos as maturity to immaturity, pity counts, as the passage quoted above indicates, as one of the cardinal virtues of the hero of the adventure tale. If the heroic faith of the past that Rowe has learned so well centers on such concepts as "sacrifice, courage, virtue", so does their restatement as sources of destruction on the very next page situate Rowe's pity as part of the hero's constitution, and part of the danger he represents for others.

Pity may be so embraced by the romantic values of past and present, of war and prewar, because at its heart, for Greene, lies the conviction he deems d efinitive of heroic self-conception, namely, that one is extraordinary and uniquely equipped to serve more, presumably, ordinary others. If

Rowe's dreams of himself as hero, both in adolescence and amnesiac adulthood, focus, as we have seen, on service to, trials endured for, a beloved other, so, too, is pity revealed as validating action in the best interests of others, even to the point of their annihilation. Thus the amnesiac Rowe, caught up in adventure-filled plans for his illicit trip to the "sick bay," is appalled by the pacifism he reads in Forester's copy of Tolstoy's What I Believe.

Such a worldview jars with Rowe's heroic persona and its need for Willi's "more violent line," but the way he articulates this to himself stresses the connections between the proper virtues of the hero and pity's own capacity to sanction any action: "why does he write as if the worst thing we can do to our fellow-man is to kill him? Everybody has to die and everybody fears death, but when we kill a man we save him from h is fear". This line of reasoning thus defends the murder of others as, indeed, for their own good, and thus consonant with heroism. So long as we act heroically, so long that is, as we act in the interests of another, any act, for Rowe, may be justified: "there was the point—not to kill for one's own sake. But for the sake of people you loved,...

It was right to risk damnation". Such thinking, that of the "immature," romantic Rowe, seems, then, very much in accord with that of the "mature," pitying Rowe who would serve his wife the poisoned milk, for her own good, to end her pain, even though "he could never know whether her fear of his act had been worse than the pain". Though he cannot, as he himself admits, ever know whether she might well have preferred "any sort of life to death", he has been able, with pity and romantic heroism both to guide him, to decide what her preference should be, and act on her behalf, to the point even of her own destruction.

As the threads of historical continuity, then, both heroism and pity serve to make of history a continuum of violence, through a shared paternalism that underwrites any action at all that can be argued to serve or to spare another. Such paternalism is also, for Greene, the very pith of the forgetting that is the very essence of the war and of the history of which it constitutes an emblematic part. As the above passages make clear, what it entails is the forgetting or repression of the other, of her actual preferences, of her capacity to decide and act upon her own "best interests." Likewise are the actual interests and weaknesses of the heroic/pitying self elided and in their place erected a form of heroic infallibility, a certain knowledge of what is best for the other that can cloud both what the other might desire and what the heroic agent might truly be seeking through such "other-centered" action—hence Rowe's post facto fears that he might well have acted to end his own pain, not his wife's.

This is, then, forgetting in Lyotard's mode, a forgetting of the other as agent that substitutes instead a certain belief in the rightness of one's own actions, as well as of one's right to undertake them. And it is such forgetting that, in its erasure of the other as a self capable of self-determination and its dictation of certain goods for all, Greene sees at the root of the twentieth-century's own genocidal reenactment of the historical nightmare. Thus, as McEwen notes, for Greene "it is dreadful to be sure of oneself", for what such certainty, in its heroic or pitying justifications, permits is an imposition of will, a quashing of the other, very much at home with the violence of war: Do you know what happens...when you wish the world to be neat and orderly and precise, a closed, untroubled place? You try to make it that way. And when people don't respond (and they don't), you end up with Belsen.

Certainly, The Ministry of Fear attempts to provide plenty of evidence that this is so. Not only does Rowe's pity drive him to murder, just as his desire for adventure implicates him in the murderous plot of Hilfe and his confederates, but also such certainty as to one's right to decide for others is the common foundation for what will become the novel's "massacre on an Elizabethan scale". Like Rowe, the Nazi spy Poole also believes that "even murder can sometimes be excused," a truth he relates, tellingly, with "an intolerable confidence," as he appeals to Rowe as another man of intelligence, a cut above the sheep who may or may not have to be excusably murdered. So, too, the idealist Dr. Forester, a man of sufficient pity that he does "not approve...of taking animal life", is nonetheless in league with Poole, Hilfe, and the others, and is "quite unmoved by the story of the Nazi elimination of old people and incurables".

Indeed, he will be party to the murder of muddled Major Stone, a crime he defends in advance as "the greatest mercy we can ask for him". Forester's own death is, in apt and illuminating fashion, brought about for his own good, with "respectable, hero-worshipping Johns" killing his idol, the fulfillment of his own romantic dreams of heroism, to protect him he was saving him from the interminable proceedings of the law courts, from the crudities of prosecuting counsel, the unfathomable ignorances of the judge, and the indignity of depending on the shallow opinion of twelve men picked at random. Even Anna Hilfe, with whom a loving Rowe ends up in the novel's conclusion, is, as herself part of her brother's ring, presented as a character of suspect, even oppressive, pity. Thus, visiting an amnesiac Rowe freed from the memory of his wife's murder, Anna refuses to tell him the truth and admits she prefers him so protected from the truth, even if it consigns him to Forester's clinic-cum-prison: "This is how you should be. This is how I like you".

If in all these characters the alchemy of pity and self-certainty yields a precipitate of murder and confinement, Willi Hilfe reveals the violence of such an imposition of will shorn even of pity's respectability. While the above instances serve to demonstrate, in Webster's words, how suffering in Greene's fiction "is made by idealists who fancy themselves God", Willi, who makes no pretense to ideals of any sort, still starkly illustrates the essence of their idealism and the ends to which it tends. For as Silverstein argues, Willi's nihilism, like Nazism itself, "only carries Rowe's sense of pity to its logical and terrifying extreme".

While Anna posits her brother's service to the Nazis as the antithesis of Rowe's pity—"they can bear pain—other people's pain—endlessly" —the narrative rather reveals Willi's mercilessness to be the obverse, not the inverse, of Rowe's quality of mercy. We have, for example, already seen how

the test for literary worth, particularly since such realism is a relatively recent development in literary history. There is also something mistaken in denying fantasy any claims to truthfulness.

Writing such different kinds of fiction, Greene and Tolkien might seem odd literary bedfellows. However - both English, both Roman Catholic, both writing over long careers during the 20th century—Greene and Tolkien, in their fiction and other writing, suggest that realism and fantasy, often contentiously opposed in critical debate, have more complex relations and can effect similar truths. Because Greene's The Power and the Glory and Tolkien's The Lord of the Rings both effect a vision of the world governed by divine imperatives, the divide they might represent between realism and fantasy becomes less precise, insofar as both works embody mythic dimensions, both suggesting the kind of revelatory power that theologian David Tracy ascribes to religious classics:

To enter the conversation of religious classics through real interpretation, therefore, is to enter a disclosure of a world of meaning and truth offering no certainty but promising some realized experience of the whole by the power of the whole. That world affords no technically controlled comprehensibility yet it does release the self to the uncontrollable incomprehensibility of an experience of radical mystery.

The Power and the Glory and The Lord of the Rings, the masterpieces of their respective authors, arguably suggest in their different literary approaches the kind of paradoxical disclosing and concealing "of the whole of reality by the power of the whole" and that essential oneness of morality, mystery, and reality that Tracy attributes to religious classics. As Greene and Tolkien together suggest, placing realism and fantasy on opposite ends of a continuum of truthfulness (and by direct implication, on a similar continuum of literary merit) is a move that ignores realism's relations with fantasy and downplays fiction's power to reveal mystery through a mythic dimension.

The surface similarities between Tolkien's trilogy and Greene's novel are striking, and here for a moment we take that view from a distance that Northrop Frye describes as the vantage point from which we can best see the archetypal organization of a work. Both the whisky priest and the ring-bearer are reluctant heroes whose journeys lead them where they had not intended to go but where they find they are compelled to go by their sense of calling, the priest because he is a priest, Frodo because he is the ring-bearer. Frodo often moves forward, particularly in the realms of Mount Doom, without hope, and the whisky priest, even when he has accepted martyrdom over escape, has little hope for his own salvation or much conviction that his death will prove honorable in the eyes of God or others.

Both journeyers also become swallowed in landscapes marked by heat, filth, desolation, and danger (Frodo through the marshes and vast, decimated territory of Mordor, the whisky priest in the harsh land of Tabasco and amid human squalor - a trash heap where he encounters his daughter, the jail where he finds communion with fellow sinners, among the great crosses and in the bitter rain as he approaches the state border). Both are pursued, Frodo by every power allied with Sauron, the whisky priest by the lieutenant and soldiers.

Both with some reluctance show mercy to figures who betray them (Frodo to Smeagol/Gollum and the whisky priest to the yellow-fanged mestizo), and this mercy proves crucial in both stories to the success of the journeyers (Smeagol/Gollum completes the destruction of the ring when Frodo wavers; the whisky priest makes his extraordinary decision to give up his life only after receiving the Yankee fugitive's scrawled note from the mestizo). Finally, both of their journeys involve a renunciation of power - Frodo gives up the Ring, and the whisky priest gives up his life. Within the narratives both become a part of stories foretold and told later (Frodo's role is prophesied, and his providential success becomes the stuff of Middle-Earth history and song; the whisky priest's life ironically becomes the story of a Catholic martyr/saint).

These parallels of their journeys, of course, exist amid great conceptual and aesthetic differences. Greene's priest is a figure living very much in what Tolkien calls the "Primary" or actual world, and this is the most crucial difference between the two works; it marks the aesthetic divide between realism of content and fantasy. Even if Greene creates what some critics have, in various ways, called "Greeneland," even if he unavoidably projects his own psychology onto his scene, he is still representing early twentieth-century Mexico.

Greene's represented world is also explicitly and historically shaped by Christianity. His whisky priest is, as R.W.B. Lewis puts it, a rogue whose particular sins as a priest (habitual drinking, begetting a child) emerge in all their mundane humanity amid other sins equally human but more theological (pride, despair).

As such, he is unlike the Halfling Frodo whose moral character is more exclusively figured in terms of how he deals with the Ring and his role as ring-bearer. The whisky priest journeys mostly alone while Frodo almost always has a companion. The sacraments of the Catholic Church have an explicit place in Greene's novel, as does worship and a more general sense that God works through nature; Tolkien's creatures in The Lord of the Rings, while the most noble among them allude to the presence of a benevolent and omnipotent Providence and sometimes show prayer-like reverence, are not religious in any modern sense of the word and do not engage in explicit worship.

Clearly there is no magic in Greene's novel, nothing fantastic in the sense of overt supernatural action, though the sacraments are certainly fantastic to those who don't believe in them; the lieutenant certainly sees them as bogus. The evil the priest encounters is always ordinary human evil - use of power to dominate others, egotism, lust, gluttony, nihilism, merciless accusation, pride, greed, sensuality - and Greene represents all of these with his characteristic ambiguity. The nihilistic lieutenant is motivated by a desire to help the poor and sometimes shows mercy to match that of the whisky priest; the pious woman in prison judges the sexual intercourse of the inmates, while the whisky priest recognizes a possible goodness in it and the worse sin in her pious judgments. On the other hand, Tolkien's most evil creatures in The Lord of the Rings — Sauron, the Orcs, the Nazgul - seem more purely and irredeemably so, though Elrond, implying the goodness of creation and the larger mythic history out of which the trilogy grows, emphasizes that "nothing is evil in the beginning. Even Sauron was not so".

Graham Greene, in fact, could imagine pure evil in the world, although his fiction has always proved more ambiguous and complex here than his extra-fictional commentary might suggest. By his own account, he first experienced literature's power to reveal the nature of reality and particularly the mystery of evil in a historical romance, Marjorie Bowen's The Viper of Milan (1906). Greene famously claims, "Bowen had given me my pattern - religion might later explain it to me in other terms, but the pattern was already there - perfect evil walking the world where perfect good can never walk again, and only the pendulum ensures that after all in the end justice is done" . Greene found Bowen's historical romance true to life because it mirrored his already acute sense of the human capacity for evil. In Greene's earliest sense of realism, mystery and the fantastic were already important. Biographer Norman Sherry has well noted Greene's early attraction to fantasy not only in his reading but also in his writing .

In 1922 Greene wrote a story for the school newspaper The Berkhamstedian tellingly titled "The Tyranny of Realism," an allegorical story that suggests a reconciliation between "Fantasie" and "Realism." In it a boy, bound before the throne of King Realism, sees a sad maiden named "Fantasie" at the King's feet. After bewailing the King for taking away his "unknown country of dark caves and hidden ways, and sun-splashed woods" and for keeping the boy's love, "Fantasie," a slave, the King, with a "little, whimsical smile" instructs the boy to try his bonds.

The bonds disappear, the King takes him to the throne, and the walls around them disappear, exposing "great, dark rolling plains, and the star-encrusted sky." In the final moment of the story, the boy sinks to his knees before the King, whose face is "the face of a God," and the boy sees that King Realism looks not at him but at Fantasie, who has taken her place on a throne beside the king. Realism and Fantasie kiss "in a long passion of joy". Sherry perceptively suggests that "the allegory is probably a pointer to Graham's hope that because he felt he must in the future write in a more realistic vein it did not mean that his fantastic imaginings could not also flourish" (Volume I 114). Greene's boyhood story reflects not only a reluctance to sacrifice fantasy to realism but also a desire to unite them.

Greene continued to dabble with fantasy during his long literary career. Characters recalling haunting childhood memories often provided the realistic frame for such forays. In the short story "The Hint of an Explanation" (1948), a provocative childhood encounter with a pitiful, evil-bent, anti-Catholic baker changes the life of the story's central figure. In "Under the Garden" (1963), a childhood "fantasy" narrative, a "memory" of a visit to two strange people living underground becomes a compelling, if ambiguous, reflection of truth and mystery for the terminally ill main character Wilditch. Even in his last novel The Captain and the Enemy (1988), Greene teases us with an ambiguously allegorical father figure dubbed "the Devil," suggesting that Greene's interest in the fantastic never died, even if he would only present these dimensions under the garb of irony and in a realistic frame, leaving the nature and imperatives of mystery ambiguous.

Graham Greene, of course, is not primarily a fantasy writer, but he did have a religious vision that found literary expression after his conversion to Roman Catholicism in 1926, particularly in the string of novels explicitly dealing with Catholic themes of sin and salvation, good and evil - Brighton Rock (1938), The Power and the Glory (1940), The Heart of the Matter (1948), and The End of the Affair (1951). Because Greene's realism here includes that wider reality embraced by Catholic belief, involving both the natural and the supernatural, the seen and the unseen, it already exceeds the limits of naturalism or radical realism. Given its theological dimension, Greene's explicitly religious fiction might seem fantastic, might even seem to fit C.S. Lewis's broad definition of literary fantasy: "any narrative that deals with impossibles and preternaturals" But Greene's commitment to referential narrative placed even his explicitly religious fiction in a more realistic mode with its own challenges. Catholic writer Flannery O'Connor recognized well the difficulty that Christian writers like Greene and her self faced in writing for an increasingly secular audience: The problem of the novelist who wishes to write about a man's encounter with... God is how he shall make the experience which is both natural and supernatural - understandable, and credible, to his reader. In any age this would be a problem, but in our own, it is a well-nigh insurmountable one.

In his realism of content, Greene rises to the challenge that O'Connor describes. Though always heterodox and doubtful in a way that O'Connor was not (Greene's fiction and life, even by his own account, attest to this), Greene still reveals in his explicitly Catholic fiction a similar gritty sacramentality, a stubborn sense that nature and human nature are the privileged sites in which and through which any kind of divine grace works.

Indeed, he was rarely heavy-handed in his narration, rarely overleapt the human and the natural to get to the divine dimension.2 His works often suggest, amid great suffering and absurdities, eternal possibilities and consequences for human action, a dramatic effect he praised in Henry James and found lacking in Virginia Woolf and Somerset Maugham. But as it was with Henry James, Greene's treatment of the spiritual dimension is subtle and grounded in the physical and psychological dimensions of character and place. Few would mistake Greene for a fantasy writer even in C.S. Lewis's terms - indeed the "preternatural" is rarely laid bare in his fiction and virtually all that he represents is wonderfully and terribly possible in the actual world.

WHILE Greene was writing The Power and the Glory in 1939, Tolkien was beginning painstaking work on his own masterpiece, one set not in twentieth-century Brighton, Mexico, Sierra Leone, or war-ravaged London, but in Middle-Earth. While Greene's aesthetic emphasis involved realism of content, Tolkien's was decidedly different from the start.3 In his essay

"On Fairy-Stories," originally written for a 1938 lecture, Tolkien describes many of his own aesthetic aspirations. Like his Oxford colleague and friend C.S. Lewis, Tolkien defended fantasy against dismissal by prevailing champions of realism of content.

Fantasy, he first explains, is etymologically and semantically connected with the "fantastic." Both involve "images of things that are not only `not actually present,' but which are indeed not to be found in our primary world at all, or are generally believed not to be found there". He then describes fantasy as a "form of Art" that represents a "Secondary World," as opposed to our "actual" or "Primary World," a form of Art remarkable for its "arresting strangeness" and inherent challenges for the writer. Fantasy and realism were not mutually exclusive modes of writing for Tolkien. They were, by necessity, mutually related: fantasy demands an "inner consistency of reality" and that inner consistency "is more difficult to produce, the more unlike are the images and the rearrangements of primary material to the actual arrangements of the Primary World".

In other words, the secondary worlds of fantasy demand their own realism of presentation. Tolkien argues, for example, that it is particularly difficult to create a credible Secondary World in which a "green sun" is not only imaginable but also believable. So if fantasy and the fantastic involve "freedom from the domination of observed `fact'", artistically they demand their own internal realism to achieve what Tolkien calls "Secondary Belief" in both the designer and the spectator, the writer and the reader, what Tolkien rightly identifies as a function of all Art.

even in distinguishing the images of Primary and Secondary worlds, Tolkien hints at their aesthetic and analogical relationship. Fantasy, he implies, is inescapably linked to the Primary world, for it is an "art which plays strange tricks with the world and all that is in it" . While this art in some sense re-imagines "the world and all that is in it" so that its images are strangely unlike the world, the likeness, the other half of analogy, nonetheless remains. Privileging both the freedom and challenges of fantasy, Tolkien also parenthetically suggests that fantasy is not detached from the Primary world at all: "That the images of fantasy and the fantastic are of things not in the primary world is a virtue not a vice". Every image of fantasy, he implies, has an imaginative footing in the Primary World, a claim consistent with Tolkien's belief that long-enduring words can lead us back, in their etymology, to concepts that once existed but have since vanished. So Tolkien reveals that, while fantasy and realism of content are clearly distinguished by the worlds they treat, good fantasy answers its own demands for realism, and the Primary world is ever related by analogy and the referentiality of language itself.

The literary bias toward realism of content that Lewis recognized in the 1960s arguably endures in the early twenty-first century. As it was then, the bias is an academic rather than a popular one. In fact, both Joseph Pearce and Tom Shippey have outlined well the recent public polls that place The Lord of the Rings as the greatest book of the twentieth century.4 Professional critics and university professors have responded quite differently, finding troubling implications in such popular adulation of a work of fantasy.

Critic Germaine Greer's recent commentary on such popular polls sums up their dismay: "The books that come in Tolkien's train are more or less what you would expect; flight from reality is their dominating characteristic" . In the 1930s Tolkien already knew well the scornful charge that fairy-stories, fantasy, science fiction, and their creators are - because they depart from realism of content - escapist by nature. Convinced that "Escape" was, in fact, sometimes the more practical or even heroic action in both art and literature, Tolkien suggests in "On Fairy-Stories" that critical denunciations of literary escapism are often fundamentally flawed, if not also disingenuous:

Why should a man be scorned, if, finding himself in prison, he tries to get out and go home? Or if, when he cannot do so, he thinks and talks about other topics than jailers and prison-walls? The world outside has not become less real because the prisoner cannot see it. In using Escape in this way, the critics have chosen the wrong word, and, what is more, they are confusing, not always by sincere error, the Escape of the Prisoner with the Flight of the Deserter.

Aesthetically, realism of content proved a prison for Tolkien, and he found his way of escape in fantasy, much as Greene found his in global wanderlust and the realistic works that grew out of it. To distinguish among kinds of escape might be a good antidote against unquestioned literary biases. As it is, realism of content remains a litmus test for literary worth in much of the academy, certainly when it comes to literature written since the end of the nineteenth century. The attendant denigration of fantasy is regrettable, for the more interesting literary picture involves both fantasy and realism and their mutual relations, relations Greene and Tolkien recognized in their common respect for myth.

In a 1963 interview with Frank Kermode, Greene himself situates The Power and the Glory in the realms of myth:

My own wish always is to produce a central figure who represents some idea of reasonable simplicity, a mythical figure, if you like. And the simplicity often gets damaged by plot making... I would like to ascend into myth, but find my boots so often muddy with plot. My own feeling is that the nearest I came to hitting the mythical element was in The Power and the Glory, where I feel the plot was sufficiently simple for the main purpose of this story to remain clear throughout.

Greene's whisky priest achieves a mythic dimension in a journey shadowed by impending capture and death. He reveals his ultimate integrity and achieves a kind of redemptive efficacy for others only when he rejects escape to the comfortable complacency that priestly life outside of Tabasco would mean, only when he accepts self-sacrifice for the sake of a criminal and his own vocation. Frodo Baggins must likewise leave the deceptive security of the Shire, just as, when he has accepted the burden of being ring-bearer, he must eventually leave Rivendell and Lothlorien and, finally, the reclaimed Shire as well.

He, too, journeys under the shadow of death and moves toward a doom that is paradoxically his and his world's only hope. As Jane Chance has noted well, Frodo goes not to obtain knowledge or gifts but "to divest himself (and the world) of this power" of the Ring.

On their journeys, both Frodo and the whisky priest discover who they are and what they live for, and the dramatic effect of both journeys suggests the kind of disclosure that David Tracy associates with religious classics - "that how we ought to live is grounded in reality itself'. In particular, mercy and self-sacrifice resonate with the very nature of Providence ("the power of the whole" and the ground of reality) implied in both works, suggesting, as many critics have already noted, the Christian dimensions of both works.

In disclaiming both topical and allegorical dimensions to his trilogy in the "Foreword to the Second Edition" of The Lord of the Rings, Tolkien places his aesthetic priority on freedom for the reader, versus what he saw as the author's "purposeful domination" through allegory (xvii). His aesthetic is consonant with the dramatic effect of The Lord of the Rings, in which domination of others through the use of power emerges as the epitome of evil (the same could be said of Greene, for whom treachery was also a definitive aspect of evil).

In speaking of myth in a 1951 letter to publisher Milton Waldman, Tolkien emphasizes a similar need for care in writing modern myths: "Myth and fairy-story must, as all art, reflect and contain in solution elements of moral and religious truth, but not explicit, not in the known form of the primary 'real' world". Describing The Lord of the Rings as "coming down from myth and legend to the earth", Tolkien also recognized it as an essentially religious story. As his now famous 1953 letter to Robert Murray, S.J. attests

The Lord of the Rings is of course a fundamentally religious and Catholic work; unconsciously so at first, but consciously so in the revision. That is why I have not put in, or have cut out, practically all references to anything like 'religion,' to cults or practices, in the imaginary world. For the religious element is absorbed into the story and the symbolism. However that is very clumsily put, and sounds more self-important than I feel.

While Greene's novel explicitly treats Christian mysteries, any particularly Christian elements of myth are only implied in The Lord of the Rings, for Tolkien's represented world is indeed pre-Christian, though its genesis obviously is not.

Frodo's journey certainly reveals the presence of a governing, if inscrutable, loving Providence and the privileging of mercy indicative of the Christian myth. Gandalf helps to shape Frodo's later behaviour toward Gollum by his early admonition: I have not much hope that Gollum can be cured before he dies, but there is a chance of it. And he is bound up with the fate of the Ring. My heart tells me that he has some part to play yet, for good or for ill, before the end; and when that comes, the pity of Bilbo may rule the fate of many - yours not the least.

Pity and mercy are bound up with "fate" and Providence in the wisdom of Gandalf, and so, too, is the notion of Gollum's possible if unlikely "cure." Gandalf implies that Elrond's later words are true, that nothing begins as evil, so that Gandalf's advice "not to strike without need" is consistent with his view of the Power that governs the world. Likewise, Greene's whisky priest, recognizing the mestizo as "Judas," must also admit that at the centre of his own faith there always stood the convincing mystery - that we were made in God's image. God was parent, but He was also the policeman, the criminal, the priest, the maniac, the judge... and God's image shook now up and down on the mule's back, with the yellow teeth sticking out over the lower lip.

The mestizo, too, he believes against belief, was made in the image and likeness of God, and even when he is actually being betrayed, the priest pities the betrayer for the sin he commits: "It was really shocking bad luck for the poor devil that he was to be burdened with a sin of such magnitude... Poor man, the priest thought, he isn't really bad enough... ". Mercy and pity are consonant with the Christian imperatives that the whisky priest accepts and that Greene's overall narrative suggests as true.

Not only imagining but acting on mysteriously motivated mercy, the whisky priest, against his own self-recognition as the worst of sinners, follows the pattern of Christ. Placing the whisky priest in the picaresque tradition as "the rogue...on his undignified flights from and toward the forces of destruction," R.W.B. Lewis was one of the earliest to recognize the nature of Greene's success at capturing the "paradoxes of sainthood". The whisky priest's mythical association with Christ - a servant of the poor, betrayed by a Judas figure into the hands of authorities and executed as a criminal, whose death suggests halting elements of redemption and resurrection - might have betrayed the artistic integrity of the novel for the sake of the pattern, a danger that Tolkien connected with allegory.

But, as R.W.B. Lewis suggests, while the pattern here is mythic in its movement, perhaps bordering on allegory, "it is nevertheless artistically redeemed by a full awareness of the grotesque disproportion between the model and its re-enactment". While for Tolkien the mythic dimension of The Lord of the Rings, a modern fantasy, demanded for its integrity a distancing from any explicit religious elements, for Greene the mythic dimension of The Power and the Glory, a work of modern Christian realism,5 demanded a different kind of distance - a represented distance between the myth and what is, between Christ and followers of Christ; in effect, realism of content. Indeed, in the early scene in the novel in which the pious woman reads modern stories of saints' lives to her children, she bristles at the thought that the "whisky priest," whom the family briefly harbored, could ever be a holy martyr like those in the stories. She worries to her husband:

"... the boy - he asks such questions - about that whisky priest. I wish we had never had him in the house."

"They would have caught him if we hadn't, and then he would have been one of your martyrs. They would write a book about him and you would read it to the children." "That man - never." "Well, after all," her husband said, "he carries on. I don't believe all that they write in these books. We are all human."

The husband proves more accurate in his reading of

characters and stories insofar as the whisky priest does become a martyr, and, to their son, a more believable one. To the husband, the sanitized stories his wife reads are unrealistic; to the boy they are boring and inaccessible. The whisky priest simply does not fit the pattern, and here lies both his credibility as a character and his paradoxical efficacy as a mythical figure.

Frodo, on the other hand, has no Christian pattern to follow or against which to be measured. When he agonizes to Gandalf, "I am not made for perilous quests. I wish I had never seen the Ring! Why did it come to me? Why was I chosen?" Gandalf can only reply, "Such questions cannot be answered.... You may be sure that it was not for any merit that others do not possess: not for power or wisdom, at any rate. But you have been chosen, and you must therefore use such strength and heart and wits as you have".

Frodo is an unlikely figure for such a "perilous quest," but he must mark out a new path. He is called, and called evidently by the same power Gandalf alludes to in connection with Bilbo's discovery of the Ring: "Behind that there was something else at work, beyond any design of the Ring-maker. I can put it no plainer than by saying that Bilbo was meant to find the Ring, and not by its maker. In which case you also were meant to have it. And that may be an encouraging thought". Bilbo's journey led him to adventures and treasures, including the Ring; Frodo's journey takes on a completely different focus. Frodo speaks the truth when he accepts the quest to destroy the Ring: "I will take the Ring... though I do not know the way".

As Gandalf anticipates, the Enemy can imagine only his own selfserving pattern: "the only measure that he knows is desire, desire for power; and so he judges all hearts. Into his heart the thought will not enter that any will refuse it, that having the Ring we may seek to destroy it. If we seek this, we shall put him out of reckoning". In concurring, Elrond notes the inscrutability of the road ahead and suggests that the ring-bearer cannot rely on the usual creaturely powers in the face of such peril:

"The road must be trod, but it will be very hard. And

neither strength nor wisdom will carry us far upon it. This quest may be attempted by the weak with as much hope as the strong. Yet such is oft the course of deeds that move the wheels of the world: small hands do them because they must, while the eyes of the great are elsewhere"

Elrond's observation about the "small" anticipates the Christian paradox of strength in weakness that both Frodo and the whisky priest prove true. But, rejecting the notion that Frodo is a "type" of Christ, Tom Shippey rightly notes that Frodo has "no supernatural dimension at all" and promises no soul-salvation. The evocative power of Frodo's journey, Shippey admits, offers, as does the trilogy as a whole, "hints of the Christian message," but the overall narrative "refuses just to repeat" that message. In refusing to impose the Christian pattern and in dramatically revealing the gap between creaturely efforts and Providential power, Tolkien suggests an aesthetic and moral impulse surprisingly similar to Greene's, considering their crucial differences. For both writers, the integrity of realism and myth demanded such distance and difference.

INDEED, the debate over what constitutes reality drives the dramatic action of Greene's novel. The whisky priest's belief in the power of the sacraments, particularly the Eucharist, remains unwavering, despite his sense of his own moral failure: "Now that he no longer despaired it didn't mean, of course, that he wasn't damned - it was simply that after a time the mystery became too great, a damned man putting God into the mouths of men: an odd sort of servant, that, for the devil". And when he does seem to despair even over the Eucharist, it is despair over the capacity of the beleaguered faith to endure among the people. Witnessing the anger and hopelessness of Maria, the mother of his daughter Brigitta, "he was aware of faith dying out between the bed and the door - the Mass would soon mean no more to anyone than a black cat crossing the path. He was risking all their lives for the sake of spilt salt or a crossed finger". What he imagines here is the kind of spiritual desolation that the lieutenant wishes to achieve, one that accurately reflects the quagmire of human suffering in Mexico. The lieutenant's view is purely political and physical:

It infuriated him to think that there were still people in the state who believed in a loving and merciful God. There are mystics who are said to have experienced God directly. He was a mystic, too, and what he had experienced was vacancy - a complete certainty in the existence of a dying, cooling world, of human beings who had evolved from animals for no purpose at all. He knew.

Convinced that the Church is perpetuating fantastic lies about human existence and driven by a hatred of priestly power and hypocrisy originating in his childhood, the lieutenant demonstrates a religious intensity in his nihilism as he considers the poor village children:

It was for these he was fighting. He would eliminate from their childhood everything which had made him miserable, all that was poor, superstitious, and corrupt. They deserved nothing less than the truth - a vacant universe and a cooling world, the right to be happy in any way they chose. He was quite prepared to make a massacre for their sakes - first the Church and then the foreigner and then the politician - even his own chief would one day have to go. He wanted to begin the world again with them, in a desert.

Penning the Police/Policing the Pen: the Case of Graham Greene's 'The Heart of the Matter'

Graham Greene's description of his conflicting intentions regarding the structure and content of The Heart of the Matter reveals the quandary of combining two novels into one. In his introduction to the 1971 edition he writes:

Two very different novels began on the same balcony with the same character, and I had to choose which to write.

One was the novel I wrote; the other was to have been an "entertainment". I had long been haunted by the possibility of a crime story in which the criminal was known to the reader, but the detective was carefully hidden, disguised by false clues which would lead the reader astray until the climax. The story was to be told from the point of view of the criminal, and the detective would necessarily be some kind of undercover agent.... When I left Wilson on the balcony and joined Scobie I plumped for the novel.

But as in Brighton Rock the ostensible shedding of one form for another - the replacement of a thriller with a "serious" novel - only succeeds in stripping away the surface trappings of an ordinary suspense or detective story, such as the focus on a crime and a subsequent investigation and pursuit, for the novel still resembles a thriller in its growing atmosphere of spying and suspicion, trust and distrust, centered on Scobie's attempts to hide his adultery and reconcile his desire to remain uncompromised with his dealings with the Syrian trader, Yusef. Scobie traces his affection for West Africa to his sense that "human nature hasn't had time to disguise itself .

Here you could love human beings nearly as God loved them, knowing the worst: you didn't love a pose, a pretty dress, a sentiment artfully assumed". Despite his love for this lack of artifice, however, Scobie too will become an inhabitant of the country of lies; his increasing need to hide his actions is directly proportionate to the breakdown of his ability to trust anyone or believe in anything: "It seemed to Scobie one of the qualities of deceit that you lost the sense of trust. If I can lie and betray, so can others". It is this special quality of distrust that is the core landscape of the novel, and though it is a topography which is displayed in other Greene works, here it finds its most emblematic representation.

The figure of a police officer becoming a symbol of dishonesty or questionable ethics is part of a larger pattern in Greene's writing of subverting the role of the forces of detection, be they officials of the police or private investigators. This subversion can take the form of implied incompetence, as with Mather in A Gun for Sale and Rennit in The Ministry of Fear, or it can be a questioning of moral authority, as with Ida in Brighton Rock or the lieutenant in The Power and the Glory. The Heart of the Matter, while it suggests Scobie's commitment to his job, also immediately challenges his efficacy and policing power. Scobie is quite self-conscious about what his work entails, and he believes that it is a vocation requiring perceptiveness and a strong sense of justice; asked by Helen Rolt how he knows about her stamp album, he replies, "'That's my job. I'm a policeman'", and in his dialogue with God he states, "I'm not a policeman for nothing - responsible for order, for seeing justice is done". Maria Couto asserts that "the novel does not explore the ineffectiveness of Scobie's role as arbiter of justice", but I would argue that Greene does indicate, on a number of occasions, Scobie's weaknesses in that area; years of being a police officer in the far reaches of Africa have left Scobie with a sense of his own deep limitations, especially in mediating local housing disputes:

At the beginning of his service Scobie had flung himself into these investigations; he had found himself over and over in the position of a partisan, supporting as he believed the poor and innocent tenant against the wealthy and guilty house-owner. But he soon discovered that the guilt and innocence were as relative as the wealth.... After that he had tried to kill these cases at birth: he would reason with the complainant and point out that the investigation would do no good and undoubtedly cost her time and money; he would sometimes even refuse to investigate. The result of that inaction had been stones flung at his car window, slashed tyres, the nickname of the Bad Man that had stuck to him through all one long sad tour. The first time we see Scobie on duty, appropriating what he perçeives to be a possible home-made bomb, his investigative instincts are subject to ridicule:

Scobie picked the bottle up. It was a dimpled Haig, and when he drew out the palm leaves the stench of dog's pizzle and nameless decay blew out like a gas escape.... He threw the bottle over the wharf, and the hungry mouth of the water received it with a single belch, but the contents were scattered on the air, and the whole windless place smelt sour and ammoniac. The policemen were silent: Scobie was aware of their mute disapproval. He should have left the bottle where it stood. When Scobie is tipped off by Yusef that diamonds will be found on board the Portuguese boat in the possession of Tallit's cousin, he has them confiscated, only to find out afterward who owns the gems:

"I would like to trust you, Yusef. Tell me the truth. Were the diamonds yours or Tallit's?" "I always want to speak the truth to you, Major Scobie. I never told you the diamonds were Tallit's."

"They were yours?"

"Yes Major Scobie."

"What a fool you have made of me, Yusef."

F. N. Lees believes in "the author's insistence on Scobie's professional merit (put beyond doubt by eventual promotion)" ; but the timing of the promotion, coming at a point in the novel when Scobie has already severely compromised himself, ironically acts as a further undercutting of his position.

Greene's technique of undermining the law authorities represents nothing new, of course, in the tradition of the detective story: "Humble, prosaic, oafish, well-meaning, slow - these are some of the adjectives called to mind by the policemen that populate detective stories. Invariably they get it wrong". But this feature is not limited to detective fiction; as D. A. Miller argues, the novel itself regularly holds the police "to their place on the periphery" in a "gradual process of marginalization". One of the ways this "marginalization" takes place in the nineteenth-century novel is through the replacement of police power with another kind of disciplinary agency; the coercive force over the individual of public opinion and social gossip, as displayed in many quintessential Victorian works, acts as a powerful regulatory substitute even when the police no longer constitute an effective institution within the world of the novel.

The title character of Felix Holt remarks on this force: "|I'll tell you what's the greatest power under heaven,' said Felix, and that is public opinion". In fact, the ascending dominance of gossip within a community can lead to an ironic situation; public opinion, which originally could be seen as a kind of grass-roots corrective to political misrule , itself becomes a force which must be fended off, as John Stuart Mill cautions: "Protection, therefore, against the tyranny of the magistrate is not enough; there needs protection also against the tyranny of the prevailing opinion and feeling".

The relationship between public monitoring and the official eye of the police is thus an essential dynamic in texts like the The Moonstone, which can be interpreted as a comprehensive displacement of the detective's function by the surrounding community, but without any " ׀collective' intentionality" on the part of that community: "Without having to serve police functions in an ex officio way, gossip and domestic familiarity produce the effect of surveillance... but a direct assumption of policing power by the community is avoided" .

The Heart of the Matter, which has been critically examined mainly in theological terms or from the perspective of its African setting and colonialism, is also a powerful example of the undermining of the police; Greene purposefully blocks and reverses Scobie's authority in several ways, as the novel charts a consistent pattern in which Scobie's investigative acumen proves dubious and he becomes the observed rather than the observer. The power of private and public surveillance and communal gossip is a potent thread in the story, from Wilson's extended monitoring of his unaware quarry and Louise's clinging presence to Father Rank's penchant for passing along secrets and Yusef's widespread sources of information that Scobie cannot nearly match.

This culminates in an overturning of Scobie's policing power by a questioning of his ability to see what is around him and also through the text's skeptical regard for his self-awareness. The notion of a "hidden detective" that Greene refers to in his introduction is not abandoned entirely; the novel traces Wilson's secret quest to investigate Scobie and stresses his desire to remain obscured: "He wanted passionately to be indistinguishable on the surface from other men". But the hidden detective here, as in other Greene works, also comes in the implied form of a faceless yet omnipotent divine hound, and it is the clear parallel between this kind of presence and that of a hidden human authority that is evoked in Miller's telling remark that "the police are only - as Gaboriau also called them - a ׀Providence au petit pied'... a ׀little providence' fully analogous to the great. What matters is that the faceless gaze becomes an ideal of the power of regulation". The "faceless gaze" inevitably applies both to Greene's authorial voice and to the divine detective at the core of the book; a poem by Rilke that Scobie reads provides a resonant articulation of the invisible "heart of the matter":

We are all falling. This hand's falling too - all have this falling sickness none withstands. And yet there's always One whose gentle hands this universal falling can't fall through.

Despite Scobie's denial of this heavenly grip - "He thought, those hands will never hold my fall: I slip between the fingers, I'm greased with falsehood, treachery" - the fact of his struggle with and studied rebellion against God's pursuit only serves to emphasize the central role of divine surveillance in the text.

Ultimately, however, The Heart of the Matter exhibits a complex attitude toward the theme of policing, for I would suggest that even with the concerted efforts on the part of the novel to undermine Scobie as a centre of authority, it also displays his elusiveness. But this paradoxical notion - that Scobie is both policed and yet evades policing - is one that provokes certain questions. If Scobie has been thoroughly monitored by the society around him, such that his adultery and even his suicide are perceived by others, in what way can we assert that he has avoided being detected by the community? A further query arises, this one regarding the issue of Scobie's resistance to divine control: Is an "escape" from God's will possible?

Thomas Docherty seems to propose this when he argues that Scobie's suicide is "a usurpation of God's position, taking God's place as the authorial proprietor and arbiter of his existence". But Greene has stated that "if God exists... He is omniscient" ; what, then, is the text's understanding of Scobie's autonomy in the face of an all-knowing deity? Finally, what is the relationship between the character and his "author-god"? Greene notes that writers "create characters over whom they exercise almost total control," and yet he also admits that Scobie somehow eluded this authorial regulation. An examination of these issues, which the latter part of this essay will begin to undertake, is pertinent not just in attempting to comprehend The Heart of the Matter, but also for the implications it has for much of the author's oeuvre, which is concerned with the limits of human knowledge and hence the undermining of the temporal process of detection, as well as the relationship between God and man.

The opening scene of The Heart of the Matter establishes Scobie as unaware of being observed. On the balcony of the Bedford Hotel, Wilson and Harris - the cable censor - peer at the street below: "Look down there," Harris said, "look at Scobie." A vulture flapped and shifted on the iron roof and Wilson looked at Scobie. He looked without interest in obedience to a stranger's direction, and it seemed to him that no particular interest attached to the squat grey-haired man walking alone up Bond Street. He couldn't tell that this was one of those occasions a man never forgets.

The force of judgment created by this overhead angle is combined with a casual interchange of condemnatory gossip, which begins with Harris's unfounded accusations regarding Scobie's interest in native women:

"He loves 'em so much," Harris said, | he sleeps with 'em." "Is that the police uniform?" "It is. Our great police force. A lost thing will they never find - you know the poem."

"I don't read poetry," Wilson said. His eyes followed Scobie up the sun-drowned street. Scobie stopped and had a word with a black man in a white panama: a black policeman passed by, saluting smartly. Scobie went on.

"Probably in the pay of the Syrians too if the truth were known." The passage introduces the immediate, if offhand, monitoring of Scobie, and also brings out two other aspects: Wilson's denial of part of his identity - his secret love of poetry - and the general disdain and skepticism regarding the competence of the police. The very nature of gossip is that it focuses attention on an object while hiding itself: What characterizes gossip, after all, is that it never "minds its own business." Gossip is always about someone else, always oriented to a story that both precedes its discourse and stands outside its frame. The opposition between someone else's story and its own discourse works to neutralize its activity, staged as mere observation. What keeps gossip from becoming the subject of a narrative, is precisely the narrative that is the subject of gossip.

The acts which are erroneously presumed here - Scobie's extra-marital liaisons and his being in the pay of the Syrians - are the very things which he must later attempt to conceal. The "party line" on Scobie is confirmed a few moments later in his conversation with the retiring Commissioner:

"Do you know the latest story they are using against you at the Secretariat?" "I suppose I'm in the Syrians' pay?" "They haven't got that far yet. That's the next stage. No, you sleep with black girls." At this point Scobie's attitude is chiefly one of unconcern, but his fear of the web of communal monitoring surfaces when one night he encounters Yusef: "If Fellowes drives by now, what a story, Scobie thought. The deputy-commissioner meeting Yusef, the store-keeper, clandestinely at night. To give help to a Syrian was only a degree less dangerous than to receive help". This caution is well founded; we find later on that he had been spotted that night by Yusef's rival, Tallit:

"The other night a police car brought Yusef home," Tallit said. "I saw it from here plainly."

"One of the drivers earning a bit on the side," Father Rank said. "I thought I saw Major Scobie. He was careful not to get out. Of course I am not perfectly sure. It looked like Major Scobie." Each compromising situation that Scobie falls into further subjects him to the scrutiny of others, as when Fraser sees him burning the Portuguese captain's letter:

Fraser said cheerfully, "Burning the evidence?" and looked down into the tin. The name had blackened: there was nothing there surely that Fraser could see - except a brown triangle of envelope that seemed to Scobie obviously foreign. He ground it out of existence with a stick and looked up at Fraser to see whether he could detect any surprise or suspicion.... Only his own heart-beats told him he was guilty - that he had joined the ranks of the corrupt police officers.

The sense of Scobie in a potentially dangerous

environment is reinforced in the description of his life at home: "He stood very still like a spy in foreign territory, and indeed he was in foreign territory now". His perpetual sense of responsibility for Louise also extends to how the gossip will affect her; at the officer's club he is cognizant of the community's spying on his wife: "He could feel the malice and snobbery of the world padding up like wolves around her. They wouldn't even let her enjoy her books, he thought". His extraordinary obsession with making sure his wife does not fall into despair or become an object of absurdity often spurs Scobie to detect each shift in her mood:

He never listened while his wife talked. He worked steadily to the even current of sound, but if a note of distress were struck he was aware of it at once.... So long as his ear-drum registered those tranquil sounds - the gossip of the club, comments on the sermons preached by Father Rank, the plot of a new novel, even complaints about the weather - he knew that all was well. It was silence that stopped him working - silence in which he might look up and see tears waiting in the eyes for his attention.

Every nuance of Louise's behaviour is subject to his examination; he can even assess other people's perceptions of his role as her husband: "He knew every one of her faults. How often he had winced at her patronage of strangers. He knew each phrase, each intonation that alienated others.... The worst was when he detected in his colleagues an extra warmth of friendliness towards himself, as though they pitied him".

But Louise proves to be just as capable of observing Scobie as the reverse, and the dynamic of the Scobies strongly echoes that of Pinkie and Rose in Brighton Rock. In each case there is vacillation between a thin web of surface serenity, which has been forged by a mutual backing away from tension, followed by an outbreak of conflict; in both novels the woman is shown as alternately complaining and yet acquiescing to her situation; and both Louise and Rose suddenly strike back at their partners with a startling display of perceptiveness, only to revert to a kind of willed but fragile optimism upon reassurances from the men. Pinkie is forced to reckon with

Rose's detective skills, and Scobie finds himself taking notice of Louise's unexpectedly accurate assessment of their marriage when they discuss the possibility of her trip to South Africa:

"I'd miss you," he said. "No, Ticki, you wouldn't," she said, and surprised him by the range of her sad spasmodic understanding. "After all," she said, "there's nobody to save for." Though Scobie, like Pinkie, remains in some ways utterly undetectable to his spouse, he is perpetually jolted by her ability to see through the veil of comforting lies he has attempted to set in place:

"Yes, she said, "I know you aren't happy either. Without me you'll have peace." This was what he always left out of account - the accuracy of her observation. He had nearly everything, and all he needed was peace.... How often he had been pitied for the austerity of the work, the bareness of the rewards. But Louise knew him better than that.

Upon her return from South Africa, in her desire to go with him to communion he feels "as though he were being urged by a kindly and remorseless gaoler to dress for execution". She will not be put off easily and continues to stalk him, suggesting that they attend communion:

"If you want to," he said. It was the moment he had known would come. With bravado, to show that his hand was not shaking, he took down a glass. "Drink?" "It's too early, dear," Louise said; he knew she was watching him closely like all the others. Even her aura of cheerful acceptance seems to him like a tricky maze: "Darling," she said, "if you aren't well, stay where you are. I don't want to drag you to Mass."

But the excuse it seemed to him was also a trap. He could see where the turf had been replaced over the hidden stakes. If he took the excuse she offered he would have all but confessed his guilt.

Thus she becomes the policeman and he the suspect to be led to trial: "|Aren't you coming, dear?' Louise asked, and again the hand touched him: the kindly firm detective hand. He rose and followed her and knelt by her side like a spy in a foreign land". Scobie's mechanical soothing of his wife is belied by the knowledge of the true pattern of their dynamic:

Again the nerve in his head tightened; unhappiness had uncoiled with its inevitable routine - first her misery and his strained attempts to leave everything unsaid: then her own calm statements of truths much better lied about, and finally the snapping of his own control - truths flung back at her as though she were his enemy. As he embarked on this last stage, crying suddenly and truthfully out at her while the angostura trembled in his hand, "You can't give me peace," he already knew what would succeed it, the reconciliation and the easy lies again until the next scene.

Their interaction sharply accentuates, among other things, the fact that Scobie is being observed and that he has memorized the art of appeasement which often involves a disregard for honesty. Years of this kind of relationship have actually molded his conception of the truth: "The truth, he thought, has never been of any real value to any human being - it is a symbol for mathematicians and philosophers to pursue. In human relations kindness and lies are worth a thousand truths. He involved himself in what he always knew was a vain struggle to retain the lies. |Don't be absurd, darling. Who do you think I love if I don't love you?'". Although he is, at least initially, "unaccustomed to lies", his marriage is a longstanding forum for the evasion of the truth. What follows from this is that Scobie's increasing concealment of his activities contains, in some respects, its seeds in his relationship with his wife.

Greene's undermining of Scobie as a detective begins with the inverted situation of others policing the policeman; he is constantly observed, gossiped about, scrutinized. But the subversion of his detecting power is also presented by mocking the duties he must perform, including searching a ship for diamonds: "To try and find a few diamonds in a liner of fifteen thousand tons was absurd: no malign tyrant in a fairy-story had ever set a goose girl a more impossible task, and yet as regularly as the ships called the cypher telegrams came in - |So and so travelling first class suspected of carrying diamonds. The following members of the ship's crew suspected.... ' Nobody ever found anything". His meeting with

Yusef also furthers the picture of Scobie as the target of gossip as well as a policeman who is reduced to guesswork:

"Oh, I had heard that you were resigning, Major Scobie." "No." "We shopkeepers hear so much but all of it is unreliable gossip." "How long will the rice shortage go on, Yusef?" "You know as much about that as I do, Major Scobie."

If Louise sometimes rises to the role of shrewd observer and even a jailer, it is Yusef who ironically recalls the Great Detective in certain comic respects; because he cannot read or write he stores all his information in his head - a parodic reminder of the cerebral ruminations of Sherlock Holmes - and his network of information is so formidable as to highlight Scobie's own woeful inadequacy as a detective. Yusef repeatedly warns Scobie that Wilson is spying on him:

"They have sent a special man from London to investigate the diamonds - they are crazy about diamonds only the Commissioner must know about him none of the other officers, not even you." "What rubbish you talk, Yusef. There's no such man." "Everybody guesses but you." "Too absurd. You shouldn't listen to rumour, Yusef." Yusef's reading of Scobie is accurate; the policeman cannot even detect as well as Father Rank, who hints that he perceives the special agent's identity and also displays his own powers of observation in trivial matters in a dialogue with Wilson:

"You ought to have been a policeman, Father." "Ah," Father Rank said, "who knows? There are more policemen in this town than meet the eye - or so they say."

"Who say?" "Careful of those sweets," Father Rank said, "they are harmless in moderation, but you've taken four already." Father Rank detects while Scobie hides secrets: the policeman and the priest reverse their expected functions. Father Rank unabashedly affirms that he is a gossip: "If a man tells me anything I assume he wants me to pass it on". On the other hand, Scobie, as the priest admits, is a person to whom people make "confession": "If people are in trouble they'd go to you, Scobie, not to me. They ask me to dinner to hear the gossip".

A detective's power is contingent on his vision; seeing

becomes, quite literally, the root element in overseeing. Mark Seltzer, in discussing Henry James's use of the techniques of surveillance, notes that police fiction is "precisely the form that most insistently manifests the twin operations of vision and supervision, of spectatorship and incrimination.... In the figure of the detective, seeing becomes the mode of power par excellence". Greene suggests that Scobie's initial refusal to acknowledge Wilson's identity is a product of his own self-deception, as Louise tells her husband's nemesis: "|Oh, I think sometimes he's got a kind of selective eye-sight.

He sees what he likes to see'". When Scobie teases Robinson over his preoccupation with medical books, the bank manager retorts that "a man's got to know what's wrong with him", which qualifies as a perfect critique of Scobie. Though he constantly reiterates the impossibility of comprehending someone else "in the confusing night he forgot for the while what experience had taught him - that no human being can really understand another" - he fails to realise how this also applies to his own murky self-awareness. Thus the adulterous relationship with Helen takes him by surprise:

It seemed to him that he had not felt so much at ease with another human being for years - not since Louise was young. But this case was different, he told himself: they were safe with each other. He was more than thirty years the older; his body in this climate had lost the sense of lust....

She stood pressed against him with her hand on his side.... She raised her mouth and they kissed. What they had both thought was safety proved to have been the camouflage of an enemy who works in terms of friendship, trust and pity.

Even his sense of responsibility wanes at the point where he blames God for his dilemma: "Take your sponge of gall. You made me what I am". The inability to fully examine his own behaviour, and his unwillingness in the first half of the novel to accept Wilson's real identity, are part of the same pattern that ultimately leads to the murder of his servant, Ali - an incident which epitomizes the relinquishing of power as it relates to the limits of vision:

It seemed to Scobie that now or never he must ask what

was Yusef's plan, but the weariness of his corruption halted his tongue....

"You must not worry, Major Scobie. I think your boy can be made quite trustworthy."

He said with relief and hope, "You mean you have a hold on him?"

"Don't ask questions. You will see."

The irony of Yusef's comment that Scobie will see resonates firmly with the reader, for the murder opens Scobie's eyes to his self-imposed blindness: "Oh God, he thought, I've killed you: you've served me all these years and I've killed you at the end of them".

Eventually Yusef's warnings and Wilson's dogged questioning and open admission that he is watching him put Scobie on guard, and the last half of the novel records Scobie's grudging acceptance of the reality that he is being spied upon; finally he asks the Commissioner, "Am I the only one who doesn't know about Wilson?". His relationship with Helen has set in motion the mindset of a man trying to cover his tracks; as he leaves her hut for the first time after they make love, he has already begun to fashion in his own mind the undetectable crime: he planned the moves ahead: he embarked for the first time in his life on the long legalistic arguments of deceit.... He looked carefully everywhere for signs of his presence: he straightened a mat and hesitated over an ash-tray. Then at the end of it all he had left his umbrella standing against the wall. It seemed to him the typical action of a criminal.

The fact of pursuit, so dominant in other Greene texts, reveals itself to Scobie in a scene at the club: "Scobie looked across the table at Helen.... Again he was aware of Wilson looking fro.m one to another of them, and Scobie drew desperately at his mind for any phrase that would end their dangerous solitude. They could not even be silent together with safety". Increasingly Scobie feels life "closing in on him". The inevitable result of this perceived pursuit is his deep suspicion of the people around him; everyone seems like a detective to the beleaguered suspect: "The door creaked gently open behind him. Scobie did not move.

The spies, he thought, are creeping in. Is this Wilson, Harris, Pemberton's boy, Ali...?". The word "trust" is the axis around which all else revolves in Scobie's mind. Yusef's conception of trust is that "You must always know more about them than they do about you", a definition that ruthlessly connects all human feelings and interactions to the dynamics of power; as he demonstrates in the case of Ali, the most "trustworthy" person is one who can never again speak. Ironically, this is Scobie's self-perception as well; once dead, he feels he will no longer plague God: "I can't go on, month after month, insulting you.... You'll be better off if you lose me once and for all". Thus Scobie feels a kinship with his pursuer, Yusef, a trust based on their sharing a life of deceit: "Now he felt an odd yearning towards his tormentor... as though concealed there was his only companionship, the only man he could trust. At least his blackmailer knew him as no one else did: he could sit opposite that fat absurd figure and tell the whole truth".

Scobie's illicit activities prompt his pervasive concern with how things look to others, and yet he is often blind to the fact that he is a bad deceiver; at the club he muses that he and Helen have evaded the detection of others: "Scobie thought with a tremor of self-disgust, how clever we've been: how successfully we've deceived the gossipers of a small colony. It oughtn't to be possible for lovers to deceive so well". He does not realise what others know and the extent to which he has been observed; returning one night from Helen's hut he meets a knowing Wilson:

"Scobie," Wilson exclaimed and the man turned. "Hullo, Wilson," Scobie said, "I didn't know you lived up here."

"I'm sharing with Harris," Wilson said.... "I've been taking a walk," Scobie said unconvincingly. "I couldn't sleep." It seemed to Wilson that Scobie was still a novice in the world of deceit. In addition to this, Yusef informs Scobie that Helen's boy is also in the Syrian's employ, and that he is now in possession of a compromising letter that Scobie has written Helen: "The formal voice suddenly stopped and the old Yusef implored again, |Oh, Major Scobie, what made you write such a letter? It was asking for trouble'". For Louise, Scobie's outlook is transparent—"He has a terrible sense of responsibility" and she has even known of his affair all along, as she admits after his death:

"Did you know all the time - about her?" Wilson asked. "It's why I came home. Mrs Carter wrote to me. She said everybody was talking. Of course he never realised that. He thought he'd been so clever." Scobie's adultery, in fact, is public knowledge; in the end even his suicide, carefully planned so that "no one must even suspect", is uncovered after Wilson inspects the diaries in a prototypical piece of police work: Wilson said, "Have you noticed that he's written in pieces about sleeplessness - afterwards?"

"How do you know?" "You've only to compare the colour of the ink. And all these records of takini his Evipan - it's very studied, very careful. But above all the col7our of the ink." He said, "It makes one think."

She interrupted him with horror, "Oh no, he couldn't have done that." Ostensibly it would seem that Wilson is left with the last word on the subject of Scobie: "His secrets were never very secret".

But The Heart of the Matter, as does much of the author's work, allows for the conflicting impulses of pursuit and evasiveness, charting both the undermining of Scobie's policing authority and the consistent spying on his activities, and yet on the other hand insinuating his resistance to being appropriated. The ability of Scobie and other Greene figures to remain impervious to efforts to detect theme - specially in the metaphorical sense of maintaining a deeply guarded self or inner life that defies perception or is opaque to others and thus remains free" - needs to be understood in several different contexts, depending on the nature of the pursuer. I should like, therefore, to analyse briefly how Greene depicts large areas of disconnection between the characters in the world of the text - with a specific focus on how this signifies Scobie's undetectability in the eyes of man - before addressing the more problematic and complicated issue of his potential to challenge his divine or literary creator.

One of the primary themes that the novel uses to convey the inherent difficulty in tracing any character is that of the fundamental unreliability of writing. Throughout The Heart of the Matter there are examples of written communications that are distorted: letters are mispelled or lost or stolen; cables informing Scobie about the illness and subsequent death of his daughter are sent in reverse order; official government telegrams are contradicted by other telegrams; Scobie's diaries are terse and cryptic; as Yusef says, "Words are very complicated". The idea of writing concealing or distorting its own meaning pervades the novel, as Scobie indirectly exhibits:

He had written down against the date October 31: Commissioner told me this morning I am to succeed him. Took some furniture to H. R. Told Louise news, which pleased her. The other life - bare and undisturbed and built of facts - lay like Roman foundations under his hand. This was the life he was supposed to lead; no one reading this record would visualise the obscure shameful scene in the garage, the interview with the Portuguese captain, Louise striking out blindly with the painful truth, Helen accusing him of hypocrisy.

The cables Scobie receives from Louise about the death of their daughter also exemplify the distortion of writing: "I got one cable just after breakfast.... The cable said, Catherine died this afternoon no pain God bless you. The second cable came at lunch-time. It said, Catherine seriously ill. Doctor has hope my diving. This was the one sent off at five. |Diving' was a mutilation - I suppose for |darling'". The cables in their proper order would have broken the news gradually, but instead they are darkly comic; "diving," intended as a term of endearment for Scobie, ironically suggests the condition of the dying girl. Scobie's letters to his wife while she is away are similar to his diaries: "He had to be accurate: he could comfort only by omission". The exactness of the writing is almost absurdly tangential to the essence of his thoughts, and Scobie encounters the same kind of obtuseness when he reads Pemberton's suicide note; the two men are linked by the impenetrable records they leave behind: "Don't go and pay the money I owe - the fellow doesn't deserve it. They may try and get it out of you. Otherwise I wouldn't mention it. It's a rotten business for you, but it can't be helped. Your loving son. The signature was |Dicky'. It was like a letter from school excusing a bad report". The assault on writing and its aspiration to meaningfulness is again manifested in the note Helen's father sends to comfort her upon her husband's death; he little realizes that his words are projections of his own world view and have no meaning for Helen, as she tells Scobie: "He's very sweet, but of course he doesn't know a thing about me".

This breakdown of all forms of communication helps to supplement the novel's picture of human beings who are profoundly isolated from one another. Louise's assumption that her husband's fate is predictable - "It's no good even praying" - is quickly refuted by Father Rank, who asserts that the Church "knows all the rules. But it doesn't know what goes on in a single human heart". The impossibility of such knowledge signals the end of human detection, and Greene contributes to the disruption of such detection by implanting contradictory clues about the same character. Scobie cannot be categorized exclusively as a saint or as "a very sick man" ; his behaviour incorporates both clear-eyed perceptions and lies, to others and to himself.

We see Scobie as a deceiver and yet a stickler for truth, as a perceptive observer - his unearthing of the Portuguese captain's letter fixed to the cap of a cistern indicates a trained eye - and yet blind to the actions of others as well as to his own motivations (what Greene calls his "inordinate pride" - Heart xv), and as a man consumed by responsibility to the people around him and yet shifting the blame to God for creating him that way. The Commisioner's somewhat affectionate appellation "Scobie the Just" may seem ironic in light of Scobie's later deceptions, but Yusef remembers that Scobie could have jailed him if not for a scrupulous regard for the truth: "You could have caught me if you had told your policeman to say something a little different. I was quite overcome with astonishment, Major Scobie, to sit in a police court and hear true facts from the mouths of policemen. You must have taken a lot of trouble to find out what was true, and to make them say it".

The enigma of Scobie signifies the difficulty of interpretation, in opposition to detective fiction that dispels discord through a structure of problem solving. Scobie misreads the theological memoir A Bishop among the Bantus to a little boy in the hospital as "a kind of detective story", to satisfy the boy's thirst for adventure, but he makes sure to tack on an unthreatening ending in which "Arthur" Bishop, the "secret agent," successfully infiltrates a pirate ring: Bishop discovers all their secret passwords and hiding-places and their plans of raids, of course, so that he can betray them when the time is ripe". Scobie thus instinctively grasps one of the cardinal principles governing the genre, that of narrative closure; the ending of a detective story is "less a resolution than an erasure: the answer to a riddle, the unmasking of a criminal, and, most important, the full explanation of everything that has happened in the preceding narrative".

But The Heart Of the Matter's secrets and distorted correspondences prevent a simple resolution or unmasking of its mysteries; it is easy neither for the characters to detect one another nor for the reader to affirm an all-encompassing understanding of the characters, especially Scobie. Scobie can be policed (in the sense of watched or regulated), but he resists being detected - literally "to be uncovered" - by his fellows, a trait that he shares with several of Greene's other protagonists. In Brighton Rock, for example, Pinkie's "young ancient poker-face... tells nothing" ; he is described as having "an air of removing his thoughts, like heavy bales and stacking them inside, turning the key on all the world".

The cryptic inner life of Querry, the cipher-like architect of A Burnt-Out Case, remains hidden even in his moment of death: "|Absurd,' Querry said, |this is absurd or else...' but what alternative, philosophical or psychological, he had in mind they never knew". His incompleted speech is an ambiguous seal on "an ambiguous man", and satisfies Greene's desire to create an enigma: "I feel X later changed to Querry must die because an element of insoluble mystery in his character has to remain". Many of Greene's novels thus call into question our capacity to interpret the world around us or even each other; an initial series of observations or impressions about a character quickly yields to the fact that man is mysterious, as Leon Rivas, the revolutionary priest of The Honorary Consul, remarks: "I have never met a simple man.

Not even in the confessional, though I used to sit there for hours on end. Man was not created simple". Often man's clouded or distorted insights are contrasted in the text with the vantage point of God, who possesses infinite wisdom. Fowler, in The Quiet American, skeptically links the very limitation of human perception to the impetus for a religious faith: "Perhaps that's why men have invented God - a being capable of understanding". His sentiment is echoed by Maurice Bendrix, who theorizes that "when we get to the end of human beings we have to delude ourselves into a belief in God, like a gourmet who demands more complex sauces with his food". But this kind of outlook notwithstanding, Greene often depicts a powerful divine agent that is experienced by certain characters in the form of an almost tangibly immanent presence, invisibly monitoring their activities.

In The End of the Affair, to cite but one instance, both Bendrix and Sarah Miles lay claim to having an exclusive understanding about why the affair ended, but neither one is privy to complete knowledge, which is reserved for an omniscient force; the novel illustrates what Greene calls God's plot-making, a divine "narrative" that conflicts with a linear structure leading to a conclusion - of which detective fiction is an example - that typifies man's ordering of reality. God transcends the boundaries of temporal knowledge; as the priest in The Power and the Glory intimates, His is a point of view unconfined by time or space: "He thought of the immeasurable distance a man travels.... And to God it was only a moment. The child's snigger and the first mortal sin lay together more closely than two blinks of the eye".

Scobie's attitude to this divine hound fluctuates from a plea to remain connected after he commits himself to maintaining the tie with Helen—"Oh God, I have deserted you. Do not you desert me" - to frustration at God's easy submission to man's pursuit: "Scobie thought: God has just escaped me, but will He always escape?...

It seemed to him for a moment cruelly unfair of God to have exposed himself in this way, a man, a wafer of bread, first in the Palestinian villages and now here in the hot port, there, everywhere, allowing man to have his will of Him". But if he is exasperated by what he experiences as God's accessibility, Scobie still cannot see Him, as he admits: "I've preferred to give you pain rather than give pain to Helen or my wife because I can't observe your suffering. I can only imagine it". The presence of God approaches him like a silent observer that has emerged from the darkness: "The other voice... spoke from the cave of his body; it was as if the sacrament which had lodged there for his damnation gave tongue". The novel's pattern of placing Scobie in view while hiding his pursuer is thus subtly repeated in his relationship with God; this kind of dynamic recalls Jeremy Bentham's scheme for a Panopticon, a circular prison centered on a main watchtower in which fully visible prisoners are constantly monitored by invisible guards.

This new form of punishment, what Michel Foucault calls "disciplinary" as opposed to "traditional" power, "leaves the domain of more or less everyday perception and enters that of abstract consciousness; its effectiveness is seen as resulting from its inevitability, not from its visible intensity.". In such an enterprise, then, the detective or pursuer becomes an invisible but constant presence, continuously asserting his unseen but nonetheless formidable power. In Greene's work the most persistent manifestation of this inexorable but abstract detection are the "beating wings" of Brighton Rock or what Scobie experiences as the sudden movement of an external force which longs to reach him before he dies: "It seemed to him as though someone outside the room were seeking him, calling him, and he made a last effort to indicate that he was here". Whether one argues that his motivations are based on monstrous pride or an oddly sacrosanct fidelity, Scobie's suicide is a means of removing himself from the faceless gaze: "And you too, God - you are ill with me.... You'll be better off if you lose me once and for all.... It will be no use then sweeping the floor to find me or searching for me over the mountains. You'll be able to forget me, God, for eternity". Though Scobie insists that his final actions result from his aversion to insulting God with his lack of penitence, the burning desire to be out of sight is also clearly revealed in his words.

Given the substantial rendering in Greene's fiction of God's omniscience, Scobie's suicide cannot mean that he is actually concealed from divine vision, and yet the "other voice from the cave" gives the vague impression that such flight is plausible: "You say you love me, and yet you'll do this to me - rob me of you for ever. I made you with love.... And now you push me away, you put me out of your reach". What this represents is Scobie's own internalization of God, a Voice that he conceives of in a very particular way as being subject to man's challenge and repudiation. Scobie's final utterance in this agonized debate - "you see, it's an impasse, God, an impasse" - reflects a defiance of divine wishes, at least insofar as he imagines such expectation; Scobie has assimilated moral theology in such a way as to turn religion, in Miguel de Unamuno's striking phrase, "into a kind of police system" .

Though the text's pattern of subverting the temporal process of detection does not extend to a questioning of God's knowledge, Greene's fiction does speculate on a reciprocal interrelation between God and man, a mutuality that exists between creator and creation; this is espoused in The Honorary Consul by Leon Rivas: "The evolution of God depends on our evolution. Every evil act of ours strengthens His night-side, and every good one helps His day-side. We belong to Him and He belongs to us". In a certain sense, then, Greene asserts the displacement of simple cause and effect and posits a deity subject to being shaped by man; the suicide can be construed in that light as a kind of policing of the divinity, who must now submit to Scobie's choices.

Finally, the other voice from the cave suggests not simply the negotiations that Scobie carries out with the divine overseer but, on another level, the constant supervision of the character by his author. The Heart of the Matter consistently demonstrates Flaubert's theory that "an author in his book must be like God in the universe, present everywhere and visible nowhere", as Scobie falls under the perpetual invisible gaze of both the eye of God and of Graham Greene.

The novel strongly brings into focus the relationship between authority, literary creation, and a sense of divinity, an interlinkage that has been deftly illuminated by Edward Said; not only does "authority" connote the power to enforce obedience or influence action, "but it presents a connection as well with author - that is, a person who originates and gives existence to something, a begetter, a beginner, father, or ancestor, a person also who sets forth written statements". Scobie's disappearance may thus be seen to have the dual aim of trying to rebel against both of his "creators," as Greene admits:

All writers, even the worst, are led into assuming a role vaguely comparable to God's, for they create characters over whom they exercise almost total control. I should add, though, that a writer is even more like a double agent than he is like God: he condemns and sustains his characters by turns. Their relationship is so ambiguous that when the characters come to elude his control - as which Scobie in The Heart of the Matter - one doesn't know whom to blame.

A critical sentiment frequently expressed with regard to Greene is that he exercises excessive control over his texts, with the effect of making "the characters subservient to some story-line which is not created by them but by some power outside them". The goal of this tight rein is to manipulate the reader into accepting a certain theological or political doctrine, an assessment of the novelist typified by one critic's lament that in The End of the Affair Greene's management of the plot in the later stages "has the effect of detaching the characters from their established logic as personalities and forcing them to serve a function outside themselves". These charges do raise legitimate issues about Greene's work: "To what extent does the need to communicate the supernatural influence, determine or undermine a novelist's narrative technique?" (Sonnenfeld 308). But even Greene's admitted penchant for authorial intervention, what he calls "the traditional and essential right of a novelist, to comment, to express his views" (Collected 116), does not produce or guarantee an iron-clad control over or regulation of his characters, a situation that he acknowledges in terms that strongly parallel Father Rivas's theology: "The fact is, one is changed by one's own books. The writer plays God until his creatures escape from him and, in their turn, they mould him".

Greene's belief that Scobie was able to evade him may be an allusion to the fact that his intent in developing the character was to show the destructive consequences of pity, but the effect on readers was quite the opposite: "To them Scobie was exonerated, Scobie was 'a good man,' he was hunted to his doom by the harshness of his wife". A further indication of Scobie's lingering ambiguousness also can be located in the various roles that he has been assigned by critics. An early reviewer of The Heart of the Matter sees it as "a kind of moral detective story. The crime is 'the worst a Catholic can commit' and the criminal ironically a professional hunter of men".

On the other hand, Gwenn Boardman suggests the possibility that the pursuit of truth in a detective story is "a search for 'the heart of the matter' of religious experience as it is in Scobie's quest", implying that Scobie is actually the novel's detective. The specific issue of whether Scobie is the man the text is hunting down or the one solving its deepest puzzle - it would seem to me that he is plainly both - serves to reframe the larger question of how to understand him by the end of the novel; as I have indicated, the answer to such a question depends in large part on the relationship between the character and those pursuing him. The Heart of the Matter, with all the tenaciousness of its mechanisms of policing, points out the large gap between mortal knowledge and the mysteries of the human heart. And in confessing to Scobie's partial autonomy even from his author, Greene implies that fiction which is invested in tracking of the minutest kind still cannot totally account for an individual's destiny. Yet I do not believe that imbuing Scobie and other protagonists with an aura of mystery entails a true loss of artistic control on Greene's part, but rather underscores yet again a reciprocity between a creator and his creation, leaving Scobie's fate to recall Tennyson's Ulysses: "Death closes all: but something ere the end/ Some work of noble note, may yet be done/ Not unbecoming men that strove with gods."

Greene remarks that Brighton Rock started in his mind "as a thriller. From the first sentence, my intention was to write a crime novel, but the novel eventually moved in quite a different direction." See Allain 148. Conor Cruise O'Brien notes that "servants, witnesses, drivers, guides, strangers, friends, each main character in turn, almost all are, or seem at some time to someone to be, untrustworthy. This is so of all of Mr. Greene's work and especially of The Heart of the Matter: the whole currency of the colony seems counterfeit". The role of the police in Victorian fiction is a complicated topic in its own right; though in the figures of Inspector Buckett and Sergeant Cuff, Dickens and Wilkie Collins clearly betray an admiration for new methods of English law enforcement, their fictional policemen remain fallible professionals subject to being undermined. In Collins's The Moonstone, for example, Cuff is a figure who possesses skill and knowledge, but he enters the scene "only after the local constable - a much more representative figure of the professional policeman in classic detective fiction - has made a hash of the affair, badly antagonizing everyone and failing even to recognize the all-important clue left near the scene of the crime.

Finally, Cuff himself is plainly wrong about who took the jewel, and how, and why". There are abundant interpretations of the novel's religious content. See, for example, Devitis, Mesnet, and Traversi. Couto comments that "The Heart of the Matter has for so long been discussed as a Catholic novel that it is quite possible to entirely overlook its subtle representation of the relationship between the colonial officer, the intermediary and the colonised". See also her analysis of colonialism, 119-27. Meyers discusses the text's African setting as well. According to the O.E.D. to detect also means "to find out the real character of," a definition that is pertinent to Scobie's ability to remain enigmatic throughout the text. Paul O'Prey argues that Scobie is the Greene character "critics disagree about most".

The Unquiet Graham Greene

President Bush's invocation of Alden Pyle reveals his dangerous naïveté.

There was something bizarre, indeed something almost surreal, about George W. Bush's recent reference to Graham Greene's novel The Quiet American in his speech to the National Convention of the Veterans of Foreign Wars. Attempting to draw a parallel between the conflict in Vietnam and the current conflagration in Iraq, Bush criticized Greene's suggestion that the "quiet American's" patriotism was dangerously naïve:

In 1955 ... Graham Greene wrote a novel called The Quiet American. It was set in Saigon, and the main character was a young government agent named Alden Pyle. He was a symbol of American purpose and patriotism-and dangerous naïveté.

Bush's unexpected sortie into the fictional world of Greene was itself dangerously naïve, especially as several commentators had already suggested that Bush is little more than a real-life incarnation of Alden Pyle. It was also both bemusing and amusing to see Bush reference a work that almost everyone presumed he had never read. Certainly, if he had read The Quiet American, he would not have made the rudimentary error of referring to Pyle as the novel's "main character," a distinction that belongs to Thomas Fowler, a disillusioned and cynical English journalist. Such is the pitiable state of American politics in these sorry days that an uncultured president relies for his semblance of erudition on equally unlettered speechwriters.

Be that as it may, The Quiet American is a good place to look at the relative merits of Messieurs Bush and Greene and serves as a meditation on the relationship between New World naïveté and Old World cynicism. If, for example, there is a great deal of George W. Bush in the transparent (and dangerous) shallowness of Alden Pyle, there is more than a hint of Graham Greene in the world-weary depths of Thomas Fowler. Pyle is certain that "Democracy," "Freedom," and "America" are not only inseparable but synonymous. It is almost as though they form an indivisible trinity as holy as the Trinity of the Christians and as worthy of praise. This quasi-religious zeal turns every war for Democracy into a jihad, with Pyle emerging as a fanatic for the cause of "America" in much the same way that the new breed of Muslim terrorists emerge as fanatics for "Islam." It must be said, however, that Pyle is much more likeable than any Islamic fanatic and is even disarmingly charming in his simple, unquestioning faith in the Motherland. Parallels with Bush are not only palpable, they positively palpitate from the pages of The Quiet American!

But what of Thomas Fowler, the wastrel whose jaded presence dominates the novel? Whereas Pyle is puritanical and abstemious, Fowler is an opium-addicted Baudelairean decadent. Whereas Pyle is an idealist-albeit an idealist enslaved by an ideology (ironically like his communist enemies)-Fowler is cynically indifferent to all ideals. Whereas Pyle is decorously prim in his dealings with women-and particularly in his chivalrous dealings with Phuong, the woman at the center of his and Fowler's desires-Fowler is unremittingly self-serving in his carnal relations, deserting his wife and children and seeing in Phuong little more than a comfortable and convenient ménage, indulging her as an addictive habit that, like opium, allows him to escape temporarily from his responsibility to reality. Whereas Pyle is motivated by an illusory heaven on earth, a heaven of "Democracy" and "Freedom" (again, ironically, like his communist enemies), Fowler shuns heaven and purgatory and desires only the adulterous hell of Paolo and Francesca in Dante's Divine Comedy. (Referring to an unwanted promotion that would force him to return to England, Fowler muses, "Dante never thought up that turn of the screw for his condemned lovers. Paolo was never promoted to Purgatory.") Pyle is willing to be a martyr for his false heaven; Fowler tells heaven (and Purgatory) to go to hell. Who then is worse: the puritanically idealistic Pyle or the morally iconoclastic Fowler? What is worse: the messianic Americanism of George W. Bush or the jaded, ethno-masochistic death wish of most of the leaders of Europe? New World naïveté or Old World cynicism? That is the question. Should we choose one or the other, selecting the better of two evils; or are we at liberty, with Mercutio in Shakespeare's Romeo and Juliet, to call down a plague on both their houses?

And what of Graham Greene himself? Is it fair to associate him too closely with his fictional anti-hero, Thomas Fowler? It is true that, like Fowler, he deserted his wife and children, and it is true that, like Fowler, he settled into a number of adulterous liaisons in the years after he left his wife. It is also true that, as with Fowler, his Catholic wife would not contemplate a divorce (though Fowler's fictional wife eventually relented). Yet these similarities, though certainly not superficial, serve only to mask the very real differences that exist between the life and beliefs of the author and those of his fictional creation. Unlike the doggedly godless Fowler, Greene was, and remained for the most part, a believing Catholic, a fact that separates him not only from Fowler but from the dogmatically godless leadership of Europe. Greene is, therefore, an enigma that warrants further investigation.

Greene's conversion to Catholicism in 1926 was influenced, in the first instance, by the fact that the woman whom he would later marry was herself a convert. It would, however, be a grave error to explain, or explain away, Greene's Catholicism as little more than an effort to please the woman he loved. Other Catholic influences were also at work, such as his evident admiration for the works of Eliot and Chesterton. Greene's early novels, such as Stamboul Train and Brighton Rock, were set in Eliotic wastelands, inhabited by hollow men, in which we nonetheless detect, as with Eliot's poems, the hinted at, haunting presence of an (almost) invisible Christ. His second novel, The Name of Action, published in 1930, employed several lines from Eliot's "The Hollow Men" as its epigraph.

Greene's admiration for Chesterton emerged in his review of Maisie Ward's biography of the writer, in which Greene described Chesterton's Orthodoxy, The Thing, and The Everlasting Man as "among the great books of the age" and similarly praised several of Chesterton's other books, including The Ballad of the White Horse and the novels The Man Who Was Thursday and The Napoleon of Notting Hill. It is also significant that Greene would always consider Newman's Apologia pro Vita Sua, a classic of conversion literature, as one of his favorite books.

If, therefore, Greene's Catholicism can be viewed as genuine, it doesn't alter the fact that his practice of the faith, and his expression of it in his works, was, at best, enigmatic, and, at worst, downright disreputable and heretical. Greene knew as much, declaring to Malcolm Muggeridge, upon the latter's reception into the Church in 1982, that he hoped "you will make a better Catholic than I have done." And yet, beguilingly and paradoxically, Greene's troubled faith, and his marital infidelity, provided the inherent tension in the labyrinthine morality plays that were his novels.

Greene deserted his family shortly after the end of World War II, leaving his wife for another woman. Vivien Greene remembered vividly the day that her husband left: "It was very difficult with the children. ... We went upstairs into the drawing room and then he left. And I thought, well, I'll probably never see him again and looked out of the window that was facing the street, and he looked back for a minute, didn't wave, but looked back." This dramatic moment clearly haunted Greene as well, for it emerges, ghost-like, in The Quiet American when Fowler turned random memories over in his mind: "a fox ... seen by the light of an enemy flare ... the body of a bayoneted Malay ... my wife's face at a window when I came home to say good-bye for the last time."

Greene's contorted conscience twisted itself agonizingly through the plot of The Heart of the Matter, the novel he wrote shortly after his desertion of his family, in which the moral convulsions of Scobie left many critics squirming. Whereas some writers, including Evelyn Waugh, Edward Sackville-

West, and Raymond Mortimer, had suggested that Scobie was a sinful saint, others had seen only the sinner: "Scobie commits adultery, sacrilege, murder (indirectly), and suicide in quick succession," one correspondent wrote. "In three of these cases he is well aware of what he is doing ... he takes communion in mortal sin because he can't bear to hurt his wife's feelings. This isn't the way a saint behaves." These views were reiterated in another review by a Father John Murphy:

> Scobie is a Catholic with a conscience of the highest sensitivity and insight whose weak will ultimately leads him to adultery, sacrilegious Holy Communions, responsibility for a murder ... and for full measure, to a suicide. ... How can you account for the fact that a man commits suicide in order, among other things, to avoid making any more bad Communions? But the answer is obvious: Because he despaired where he should have repented.

Another member of the Catholic clergy, in this case a bishop, reminded the author of The Heart of the Matter that "adultery is adultery whatever attempts may be made to disguise it by not using the hard word." Equally ruthless in his criticism was George Orwell, who opined that if Scobie "really felt that adultery is mortal sin he would stop committing it. ... If he believed in Hell, he would not risk going there merely to spare the feelings of a couple of neurotic women."

At the other end of the critical spectrum, the Jesuit C.C. Martindale described The Heart of the Matter as "a magnificent book," adding that its effect on one "hard-headed man to whom this book was given" had been to serve as "the last necessary stimulus" to his becoming a Catholic. Another correspondent wished it to be "put on record ... that one great sinner was so moved by Mr Greene's last book that he has completely changed his way of life and returned to the practice of the Faith."

Greene's own response to the critical reaction indicated that these repentant sinners, rather than the novel's detractors, had the deepest affinity with his own understanding of the novel: "I did not regard Scobie as a saint," he wrote to Waugh, "and his offering his damnation up was intended to show how muddled a mind of good will could become when once 'off the rails.'" Ironically these words would become prophetically autobiographical. The longer Greene remained "off the rails," the more muddled he became in his approach to Catholicism.

By the time that Greene wrote his play "The Potting Shed" in 1957, even old friends and allies, such as Evelyn Waugh, were losing patience with his heterodox dabblings. The play was "great nonsense theologically," Waugh complained, "and will puzzle people needlessly." Three years later, after Greene wrote to Waugh of how his latest novel, A Burnt Out Case, was intended "to give expression to various states or moods of belief or unbelief" and that the characterization of the doctor had represented "a settled and easy atheism," Waugh replied impatiently that many would see the novel "as a recantation of faith": "To my mind the expression 'settled and easy atheism' is meaningless, for an atheist denies his whole purpose as a man-to love and serve God. Only in the most superficial way can atheists appear 'settled and easy.'"

As Waugh observed Greene's descent from the realm of reason and creed to that of mere mood, one wonders whether he was reminded of the wit of his friend Ronald Knox who had written half a century earlier of the similar descent from faith to "feeling" of Anglican Modernists who "... temp'ring bigot Zeal, Corrected 'I believe' to 'One does feel...'"

In his last years, Greene showed a few tentative signs of returning to a more orthodox practice of the faith, though it would be an exaggeration to describe his Catholicism as "settled and easy." "I've betrayed a great number of things and people in the course of my life," he stated in 1979, "which probably explains this uncomfortable feeling I have about myself, this sense of having been cruel, unjust. It still torments me often enough before I go to sleep."

It is in this tormented light that we must view Graham Greene's relationship with his faith, his life, and his work. He never felt comfortable with Catholicism, but then he never felt comfortable with anything else either. Like St. Thomas the Apostle, whom Greene chose as his confirmation saint, he was a doubter. He doubted others, he doubted himself, and he doubted God. And yet the profundity of his novels never resides in the doubt itself but in the ultimate doubt about the doubt. It was this doubt about doubt that kept him clinging desperately to the Catholic faith. Greene was paradox personified. He was a pessimistic pessimist in the positive sense in which he was always pessimistic about his own pessimism and in the positive sense in which these two negatives made a contribution to the true moral depth of his work.

The Third Spring: G. K. Chesterton, Graham Greene, Christopher Dawson, and David Jones.

In 1852, John Henry Newman preached a sermon at the first Provincial Synod of Westminster in which he spoke of the restoration of the Catholic hierarchy in Britain as the coming of a "Second Spring... a restoration in the moral world, such as that which yearly takes place in the physical" (Sermons Preached on Various Occasions). Accompanying the more juridical aspects involved in this budding season of British Catholicism was the fact that a good number of British intellectuals had also turned to Rome, among whom were notables such as Coventry Patmore, Alice Meynell, Oscar Wilde, and, of course, Newman himself.

For Newman in particular, the decision for Roman Catholicism meant more than simply his acknowledgment that only Rome had preserved the historical link to the apostolic church and to Jesus himself. Rome alone, he had decided, was the church's only hope for standing strong against 19th-century liberalism's disregard of dogma, authority, and tradition, and its naive belief in inevitable human and historical progress. Ironically, Newman, with his theories of the authority of the laity and his notions of doctrinal development, was often suspect within his new church. However, his conviction that liberalism's path led ultimately to the betrayal of Christianity never wavered.

In this scholarly yet readable book, Schwartz builds on Newman's image of a "Second Spring," naming an early 20th-century movement in British Catholicism a "Third Spring."

In this new springtime, what most attracted the "considerable number of intellectuals" who joined the Catholic Church was its strong opposition to modernity, liberalism in doctrine, and secularism. "Thinkers drawn to the church," S. says, "were... almost exclusively those enticed by its own increasingly radical rebuttal of prevalent norms".

Christianity's task, they were convinced, was not to reconcile itself with contemporary culture, but to take a countercultural, prophetic stance that preserved the truth of Christian tradition. The book focuses on four thinkers—all men—who illustrate in a particularly vivid way this early 20th-century, general countercultural pattern of women and men attracted to Catholicism.

They are the journalist, poet, and novelist G. K. Chesterton, the novelist Graham Greene, the historian Christopher Dawson, and the poet David Jones. While each is unique, all shared a distaste for what they considered a doctrinally weak Anglicanism, a suspicion of modern relativism, and a love for Catholicism's strong authority and rich tradition.

Chesterton is described as a seeker who found wonder and joy in life, and found these deepened by his Catholic faith, wherein lay true safety and sanity in an age of "Progress, industrialism and imperialism". Despite the fact that he had difficulty with a number of the Church's dogmatic teachings, Greene felt deeply that the Church's greatest strength was its "contrarian ethic". Dawson saw Catholicism as "the sole avatar of faith that had retained its subversive legacy", and Jones was convinced that only Rome's doctrine and authority could effectively rebel "against dehumanizing modern technocracy".

The three who lived into the Second Vatican Council felt betrayed and disillusioned by some aspects of the Church's commitment to aggiorna-mento, especially regarding liturgical reform. "I thought the Church and I wanted the same thing," a frustrated Greene cried out. However, some rethinking of Vatican II during the pontificate of John Paul II, as well as contemporary movements such as Pentecostalism, S. suggests, might be proving his subjects' conviction to be correct. In any case, he says, their prophetic stance still poses a challenge that is constantly proving relevant in today's rootless world.

Some years ago in America magazine, Avery (now Cardinal) Dulles wrote that Christianity is always in some sense countercultural. Christianity also, however, signifies much more than a prophetic stance against this age. There exists a specifically "Catholic imagination" that embraces the world, its goodness, and its cultures, as sacraments of God's presence in a creation that is nevertheless shot through with imperfection and evil. S. does not totally deny this Catholic imagination to his subjects, but it is clear that his interest in their lives and witness lies elsewhere.

Graham Greene, RIP

GRAHAM GREENE's novels were driven by a strong plot-line, and he could also share the reader as a cat shakes a rat with sudden revelations and reversals, sometimes involving an ambiguous divine intervention. In this vein, he wrote four very good novels, Brighton Rock (1938), The Power and the Glory (1940), The Heart of the Matter (1948), and The End of the Affair (1951). All were critical and popular successes, and led to his international celebrity after World War II. But there is the problem of his sensibility. He had a powerful tropism toward the sordid. When he became a Catholic at the age of 22, he became in effect a Jansenist, and seems always to have been a world-disgusted puritan.

His characters typically are alcoholic priests, weak adulterers, defeated tropical administrators, marginal masses of all sorts. He could not bring himself to believe in a clean shirt or clean fingernails. Greeneland was but half a world, and a tiresome one at that. There is little point in dwelling on Greene's tedious anti-Americanism. His puritanism reinforced an instinctive hatred of American "materialism," i.e., high standard of living. After the war, England, shorn of its pre-war status and power, often exhibited the "genteel poverty" syndrome—envy of the successful. Greene shared this syndrome. He sourly favored the East, as morally more pure.

Greene much disliked being categorized as a "Catholic

novelist." He considered himself a novelist who was also a Catholic, and who sometimes made religious issues the subject matter of his narratives. He meant that an atheis could presumably have treated religious issues in a similar way. Indeed, Greene several times remarked that he had a great deal of difficulty believing in God. But given his fascination with religious themes, one might be forgiven for wondering if he was a sort of reverse hypocrite, pretending to a wavering faith when he was really a firm believer all the time.

Diary: I Am Shown the outside of All Saints Terrace, Where Graham Greene Had Lodgings, and Which Served as the Model for Many Disreputable Houses in His Work. There Is No Plaque.

By David Lodge

To Nottingham, to give the first Graham Greene Memorial Lecture. I don't give many lectures these days, but David Belbin, head of the MA in Creative Writing at Trent University, enticed me by invoking Greene's connections with Nottingham. Greene spent four months here in 1925, at the age of 21, learning the craft of sub-editing as an intern on the Nottingham Journal. It was the furthest north he had ever been, his first experience of a predominantly working-class industrial city, and he didn't much like it. "There's absolutely nothing worth doing in this beastly place," he wrote to his fiancee Vivien in Oxford. No excitement, no interest, nothing worth a halfpenny curse."

But the screenwriter Michael Eaton, a Nottingham man, argues it was here that the novelist discovered "Greeneland", that gloomy, seedy country of the mind where most of his stories unfold. One of Greene's best "Entertainments", A Gun For Sale, is set in Nottingham, as is his play The Potting Shed. Mike and David show me the outside of All Saints Terrace, where Greene had lodgings, and which served as the model for many dingy and disreputable houses in his work. There is no plaque.

Greene arrived in Nottingham as an atheist with an Anglican background and left as a Roman Catholic. To please his devoutly Catholic fiancee, he took instructions at the cathedral of St Barnabas from the happily named Fr Trollope, a former actor who had a knack of making converts. Greene was one of 150 he received into the Church in ten years. Visiting the cathedral, I am struck by its similarity to the Catholic cathedral of St Chad in Birmingham, where I live, and not surprised to discover that like St Chad's it was the work of Pugin, or that the architect considered it one of his finest buildings: it is a gem, and beautifully maintained.

One tends to think of Nottingham as being to the East Midlands as Birmingham is to the West Midlands, but they are very different. Birmingham is four times larger and the surrounding conurbation sprawls as far as Wolverhampton. Nottingham is much more compact—you can see open country from hills near the city centre—and architecturally more low-profile, more intimate and more old-fashioned.

The Victorian railway station reminds me of Birmingham's Snow Hill when I arrived there 40-odd years ago, before it was rebuilt in a soulless modern style. Nottingham feels like a well-balanced urban environment, and the people I meet like living there. All the more surprising, then, that it is declared "crime capital" of England in a survey reported on the day of my visit, whereas Birmingham comes out rather well. The council leader questions the statistical basis of the survey, and the people I speak to think it paints an exaggerated picture, but nobody can give me a convincing explanation for what is an alarming phenomenon. It's a challenge waiting for some sociologist to take up.

The venue for my lecture is the grand Victorian Arkwright Building, formerly the Nottingham University College where D H Lawrence studied to be a teacher, and now part of Trent, one of the largest of the new universities. The MA in Creative Writing, though lacking the glamour of East Anglia's famous course, is thriving. When I started out as a university teacher in 1960 there were no such courses in Britain, and their ubiquity in the US was sneered at by our academic and literary establishments.

Now most British universities offer them, and a National

Academy of Writing is due to open in Birmingham next year. There are several reasons why universities have changed their attitude: the replacement of the old finals exams by a modular course system; the transformation of higher education into a buyer's market; and, perhaps, a reaction against the aridity of much academic criticism and theory. It is noticeable how many emerging novelists have taken such courses, and how many writers support themselves by teaching them. It's a significant development that is changing our literary culture in ways yet to be measured and analysed.

David Lodge's The Year of Henry James: the story of a novel; with other essays on the genesis, composition and reception of literary fiction is published this week by Harvill Secker

Characteristic Twist: "I began to believe in Heaven because I believed in Hell."

Some kind of breakdown occurred at sixteen, perhaps the result of tension at school. He lived for six months with self-proclaimed Jungian analyst Kenneth Richmond and his attractive wife, Zoe. Richmond was a quack with no formal training. And something happened between Greene and Zoe. Rumors circulated that one of the Richmond children was Greene's—an unpromising start for a man prone to impossible romantic longings.

Seemingly as a defence against depression, Greene became filled—as he would be throughout his life—with wanderlust. While an Oxford undergraduate, Greene got himself hired to do espionage in Ireland and in French-occupied Germany in exchange for free travel. He briefly joined the Communist party, partly in the hope of a free trip to Moscow (though he may well have been working, West believes, for British intelligence as a double agent).

Greene had always been interested in Catholicism, and when he married Vivienne Dayrell Browning, a Catholic convert, he converted as well. Yet nothing—love, religion, foreign travel, intrigue—could ever quiet some deep restlessness within Greene. It was not mere youthful bravado that made him write to Vivienne during their courtship: "The only thing worth doing at the moment seems to be to go and get killed somehow in an exciting manner." He had played Russian roulette at home after his psychoanalysis and perhaps later at Oxford.

Nonetheless, he was beginning to make his way. After a couple of flops, Greene deliberately courted success with Stamboul Train (1932), a book aimed at moviegoers. But he hit his full stride with The Power and the Glory (1940), the story of a whiskey priest during the Mexican Revolution, tormented by his own cowardice and weakness, who eventually dies, after one act of religious heroism, in front of a Communist firing squad.

In The Heart of the Matter (1948) and The End of the Affair (1951), the other two books in what is sometimes thought of as a trilogy of his middle years, Greene began writing about a question closer to home: adultery and its effects on religious belief. Though Greene and his wife lived together for a dozen years and had two children, around 1940 he began an affair with Dorothy Glover. He later claimed that the strain of overwork broke up the marriage, but it seems truer to say that a side of Greene's personality had opened up that would always torment him.

Greene quoted Charles Peguy as an epigraph to The Heart of the Matter: "The sinner is at the very heart of Christianity.... No one is as competent as the sinner in Christian affairs. No one, except the saint." Some readers thought that the honorable police officer Scobie in that novel was meant as a portrait of a saint. But Scobie's dilemma, torn as a Catholic between his duties to his wife and his promises to a desperate young woman with whom he is having an affair, may reflect an ambivalence in Greene himself. Scobie's solution—disguised suicide—recalls a constant temptation.

Without breaking off either his marriage or his affair with Clover, in 1946 Greene began a simultaneous affair with a stunningly beautiful Catholic convert, Catherine Walston, who was also his goddaughter. He dedicated The End of the Affair to her. In the book, a writer is having an affair with a neighbor's wife. He and the neighbour have a strange friendship, as did Greene and Catherine's husband. When a German bomb hits the building where the lovers are meeting, the woman spontaneously prays to God that she will change her life if only her lover is not dead. Almost miraculously, he is not. But this sets off a titanic tug-of-war in several characters' souls about the relative claims of human and divine love.

The End of the Affair was a scandalous success, so much so that some Catholic wags complained that it gave the impression Christ had said: "If you love me, break my commandments." Greene and Walston were certainly busy doing that. Greene began rationalizing the affair, even getting advice from some priests that it was all right to go to confession again and again knowing he would immediately resume the liaison. Greene's earlier sense of the acute tension between earthly and heavenly impulses gradually slid into a much more lax Catholicism.

This character flaw weakened his art, as he himself might have predicted. One of his central contentions as a literary critic was that after the seventeenth century the novel had degenerated because of a lack of religious seriousness. Only in the nineteenth century, when orthodox religious belief reappeared, were the fullness and depth of the human soul again available to writers. For all their vagaries about religion, Dickens, Hardy, Conrad, Lawrence, and James had all benefited from it. By contrast, he argued, Virginia Woolf and E. M. Forster's characters "wandered like cardboard symbols through a world that was paperthin."

Politics began to replace the drama of the soul in Greene's writings by the 1950s. The Quiet American (1956), though not as purely anti-American as often thought, does foreshadow a growing indulgence towards communism. Our Man in Havana (1958) pokes fun at the world of espionage. Behind this "entertainment," however, hangs a sense of foreboding about British, American, and other shadowy intelligence forces. Greene was primed for the advent of Fidel Castro, whom he would later defend.

Greene's only other truly important novel, A Burnt-Out Case, is set in a leper colony in Africa where the architect Querry has fled following the failure of his gift as a designer of churches. Believing in nothing, he tries to help with the patients and is mistakenly characterized as a saint by the European media. Perhaps Greene was feeling unworthy of veneration himself. A Burnt-Out Case was the last gasp of a great talent. The later novels—The Honorary Consul , Monsieur Quixote (1982)—all lack the spiritual depth and emotional fireworks of vintage Greene. They lapse into sloppy ideology and gestures toward a vague liberation theology.

In a 1987 speech Greene gave in Moscow, he claimed to have observed a new thing: "We are fighting—Roman Catholics are fighting—together with Communists, and working together with Communists. We are fighting together against the Death Squads in El Salvador. We are fighting together against the Contras in Nicaragua. We are fighting together against General Pinochet in Chile." Gorbachev, who was present at this speech, was only two years away from pulling the plug on the Latin Communists, their Catholic sympathizers, and his own USSR. Greene concluded: "I even have a dream, Mr. General Secretary, that perhaps one day before I die, I shall know that there is an Ambassador of the Soviet Union giving good advice at the Vatican."

W. J. West raises the possibility that Greene may have been working as a double agent with British Intelligence all this time, giving the impression of left-wing sympathies for information-gathering purposes. But that seems quite improbable on West's own showing.

Just before the re-election of Ronald Reagan in 1984, for example, Greene told a Spanish priest that, if he died, he wanted it known that he would have become a Communist if Reagan were returned to office. Around the same time, Greene told Malcolm Muggeridge that Russia only destroyed the Church's body, while America destroyed its soul. Norman Sherry remarks, "How could his subtle mind engage in such intellectual folly?"

In the end, it's baffling. Greene's insight into the human

soul could be as acute as any contemporary's. But his trajectory presents a cautionary tale. Before communism started to break up, Greene had openly admired those Polish Catholics who collaborated with the Communist regime. Such political misjudgments, along with his desire to absolve himself for his own sins, made him unsympathetic to the vision of the human person held up by John Paul II. It comes as no surprise that Greene characterized the Pope's views on sexual matters as "unimaginative and unkind."

Greene's character flaws and Cold War fantasies led to the extinction of a great gift. He went from being the premier English novelist of the soul to an enabler of later and lesser lights who let their appetites and resentments rule their talents. Someday, we will be in a better position to winnow the wheat from the chaff in Greene's rich oeuvre. For the moment, however, he is a sad reminder of much that went awry in the second half of our century.

ROBERT ROYAL is President of the Faith and Reason Institute in Washington, D. C.

Graham Greene, Evelyn Waugh and Mexico.

By Michael G. Brennan

"It is before you cross a frontier that you experience fear" (Graham Greene)

IN 1951, the year in which The End of the Affair was published, Graham Greene also contributed a five-page introduction to John Gerard: The Autobiography of an Elizabethan, translated by Father Philip Caraman, S.J.—a composition which passes unnoticed in the three major biographies of Greene by Norman Sherry, Michael Shelden, and W.J. West. This introduction (also overlooked by most of Greene's modern-day literary critics) may, at first sight, appear merely of incidental interest to his career as a novelist. It puts on record Greene's intense admiration for the heroism and spiritual fortitude of Jesuit missionaries, both during the brutal Elizabethan persecutions of the 1580s and during the 1920s in modern Mexico.

On one level, Greene's willingness to attach his name (a

potent marketing-device after the international success of The Heart of the Matter in 1948) to this translation was doubtless intended as a straightforward act of personal friendship. The translator was a respected member of an extensive London circle of Catholic literati, including Evelyn Waugh and Greene's then mistress, Catherine Walston, and the idea for a new translation of Gerard's work had come from Father Martin D'Arcy, the Provincial of the English Jesuits. However, on a deeper level, the vicissitudes of the Elizabethan Jesuit missionaries also seem to have exerted a strong emotional appeal, both heroic and spiritual, for Greene.

His introduction to Caraman's translation at first casts Gerard's gripping narrative of his return to England, followed by his capture, interrogation and torture, as a kind of exciting "adventure" story. But this tone is then recast within a more somber and devotional framework: "(it would be more accurate, when we remember his narrow escapes, his disappointments and betrayals, the long terrible scene of his torture, to call it his Passion)".

This concept of delineating the "Passion" of the missionary priest is both powerful and arresting; and it is one which took firm root in Greene's creative imagination during the second half of the 1930s. A key text—perhaps the most important one—in considering the formulation of this spiritual concept in his writings is Greene's first-hand account of the effects of the repression of the Catholic Church in Mexico, as recorded in The Lawless Roads (1939), a volume which is often categorized, rather flatly, as one of his major "travel" books. It seems now mainly prized either for its spectacularly vivid realizations of the oppressive landscapes of Mexico; or for its documentary relevance to the rise of Mexican socialism; or, most commonly for modern literary critics, on account of its germinal role in the inspiration of Greene's most powerful and memorable depiction of the personal agonies and "Passion" of the ordinary, flawed man through the sufferings of the whisky priest in The Power and the Glory (1940).

But The Lawless Roads (and it is significant that it was

compiled soon after the intense preoccupation with hell, damnation, and the elusiveness of redemption in Brighton Rock) should also be considered for the insight it offers into the development of Greene's own understanding of his personal but often doctrinally unorthodox adherence to a Catholic faith. Within the context of Greene's exploration of his own often conflicting religious emotions in his fictional writings, The Lawless Roads becomes a pivotal text, drawing together many of the preoccupations of Brighton Rock and, at the same time, preparing the author for the intense devotional potency of The Power and the Glory.

Greene himself admitted in Ways of Escape and The Other Man that, following his conversion in 1926 (motivated primarily by a desire to please his future wife, Vivien Dayrell-Browning), his own Catholicism had hardly exceeded a dutiful formal observance of the statutory devotions. Only through his 1938 visit to Mexico (and also, to a lesser extent, in response to Franco's attack on Republican Spain), did he finally achieve a more personal and emotional engagement with what, through Brighton Rock, had already become for him the three key polarities of Catholicism: heaven and hell, love and hate, salvation and damnation. In the torrid and murderous landscapes of The Lawless Roads, an environment perfectly matched to his idiosyncratic tastes for the extremities of the human condition, Greene finally found a world which demanded from him a more intense personal engagement with Catholicism. This engagement, however, did not blend seamlessly with his initial purposes as a writer in going to Mexico. The Lawless Roads, unlike his earlier "travel" work, Journey Without Maps (1936), is distinctive for a striking unevenness of structure, at least for an overtly journalistic work which purports to have a clear documentary purpose.

It opens, for example, not in South America (or even with Greene's outward voyage from Europe) but rather with a series of puzzling internalized reminiscences about Greene's school days and childhood fears. The first readers in 1939 of The Lawless Roads—many of whom would perhaps have been drawn to it by the success of Brighton Rock—were offered a disturbing "Prologue" which took them not to Mexico but first to the hellish landscapes of Berkhamsted School and its renowned "green baize door."

This was a world in which on one side his parents' quarters, smelling of "books and fruit and eau-de-Cologne" seem to represent a calm, socially ordered middle-class England; and on the other, the lawless iodine and ink-stained schoolrooms, presided over by the bullying Collifax, become a kind of allegorical Mexico: "one was aware of fear and hate, a kind of lawlessness—appalling cruelties could be practiced without a second thought... Hell lay about them in their infancy. There lay the horror and the fascination." But—and the relevance of this "Prologue" to the subsequent chapters of The Lawless Roads now comes into clearer focus—it is only through this schoolboy world of extremities that the author can first experience the peace and solace of what he denotes as pure "faith."

Retreating into the school gardens, a kind of tainted Eden, from the fearful dichotomy symbolized by the "green baize door," the young boy finds: Faith came to one—shapelessly, without dogma, a presence above a croquet lawn, something associated with violence, cruelty, evil across the way. One began to believe in heaven because one believed in hell, but for a long while it was only hell one could picture with a certain intimacy. Such language, of course, pointedly echoes that of Brighton Rock. It is as though the thoughts of Pinkie had contaminated Greene's drafting of the "Prologue" to The Lawless Roads.

This, of course, is entirely understandable since, as he notes in Ways of Escape the page-proofs of Brighton Rock were actually corrected by Greene during his Mexican journey. Although The Lawless Roads is habitually paired with The Power and the Glory, its "Prologue" suggests that it may also be regarded as a self-conscious continuation of the three central spiritual dichotomies of Brighton Rock. As The Lawless Roads develops, specific political and geographical descriptions of Mexico are increasingly interrupted by the author's apparently incidental spiritual musings and anxieties. The first chapter (maintaining the motif of the "green baize door") is starkly titled "The Border", and Greene frequently reiterates its symbolic significance: "It is before you cross a frontier that you experience fear".

The transitory peace experienced by the child on the croquet lawn at Berkhamsted is momentarily regained when Greene observes in Orizaba the celebrations of "Saint's Night" on one of those evenings "that conspire for happiness... during a few hours you experience peace". Finding himself in a strange land, it is as though the author's primary struggle lay not in physically locating himself in an alien and hostile landscape—the renowned precision and visual potency of his descriptions of Mexico are those of the cool, controlling artist's eye.

Physically speaking, he seems entirely in command of his own geographical placement. But, at the same time, there are touches of uncertainty and questioning about exactly what moral and spiritual lessons should be drawn from this testing experience. The classrooms of Berkhamsted and Pinkie's Brighton constantly intrude into the alien environment of Marxist Mexico: "No hope anywhere: I have never been in a country where you are more aware all the time of hate... There has always been hate, I suppose, in Mexico, but now it is the official teaching". It is as though the narrative of the objective journalist is repeatedly and bewilderingly thrown by the sheer intensity of what he sees and hears about the fortitude of the hunted priests and their congregations during the religious suppressions. As the political and geographical details of The Lawless Roads rapidly encompass the extremes of climate, politics, and religion, so they are increasingly utilized as a framework for a rather more self-questioning narrative of the author's own spiritual education and, it might even be suggested, of his private "Passion" leading for the first time to his emotional engagement with religious belief.

"The haunted, trapped, murdered priest is our contemporary" (Evelyn Waugh) WHY, then, link The Lawless Roads of the late-1930s to Father Caraman's 1951 translation of the autobiography of an Elizabethan Jesuit? The first and indisputable reason is that Greene himself explicitly makes the connection between the two works. Quoting from Gerard's own account of his nerve-racking arrival back on the east coast of England as a young Jesuit missionary, Greene comments in his 1951 introduction:

That homecoming has been enacted in many countries during our half-century since Father Pro landed at Vera Cruz in his bright cardigan and his striped tie and his brown shoes, but here, in Gerard's narrative, it is happening in our own Norfolk, to us. (viii) The Jesuit Miguel Pro had returned to his native Mexico in July 1926 at the age of twenty-five: "He came back to his own country from a foreign seminary much as Campion returned to England from Douai," The Lawless Roads reports. The description of Father Pro's habitual disguise (for the garb of a priest would have provoked instant arrest) in his introduction to Caraman's translation also draws directly from the same paragraph in The Lawless Roads:

He may well have worn the same disguise when he landed (the equivalent of Campion's doublet and hose): a dark lounge suit, soft collar and tie, a bright cardigan. Most priests wear their mufti with a kind of uneasiness, but Pro was a good actor. In both descriptions, the English martyr Edmund Campion acts as a model for Greene's understanding of the physical and spiritual heroism of Father Pro. Just as Campion's memory was revered by English Catholics after his execution at Tyburn in December 1581 (and also served as an inspiration for the young missionary priests, including Father John Gerard, who followed him), so the official photographs of Father Pro's execution, intended to publicize the government's successful repression of the Catholic Church, served only to bolster the religious fervor of the common people.

The possession of the image of him, "praying for his enemies by the pitted wall, receiving the coup de grace" soon attained an iconic status among the Mexican peasantry, a gesture of silent resistance, made all the more powerful by futile government attempts to prohibit the possession of such photographs. But simply noting the fact that Greene himself makes a direct comparison between Campion and Father Pro is only the first stage in an appreciation of the significance of this connection between The Lawless Roads and Father Gerard's autobiography.

The symbolic and devotional act of a missionary willingly crossing over a frontier into a dangerous and hostile territory becomes in The Lawless Roads the central motif for Greene's personal understanding of the power and pervasiveness of Roman Catholicism in the face of brutal repression. Only through an understanding of the sheer power of hate, cruelty and violence—and a stoical testing of oneself against their pains—can a faith in goodness and love finally come to fruition. Such a duality is, of course, not only central to The Lawless Roads but also to Brighton Rock and The Power and the Glory. The reiterated juxtapositioning of Campion and Pro, a sixteenth-century Englishman and a twentieth-century Mexican, effectively formulates a strong sense of the timeless battle of the soldiers of St. Ignatius of Loyola against the forces of evil. "For Mexico remained Catholic," Greene notes at the end of the "Prologue" to The Lawless Roads, "it was a war... for the soul of the Indian".

The England of Queen Elizabeth I and the Mexico of President Calles constantly interact with one another in The Lawless Roads. At first, in the "Preface," the hints are merely subliminal, almost trivial. Greene playfully recalls Berkhamsted's mundane "Tudor Cafe" and its photographer's shop with the the genuine "diamonded Elizabethan pane" of glass. But by the end of the first chapter, "The Border," Campion and Pro stand heroically alongside one another: "They had killed Campion, they said, for treason, not for his religion, and they said the same of Pro in 1927". The same point is picked up in the third chapter, describing Greene's impressions of Mexico City, but now in a tone of passionate spiritual conviction:

> For the State puts its own interpretation on the word treason—and never punishes anyone for his religion. It is the technique the totalitarian State has always employed: in the time of Elizabeth in England, just as much as in Mexico, Russia, or Germany today, and Campion's reply is still a valid one,

"In condemning us you condemn all your own ancestors—all the ancient priests, bishops, and kings... For what have we taught, however you may qualify it with the odious name of treason, that they did not uniformly teach? To be condemned with these lights—not of England only, but of the world—by their degenerate descendants is both gladness and glory to us." Greene's preoccupation during the latter half of the 1930s with the Jesuit missions seems to have relied heavily upon two major sources: Evelyn Waugh's popular biography, Edmund Campion, published in 1935 (the year in which both John Fisher and Thomas More were canonized 400 years after their executions); and a now long forgotten volume by the Jesuit Father Wilfred Parsons on the suppression of the Catholic Church in Mexico, entitled Mexican Martyrology (1936).

Before considering Waugh's handling of Campion's life and martyrdom, it is also worth briefly recalling the important personal connection which links Edmund Campion directly to Father Caraman's translation of Gerard's autobiography. In July 1930 Waugh had been on the lookout for a Jesuit priest to instruct him in the Catholic faith. His friend, Olivia Plunket Greene, had found him Father Martin D'Arcy, and Waugh was duly received into the Church on September 29. In 1934 the lease on the Jesuit's college at Oxford, Campion Hall, was coming up to expire and a decision had been retaken to build a new institution off St. Aldate's. Father D'Arcy was then its Master and, as Martin Stannard has explained, Waugh wished to offer his literary skills as a way of offering thanks to his former instructor, "to whom, under God, I owe my faith." Furthermore, Waugh had at first been considering writing a life of Pope Gregory XIII (who founded a system of seminaries for Roman Catholic priests and supported the Irish rebels against Queen Elizabeth I's anti-Catholicism) but was deflected from this project by Father D'Arcy who suggested Campion as a preferable subject matter.

Given that D'Arcy also advised Father Caraman to translate Gerard's autobiography (and was instrumental in drawing Greene into this latter project since they were close friends by the early-1950s), it becomes apparent that the interest of two of England's most influential twentieth-century novelists in commemorating the historical achievement of the Jesuit missions was far from being merely a random coincidence. If, as can be argued, both Waugh and Greene were drawn into a deftly orchestrated literary campaign on behalf of the Jesuits, then Father D'Arcy's impact on their respective literary careers, from the mid-1930s until the early-1950s, should be regarded as of the utmost significance.

Waugh writes in Edmund Campion not only as a well-briefed journalist/historian but also as a fervent devotee of the Roman Catholic faith. His depiction of Campion as the prototype English Jesuit martyr (he had, in fact, taught at Douai the first of the seminarian martyrs, Cuthbert Mayne) is a potent, at times almost lyrically written, piece of Jesuit hagiography. At the same time, it also aims at providing a broad English readership (and not necessarily an exclusively Catholic one) with a clear sense of the essential character and quality of the man.

But, despite his genuine concern to document the full span of his subject's life, for Waugh the essence of Campion's achievement lies in his unifying and unwavering commitment to the one culminating act of his mission - a resolutely embraced martyrdom. For example, from the chronology of his early years at Douai, Waugh places strongest emphasis upon the fortuitously still-surviving copy of the Summa used by Campion at the college, with the word "Martyrium"—glossed by Waugh as "the single mot prophete et radieux"—annotated in Campion's own hand against an argument on baptism by blood. Similarly, the final chapter, starkly entitled "Martyr", painfully details the agonies of Campion's torture, hanging, and mutilation but, as it draws to a triumphant conclusion, Waugh breaks joyfully into an unashamed hymn of praise. An onlooker, Henry Walpole, is splashed by a spot of Campion's blood as the butcher throws his disemboweled entrails into a cauldron of boiling water:

In that moment he was caught into a new life; he crossed the sea, became a priest, and, thirteen years later, after very terrible sufferings, died the same death as Campion's on the gallows at York. And so the work of Campion continued; so it continues. He was one of a host of martyrs, each, in their several ways, gallant and venerable... to each succeeding generation, Campion's fame has burned with unique warmth and brilliance; it was his genius to express, in sentences that have resounded across the centuries, the spirit of chivalry in which they suffered, to typify in his zeal, his innocence, his inflexible purpose, the pattern which they followed.

In his favorable review of Waugh's biography, published in the November 1935 issue of the Spectator (and often reprinted as a preface to later editions of Edmund Campion) Greene himself picks up on this description of Walpole's "anointing" with Campion's blood, using it to demonstrate a resolute "continuity of culture" for the Jesuit missions. He was also very much struck by that peculiar blending of extreme heroism and playfulness, characteristic of young men about to cross a geographical frontier into alien, dangerous territories:

The graduates from Douai crossed the Channel to martyrdom with the same enthusiasm, the same rather childish release of spirits in practical jokes, as recruits in the first months of the First World War. The similarity ends at the Channel ports. For these recruits there were no leave trains. They had simply to stay in the line until death... For both Greene and Waugh, this poignant sense of a playful bravado served only to accentuate their personal awareness of the heroic, unquestioning self-sacrifice of the missionaries. In this 1935 review Greene was inspired by Campion's story to recall the experiences of young Englishmen in the trenches of France and Belgium.

But, by the time the second edition of Edmund Campion was published in 1946, Waugh had much more immediate battlefields to call upon. In the aftermath of the Second World War, Waugh felt, like Greene, that the memory of Campion's personal via dolorosa provided a clear model for a more modern devotional understanding of Father Pro's fortitude and self-sacrifice. In his 1946 preface Waugh wrote: "We know that his Campion's age was a brief truce in an unending war. The Martyrdom of Father Pro in Mexico re-enacted Campion's in faithful detail." By this date Father Pro's fate was, in one sense, merely part of the past history of a distant land. Nevertheless, Waugh's new preface was now able, pointedly, to reiterate the timeless moral significance of the sacrifice of all Jesuit martyrs, whether murdered in England, Mexico, or elsewhere, for an English readership still reeling from the recently discovered Western-European horrors of the Second World War: We have seen the Church drawn underground in country after country. In fragments and whispers we get news of other saints in the prison-camps of Eastern and Southern Europe, of cruelty and degradation more savage than anything in Tudor England, of the same, pure light shining in the darkness, uncomprehended.

The haunted, trapped, murdered priest is our contemporary and Campion's voice sounds across the centuries as though he were walking at our elbow. 3. "Mexico is a state of mind" (Graham Greene) WHILE the fervent admiration of Greene and Waugh for Father Pro's heroic self-sacrifice ensured that the life and death of this incidental figure in Mexican history was very well known to Catholic English readers of the 1940s onwards, it is important to recognize that neither writer seems to have expressed any significant level of personal interest in South American politics or religion before the mid-1930s. Greene did briefly mention in a letter of 1927 to his future wife, Vivien, that he had seen an article on the Mexican martyrs, although this seems to be as far as his knowledge of such matters then went (Sherry 1.698). But in May, 1936, the situation rapidly changed for Greene.

His powerful Journey Without Maps , was published on May 11 and created for him, virtually overnight, the reputation of a writer who was willing to undergo extreme physical hardship in dangerous places for the sake of his art. The seeds of Greene's desire to visit Mexico may have already been sown by this stage, but the positive public response to his Journey Without Maps brought them into confident fruition. By May 24, 1936 he was writing to his brother, Hugh Greene: "Later in the new year I may be getting off to Mexico; negotiations are on hand for a book on the Mexican Revolution and the Catholic church."

As Norman Sherry notes, these discussions were being held with Sheed and Ward, the publisher of Waugh's Edmund Campion; and by July Greene's agent seems to have secured him the promise of a book contract and a 500 pounds sterling advance. Although Sheed and Ward eventually grew cold over the project, Greene then secured the interest of Longman in England and Viking in North America. At the very end of January, 1938 he embarked with his wife, Vivien, on the Normandie for New York.

After a week of frenetic party-going, shopping, and business meetings, the Greenes headed south to Washington, where Greene sought an interview at Georgetown University with Father Parsons, the author of Mexican Martyrdom. Although, in later years, Greene was rather hazy over their meeting (which in his own autobiography Parsons confirmed did take place), he had certainly read his book and almost certainly had it with him as he began his own journey through the country. Norman Sherry suggests (I.663-4, 704) that Greene also probably read some other works on the Mexican situation, including Francis McCullagh's Red Mexico and F.C. Kelley's Blood-Drenched Altars, but Parsons's Mexican Martyrdom almost certainly had the greatest impact upon his creative thought.

Tracing the arrival in 1569 of the Jesuits in Mexico—which "more than Russia, more than Spain is a proving ground for human destiny" —Parsons notes how they had successfully established some thirty-two colleges by 1767. But the primary purpose of his documentary survey was the persecutions of the 1920s, when "the priests and people suffered... a silent epic", leading to an estimated 100 priests having been executed by firing squad by 1928. Emphasizing the timelessness of these horrors, Parsons relates both written and verbal reports of numerous examples of the brutality meted out to captured priests, beginning with Father Gonzalo de Tapia, "that proto-martyr of the Jesuits in Mexico," who was murdered by the native Indians in 1594. He also catalogues the obscene range of mutilations (powerfully reminiscent of the disfiguring and disemboweling of Campion) performed by their executioners upon the priests of the 1920s.

There are, inevitably perhaps, several passages in Parsons's Mexican Martyrdom which directly influenced not only The Lawless Roads but also The Power and the Glory. With reference to this latter work, for example, Parsons describes the hunting down and execution of the Augustinian priest, Father Elias Nieves in the spring of 1928 by a pursuing captain who, unlike so many of his compatriots (but like Greene's idealistic and fiercely secular lieutenant), "was seagreen incorruptible". Father Nieves's captain and the whisky priest's lieutenant are strikingly similar characters: both are clearly motivated by a desire to improve the lot of their poor compatriots, and neither is entirely devoid of compassion for his prisoner.

Both try to persuade their priest to recant, show compassion during his imprisonment, and ensure that, at the moment of execution, their victim is mercifully dispatched by a single shot from their own revolvers. The fourth chapter of Parsons's book is devoted entirely to Father Pro, tracing how he had been rapidly embraced by the "Christian world" as a "martyr" on account of the government's ill-conceived circulation to international news agencies of the photographs of his execution. He also quotes the young Mexican's Campion-like embracing of his fate in one of his own letters:

Already the splendor of the Resurrection is felt because the blackness of the Passion is almost at its thickest. From all sides we receive news of attacks and reprisals; the victims are many; the number of martyrs grows every day. Oh, if only I should draw a winning number. Most potently, as the day on which Father Pro had been executed drew to a close, that night at his family home "a Jesuit priest, defying the law in cassock and surplice, led the prayers" —a clear precursor to the concluding scene of The Power and the Glory when, after the execution of the whisky priest, the next, unnamed missionary quietly arrives at the house of the young boy and his mother.

Once in Mexico (Vivien was sent home to England from New Orleans), Greene usually travelled alone and often in gruelling conditions which are vividly described in The Lawless Roads. Commendably, he managed to cover a broad geographical sweep of the country and powerfully documented the disturbing treatment of the Catholic Church by President Calles. But as one begins to read through the early chapters, another more emotional concern with the timeless universality of the author's observations begins to surface.

In the first chapter, "The Border," Greene whiles away his spare time at Laredo by reading Trollope's Barchester Towers, sharply reminding himself of the universality of the struggle of good against evil: "The world is all of a piece, of course; it is engaged everywhere in the same subterranean straggle... between the two eternities of pain and—God knows the opposite of pain, not we".

The strange landscapes of Greene's childhood school memories in the "Preface" to The Lawless Roads grow entirely relevant as Barchester and Laredo become polarized in the same way as the two sides of the green baize door at Berkhamsted School: on one side the calmly ordered world of suburban English life, on the other the torrid and anarchic world of the schoolrooms. At that moment the recent persecutions in Mexico become primarily for Greene an uncomfortable reminder of the universality of intolerance: "So many years have passed in England since the war began between faith and anarchy: we live in ugly indifference. Over here lay the grave of Pro, Tabasco with every church destroyed, and Chiapas, where the Mass was forbidden".

As this first chapter draws to a close there is an even more intense, almost hallucinatory, blending of Laredo and Barchester. As the rain falls heavily outside Greene's tacky hotel onto the desolate Nuevo Leon plain, a drunken voice is heard singing in Spanish. Greene attempts to concentrate on his novel, but he finds that these sounds impinge insistently upon the reassuringly comfortable images of Mr. Arabin's High Church Anglicanism, breakfast at the archdeacon's, and the Barchester spires. As the two environments of Mexico and

England finally blend into one greater whole, the martyrdom of Father Pro (killed like Campion for his "treason," not for his "religion") takes Greene back in time to an England even before the Elizabethan persecutions: "Pro speaks with the psychology of Thomas of Canterbury, who also was in love with the good death".

Another incidental but curiously memorable Anglo-Mexican linkage is first encountered during his brief visit to Villahermosa. Strangely, on his arrival the chief of police casually informs him: "'You've come home. Why, everybody in Villahermosa is called Greene—or Graham'." He naturally enquires whether Englishmen live in the town but is simply informed in cryptic fashion: "'The Greenes are Mexicans'". He then meets up with an elderly Scotsman "who had never been out of Mexico" called Dr. Roberto Fitzpatrick. For Greene, still in the early stages of his itinerary, this transatlantic name-blending (which is far from uncommon in the colonial history of South America) serves only to compound a growing sense of unease over preserving his own identity as a solitary Englishman in Mexico:

He had been absorbed nearly as completely as the Greenes and Grahams, and there was something rather horrifying and foreboding in this—for an unabsorbed Greene. By this stage in The Lawless Roads, as the memories of Campion and Pro mingle interchangeably with one another, and the unseen Greenes of Villahermosa confuse a Greene from Berkhamsted, even individual historical identity has become a more fluid, imaginative concept than is usually denoted by traditional western nomenclature and geographical placement.

The insistent movement in The Lawless Roads from the specific to the universal underlies what is probably the most powerful, disturbing, and prophetic message for a book published in February 1939. In the "Epilogue," the lessons of Mexico of the 1920s are brought sharply into a Western-European focus as Greene recalls his embarkation in mid-1938 at Veracruz for Havana and then the Atlantic crossing to Lisbon. Through newspaper and radio reports, the "shadow of the Spanish war stretched across the South Atlantic and the

Gulf". The boat itself, a German ship carrying a diversity of nationalities, becomes a microcosm both of the challenges faced by Greene as a traveller in Mexico and of the Western-European world to come:

There is something dauntingly world-wide about a ship, when it is free from territorial waters. Every nation has its own private violence, and after a while one can feel at home and sheltered between almost any borders. The dangerous frontier which now must be crossed is that posed by the national socialism of late-1930s Germany. Although the races on board are mixed , it is the Germans who gradually predominate in Greene's account. He mentions in passing a "German stewardess," and a "German ex-officer," but most prominent are two other figures. The first is a "young German farmer... from Chiapas, who... hated Christianity" and refers with admiration to recently deceased General Erich Ludendorff, who had played a major role in German military strategy during the First World War. In debating the Mexican religious suppressions with Greene, the German farmer declares in confidently ungrammatical English:

"I see you do not know the works of Ludendorff. Listen to me. The Christians have only winned because they have killed all not Christian. Once we had nothing to give people, only Religion. Now we give the Nation. But we are not atheists like the Reds, We have a God, one God." "The old Jewish Jehovah?" "No, no. A Force.

We do not pretend to know what he is. A Principle." Greene notes that the Mexican volunteers for the Spanish Civil War "listened politely to the new Germany." Incidentally, he mentions in Ways of Escape that they provided him with the plot-line for a later novel ("the Franco volunteers on the German ship I took back to Europe began a train of thought which ended in The Confidential Agent"). But the fanatical views of the young farmer neatly encapsulate the threat of the European horrors to come. The recently deceased Ludendorff had become a widely respected member of the Nazi party, publishing his influential advocacy of Der Totale Krieg in 1935.

A gently insistent voice of opposition to such views comes from yet another German passenger, a prisoner called Kruger who had once deserted from a German ship. The other passengers openly discuss the threat posed by Hitler with him, even though he "never for a moment disguised his opinion of National Socialism." It turns out that he had left Germany in 1913 because of the then impending First World War but, ironically and entirely against his will, he finds himself in 1938 being repatriated and "carried remorselessly on towards Hamburg and prison". As the ship finally approaches Western-Europe and its safe arrival at Lisbon is expected for the following day, the lessons of violence and repression taught by Mexico prompt Greene only to look forward in time: "Violence came nearer—Mexico is a state of mind". "Notes on Anarchy" (Evelyn Waugh)

JUST as Waugh's Edmund Campion had inspired Greene's view of the Jesuit missionaries in The Lawless Roads, so Greene s perspectives on the Mexican repression were certainly familiar to Waugh as he compiled his own study of Mexico, published in 1939 with the pungent title, Robbery Under Law for the English market and the rather more neutral rifle, Mexico: An Object Lesson for North American copies. Waugh had been commissioned by the Cowdray Estate (then a prominent player in the Mexican oil industry) to expose the expropriation of British holdings by the socialist government. Unlike Greene, Waugh based himself mainly in Mexico City and opened with the frank words: "The succeeding pages are notes on anarchy". Waugh had carefully studied Greene's The Lawless Roads but was at pains to emphasize that he was writing an entirely different kind of book: Nor will I plagiarize from Mr.Graham Greene's harrowing description of his recent expedition through Tabasco and Chiapas'.

My own experiences, I am afraid, were definitely homely. For the first two-thirds of his volume Waugh provides the reader with a diligently documented history of Mexican politics from the nineteenth-century onwards. As he begins to deal with the 1920s, he traces how the repression of the Catholic Church was first instigated as an attempt by Generals

Obregon and Calles to appease two powerful labour unions, the C.R.O.M. and its successor the C.T.M. syndicate. Even though it is penned in Waugh's characteristically elegant prose style, the first two hundred pages of Robbery Under Law, it has to be admitted, read rather like a resolutely factual history lesson. Even the fate of Father Pro is only briefly mentioned and, in conjunction with the somewhat wry end of General Obregon:

In 1925 the churches were closed throughout the country; countless outrages against the religious took place during an officially supported persecution, the most famous incident of which was the execution of Father Pro, a Jesuit; there was an armed revolt by the Cristeros (followers of El Cristo Rey—Christ the King). Obregon was assassinated, with unsolicited help from his own party, by a religious cartoonist named Tocal, in 1928. Waugh then presses relentlessly onwards through his account of the regimes of Calles and Cardenas. The intended central destination of Robbery Under Law—from which a more specifically religious itinerary could only have distracted—comes on the following page when Waugh records: "In March 1938 he Cardenas took the grave step of confiscating the whole oil industry". And so Waugh's potted survey of Mexican history and politics continues for the next one hundred and fifty or so pages.

But then, entirely unexpectedly, it seems as though the author could himself take no more of these firmly factual perspectives. In a marked change of both direction and tone, Waugh's personal preoccupations (as opposed to those he was being generously paid to express) finally break through, radically redefining the narrative progression of the rest of the work. The lengthy seventh chapters in Robbery Under Law, "The Straight Fight," runs from pages 206 up to 256; and it is within this concluding third of the book that Waugh's Mexico finally converges with Greene's in The Lawless Roads. The chapter begins with a rhetorical acknowledgement of the common charge that Catholics "intrude their religion into everything" enabling Waugh unashamedly to adopt the very same tactic. Having dutifully dealt with the oil expropriation question in some considerable detail, he can at last categorically insist: "It is not land or oil or race or political organization but religion which is the single, essential question of the nation".

Shaking off, as it were, the shackles of the Cowdray Estate's demands, he even begins to refer back to selected passages from Greene's The Lawless Roads. He recalls, for example, Greene's delineation of Father Pro's civilian disguise in his own description of a local priest: "a dusty fellow in lay clothes like an impoverished ranchero to look at". He lavishes praise on the pioneering work of early Spanish missionaries among the Aztec natives ; and he records how even "Mr. Gruening, the leading apologist for the revolution" in Mexico, admitted that "the Jesuits were a fairly decent lot. They were kept in order". He celebrates the establishing of a large seminary in Texas which had supplied many priests in recent years to Mexico (like Douai sending its students back to England); and he notes that secret seminaries were even beginning to spring up in Mexican cities. His greatest enthusiasm is reserved for his lengthy description of the cult of the Virgin of Guadalupe—also reverentially described by Greene in The Lawless Roads —which he represents, alongside the martyrdom of Father Pro, as one of the two key gestures of irrepressible Catholic resistance in Mexico: "Pro is the inspiration of thousands through whom the Mexican Church is still alive".

Waugh postulates in Robbery Under Law: "The Church for her life, has to have a priesthood, an order of men peculiarly educated and consecrated for a specific work". This assertion, within the context of both The Lawless Roads and Robbery Under Law, yet again brings to mind the Jesuit missionary priests, as exemplied by Fathers Campion, Gerard, and Pro. There were, of course, also other kinds of priests in Mexico. The Scotsman Fitzpatrick at Villahermosa tells Greene about a priest at Chiapas who had fled his duties and was once so drunk that he tried to christen one of Fitzpatrick's sons with the name Brigitta: "`he was just what we call a whisky priest,'" Fitzpatrick remarks, and was deemed "little loss" by the locals.

Greene, however, adds the telling aside: "but who can judge what terror and hardship and isolation may have excused him in the eyes of God?".

Within this context, the powerful focus on the Jesuit missionary priest in both The Lawless Roads and Robbery Under Law also reminds us that there are two central but distinct examples of priesthood in The Power and the Glory. The dominating figure of the frightened whisky priest (who is clearly based upon Fitzpatrick's story in The Lawless Roads) shares in Campion's and Pro's glorious fate, executed like them, as is emphasized in the final pages of The Power and the Glory. Greene, however, is careful not to end his novel with this single scene of martyrdom; and, no less importantly, upon such a flawed and compromised figure.

Instead, as the whisky priest dies (and unknown to those who think that they have finally eradicated the threat that he embodies), so a mother is fervently teaching her young son of the execution of a Father Juan who had "spent his last night preparing for martyrdom." Her children also recall a priest who once stayed with them, a member of "el Cristo Rey," according to their mother, who is now venerated as another "of the martyrs of the Church."

The whisky priest's narrative is undoubtedly the dominant one in The Power and the Glory. But if the religious message of this novel is viewed as an organic progression from Greene's spiritual thinking in The Lawless Roads (and, by association, also held in comparison with Waugh's Robbery Under Law), then its conclusion becomes a triumphant confirmation in like Waugh's Edmund Campion and Father Caraman's translation of John Gerard's autobiography—of the endless renewal of the missionary cycle.

The boy is later awakened by a knock on the door. There he finds a "stranger... a tall pale thin man with a rather sour mouth, who carded a small suitcase." He quietly tells the puzzled boy: "I have only just landed. I came up the river tonight". Intended as both the successor and a counterpoint to the whisky priest, he is also the direct descendant of Campion and Pro. In terms of the chronological progression of Greene's own writings, he is also the fictional precursor to Greene's admiration over a decade later for the heroism and self-sacrifice of Father John Gerard.

Penning the police/policing the pen: the case of Graham Greene's 'The Heart of the Matter.'

By Elliott Malamet

Graham Greene's description of his conflicting intentions regarding the structure and content of The Heart of the Matter reveals the quandary of combining two novels into one. In his introduction to the 1971 edition he writes:

Two very different novels began on the same balcony with the same character, and I had to choose which to write.

One was the novel I wrote; the other was to have been an "entertainment". I had long been haunted by the possibility of a crime story in which the criminal was known to the reader, but the detective was carefully hidden, disguised by false clues which would lead the reader astray until the climax. The story was to be told from the point of view of the criminal, and the detective would necessarily be some kind of undercover agent.... When I left Wilson on the balcony and joined Scobie I plumped for the novel. (xiii) But as in Brighton Rock the ostensible shedding of one form for another - the replacement of a thriller with a "serious" novel - only succeeds in stripping away the surface trappings of an ordinary suspense or detective story, such as the focus on a crime and a subsequent investigation and pursuit, for the novel still resembles a thriller in its growing atmosphere of spying and suspicion, trust and distrust, centered on Scobie's attempts to hide his adultery and reconcile his desire to remain uncompromised with his dealings with the Syrian trader, Yusef.

Scobie traces his affection for West Africa to his sense that "human nature hasn't had time to disguise itself.... Here you could love human beings nearly as God loved them, knowing the worst: you didn't love a pose, a pretty dress, a sentiment artfully assumed". Despite his love for this lack of artifice, however, Scobie too will become an inhabitant of the country of lies; his increasing need to hide his actions is directly proportionate to the breakdown of his ability to trust anyone or believe in anything: "It seemed to Scobie one of the qualities of deceit that you lost the sense of trust. If I can lie and betray, so can others". It is this special quality of distrust that is the core landscape of the novel, and though it is a topography which is displayed in other Greene works, here it finds its most emblematic representation.

The figure of a police officer becoming a symbol of dishonesty or questionable ethics is part of a larger pattern in Greene's writing of subverting the role of the forces of detection, be they officials of the police or private investigators. This subversion can take the form of implied incompetence, as with Mather in A Gun for Sale and Rennit in The Ministry of Fear, or it can be a questioning of moral authority, as with Ida in Brighton Rock or the lieutenant in The Power and the Glory. The Heart of the Matter, while it suggests Scobie's commitment to his job, also immediately challenges his efficacy and policing power. Scobie is quite self-conscious about what his work entails, and he believes that it is a vocation requiring perceptiveness and a strong sense of justice; asked by Helen Rolt how he knows about her stamp album, he replies, "|That's my job. I'm a policeman'", and in his dialogue with God he states, "I'm not a policeman for nothing - responsible for order, for seeing justice is done". Maria Couto asserts that "the novel does not explore the ineffectiveness of Scobie's role as arbiter of justice", but I would argue that Greene does indicate, on a number of occasions, Scobie's weaknesses in that area; years of being a police officer in the far reaches of Africa have left Scobie with a sense of his own deep limitations, especially in mediating local housing disputes:

At the beginning of his service Scobie had flung himself into these investigations; he had found himself over and over in the position of a partisan, supporting as he believed the poor and innocent tenant against the wealthy and guilty house-owner. But he soon discovered that the guilt and innocence were as relative as the wealth.... After that he had tried to kill these cases at birth: he would reason with the complainant and point out that the investigation would do no good and undoubtedly cost her time and money; he would sometimes even refuse to investigate. The result of that inaction had been stones flung at his car window, slashed tyres, the nickname of the Bad Man that had stuck to him through all one long sad tour. The first time we see Scobie on duty, appropriating what he perceives to be a possible home-made bomb, his investigative instincts are subject to ridicule:

Scobie picked the bottle up. It was a dimpled Haig, and when he drew out the palm leaves the stench of dog's pizzle and nameless decay blew out like a gas escape.... He threw the bottle over the wharf, and the hungry mouth of the water received it with a single belch, but the contents were scattered on the air, and the whole windless place smelt sour and ammoniac. The policemen were silent: Scobie was aware of their mute disapproval. He should have left the bottle where it stood.

When Scobie is tipped off by Yusef that diamonds will be found on board the Portuguese boat in the possession of Tallit's cousin, he has them confiscated, only to find out afterward who owns the gems:

"I would like to trust you, Yusef. Tell me the truth. Were the diamonds yours or Tallit's?"

"I always want to speak the truth to you, Major Scobie. I never told you the diamonds were Tallit's."

"They were yours?"

"Yes Major Scobie."

"What a fool you have made of me, Yusef."

F. N. Lees believes in "the author's insistence on Scobie's professional merit (put beyond doubt by eventual promotion)" ; but the timing of the promotion, coming at a point in the novel when Scobie has already severely compromised himself, ironically acts as a further undercutting of his position.

Greene's technique of undermining the law authorities represents nothing new, of course, in the tradition of the detective story: "Humble, prosaic, oafish, well-meaning, slow - these are some of the adjectives called to mind by the policemen that populate detective stories. Invariably they get it wrong". But this feature is not limited to detective fiction;

as D. A. Miller argues, the novel itself regularly holds the police "to their place on the periphery" in a "gradual process of marginalization". One of the ways this "marginalization" takes place in the nineteenth-century novel is through the replacement of police power with another kind of disciplinary agency; the coercive force over the individual of public opinion and social gossip, as displayed in many quintessential Victorian works, acts as a powerful regulatory substitute even when the police no longer constitute an effective institution within the world of the novel.

The title character of Felix Holt remarks on this force: "|I'll tell you what's the greatest power under heaven,' said Felix, and that is public opinion". In fact, the ascending dominance of gossip within a community can lead to an ironic situation; public opinion, which originally could be seen as a kind of grass-roots corrective to political misrule , itself becomes a force which must be fended off, as John Stuart Mill cautions: "Protection, therefore, against the tyranny of the magistrate is not enough; there needs protection also against the tyranny of the prevailing opinion and feeling". The relationship between public monitoring and the official eye of the police is thus an essential dynamic in texts like the The Moonstone, which can be interpreted as a comprehensive displacement of the detective's function by the surrounding community, but without any "|collective' intentionality" on the part of that community: "Without having to serve police functions in an ex officio way, gossip and domestic familiarity produce the effect of surveillance... but a direct assumption of policing power by the community is avoided" . The Heart of the Matter, which has been critically examined mainly in theological terms or from the perspective of its African setting and colonialism, is also a powerful example of the undermining of the police; Greene purposefully blocks and reverses Scobie's authority in several ways, as the novel charts a consistent pattern in which Scobie's investigative acumen proves dubious and he becomes the observed rather than the observer.

The power of private and public surveillance and communal gossip is a potent thread in the story, from Wilson's extended monitoring of his unaware quarry and Louise's clinging presence to Father Rank's penchant for passing along secrets and Yusef's widespread sources of information that Scobie cannot nearly match. This culminates in an overturning of Scobie's policing power by a questioning of his ability to see what is around him and also through the text's skeptical regard for his self-awareness. The notion of a "hidden detective" that Greene refers to in his introduction is not abandoned entirely; the novel traces Wilson's secret quest to investigate Scobie and stresses his desire to remain obscured: "He wanted passionately to be indistinguishable on the surface from other men".

But the hidden detective here, as in other Greene works, also comes in the implied form of a faceless yet omnipotent divine hound, and it is the clear parallel between this kind of presence and that of a hidden human authority that is evoked in Miller's telling remark that "the police are only - as Gaboriau also called them - a |Providence au petit pied'... a |little providence' fully analogous to the great. What matters is that the faceless gaze becomes an ideal of the power of regulation". The "faceless gaze" inevitably applies both to Greene's authorial voice and to the divine detective at the core of the book; a poem by Rilke that Scobie reads provides a resonant articulation of the invisible "heart of the matter":

We are all falling. This hand's falling too - all have this falling sickness none withstands. And yet there's always One whose gentle hands this universal falling can't fall through.

Despite Scobie's denial of this heavenly grip - "He thought, those hands will never hold my fall: I slip between the fingers, I'm greased with falsehood, treachery" - the fact of his struggle with and studied rebellion against God's pursuit only serves to emphasize the central role of divine surveillance in the text.

Ultimately, however, The Heart of the Matter exhibits a complex attitude toward the theme of policing, for I would suggest that even with the concerted efforts on the part of the novel to undermine Scobie as a centre of authority, it also displays his elusiveness. But this paradoxical notion - that

Scobie is both policed and yet evades policing - is one that provokes certain questions. If Scobie has been thoroughly monitored by the society around him, such that his adultery and even his suicide are perceived by others, in what way can we assert that he has avoided being detected by the community? A further query arises, this one regarding the issue of Scobie's resistance to divine control: Is an "escape" from God's will possible?

Thomas Docherty seems to propose this when he argues that Scobie's suicide is "a usurpation of God's position, taking God's place as the authorial proprietor and arbiter of his existence". But Greene has stated that "if God exists... He is omniscient" ; what, then, is the text's understanding of Scobie's autonomy in the face of an all-knowing deity? Finally, what is the relationship between the character and his "author-god"? Greene notes that writers "create characters over whom they exercise almost total control," and yet he also admits that Scobie somehow eluded this authorial regulation. An examination of these issues, which the latter part of this essay will begin to undertake, is pertinent not just in attempting to comprehend The Heart of the Matter, but also for the implications it has for much of the author's oeuvre, which is concerned with the limits of human knowledge and hence the undermining of the temporal process of detection, as well as the relationship between God and man.

The opening scene of The Heart of the Matter establishes Scobie as unaware of being observed. On the balcony of the Bedford Hotel, Wilson and Harris - the cable censor - peer at the street below:

"Look down there," Harris said, "look at Scobie." A vulture flapped and shifted on the iron roof and Wilson looked at Scobie. He looked without interest in obedience to a stranger's direction, and it seemed to him that no particular interest attached to the squat grey-haired man walking alone up Bond Street. He couldn't tell that this was one of those occasions a man never forgets.

The force of judgment created by this overhead angle is combined with a casual interchange of condemnatory gossip, which begins with Harris's unfounded accusations regarding Scobie's interest in native women:

"He loves 'em so much," Harris said, | he sleeps with 'em." "Is that the police uniform?" "It is. Our great police force. A lost thing will they never find - you know the poem."

"I don't read poetry," Wilson said. His eyes followed Scobie up the sun-drowned street. Scobie stopped and had a word with a black man in a white panama: a black policeman passed by, saluting smartly. Scobie went on.

"Probably in the pay of the Syrians too if the truth were known." The passage introduces the immediate, if offhand, monitoring of Scobie, and also brings out two other aspects: Wilson's denial of part of his identity - his secret love of poetry - and the general disdain and skepticism regarding the competence of the police. The very nature of gossip is that it focuses attention on an object while hiding itself:

What characterizes gossip, after all, is that it never "minds its own business." Gossip is always about someone else, always oriented to a story that both precedes its discourse and stands outside its frame. The opposition between someone else's story and its own discourse works to neutralize its activity, staged as mere observation. What keeps gossip from becoming the subject of a narrative, is precisely the narrative that is the subject of gossip.

The acts which are erroneously presumed here - Scobie's extra-marital liaisons and his being in the pay of the Syrians - are the very things which he must later attempt to conceal. The "party line" on Scobie is confirmed a few moments later in his conversation with the retiring Commissioner:

"Do you know the latest story they are using against you at the Secretariat?" "I suppose I'm in the Syrians' pay?" "They haven't got that far yet. That's the next stage. No, you sleep with black girls." At this point Scobie's attitude is chiefly one of unconcern, but his fear of the web of communal monitoring surfaces when one night he encounters Yusef: "If Fellowes drives by now, what a story, Scobie thought. The deputy-commissioner meeting Yusef, the store-keeper, clandestinely at night. To give help to a Syrian was only a degree less dangerous than to receive help". This caution is well founded; we find later on that he had been spotted that night by Yusef's rival, Tallit: "The other night a police car brought Yusef home," Tallit said. "I saw it from here plainly."

"One of the drivers earning a bit on the side," Father Rank said. "I thought I saw Major Scobie. He was careful not to get out. Of course I am not perfectly sure. It looked like Major Scobie."

Each compromising situation that Scobie falls into further subjects him to the scrutiny of others, as when Fraser sees him burning the Portuguese captain's letter:

Fraser said cheerfully, "Burning the evidence?" and looked down into the tin. The name had blackened: there was nothing there surely that Fraser could see - except a brown triangle of envelope that seemed to Scobie obviously foreign. He ground it out of existence with a stick and looked up at Fraser to see whether he could detect any surprise or suspicion.... Only his own heart-beats told him he was guilty - that he had joined the ranks of the corrupt police officers.

The sense of Scobie in a potentially dangerous environment is reinforced in the description of his life at home: "He stood very still like a spy in foreign territory, and indeed he was in foreign territory now". His perpetual sense of responsibility for Louise also extends to how the gossip will affect her; at the officer's club he is cognizant of the community's spying on his wife: "He could feel the malice and snobbery of the world padding up like wolves around her. They wouldn't even let her enjoy her books, he thought". His extraordinary obsession with making sure his wife does not fall into despair or become an object of absurdity often spurs Scobie to detect each shift in her mood:

He never listened while his wife talked. He worked steadily to the even current of sound, but if a note of distress were struck he was aware of it at once.... So long as his ear-drum registered those tranquil sounds - the gossip of the club, comments on the sermons preached by Father Rank, the plot of a new novel, even complaints about the weather - he knew that all was well. It was silence that stopped him working -

silence in which he might look up and see tears waiting in the eyes for his attention.

Every nuance of Louise's behaviour is subject to his examination; he can even assess other people's perceptions of his role as her husband: "He knew every one of her faults. How often he had winced at her patronage of strangers. He knew each phrase, each intonation that alienated others.... The worst was when he detected in his colleagues an extra warmth of friendliness towards himself, as though they pitied him".

But Louise proves to be just as capable of observing Scobie as the reverse, and the dynamic of the Scobies strongly echoes that of Pinkie and Rose in Brighton Rock. In each case there is vacillation between a thin web of surface serenity, which has been forged by a mutual backing away from tension, followed by an outbreak of conflict; in both novels the woman is shown as alternately complaining and yet acquiescing to her situation; and both Louise and Rose suddenly strike back at their partners with a startling display of perceptiveness, only to revert to a kind of willed but fragile optimism upon reassurances from the men. Pinkie is forced to reckon with Rose's detective skills, and Scobie finds himself taking notice of Louise's unexpectedly accurate assessment of their marriage when they discuss the possibility of her trip to South Africa:

"I'd miss you," he said. "No, Ticki, you wouldn't," she said, and surprised him by the range of her sad spasmodic understanding. "After all," she said, "there's nobody to save for." Though Scobie, like Pinkie, remains in some ways utterly undetectable to his spouse, he is perpetually jolted by her ability to see through the veil of comforting lies he has attempted to set in place:

"Yes, she said, "I know you aren't happy either. Without me you'll have peace." This was what he always left out of account - the accuracy of her observation. He had nearly everything, and all he needed was peace.... How often he had been pitied for the austerity of the work, the bareness of the rewards. But Louise knew him better than that.

Upon her return from South Africa, in her desire to go with him to communion he feels "as though he were being urged by a kindly and remorseless gaoler to dress for execution". She will not be put off easily and continues to stalk him, suggesting that they attend communion:

"If you want to," he said. It was the moment he had known would come. With bravado, to show that his hand was not shaking, he took down a glass. "Drink?"

"It's too early, dear," Louise said; he knew she was watching him closely like all the others.

Even her aura of cheerful acceptance seems to him like a tricky maze: "Darling," she said, "if you aren't well, stay where you are. I don't want to drag you to Mass."

But the excuse it seemed to him was also a trap. He could see where the turf had been replaced over the hidden stakes. If he took the excuse she offered he would have all but confessed his guilt.

Thus she becomes the policeman and he the suspect to be led to trial: "| Aren't you coming, dear?' Louise asked, and again the hand touched him: the kindly firm detective hand. He rose and followed her and knelt by her side like a spy in a foreign land". Scobie's mechanical soothing of his wife is belied by the knowledge of the true pattern of their dynamic:

Again the nerve in his head tightened; unhappiness had uncoiled with its inevitable routine - first her misery and his strained attempts to leave everything unsaid: then her own calm statements of truths much better lied about, and finally the snapping of his own control - truths flung back at her as though she were his enemy. As he embarked on this last stage, crying suddenly and truthfully out at her while the angostura trembled in his hand, "You can't give me peace," he already knew what would succeed it, the reconciliation and the easy lies again until the next scene.

Their interaction sharply accentuates, among other things, the fact that Scobie is being observed and that he has memorized the art of appeasement which often involves a disregard for honesty. Years of this kind of relationship have actually molded his conception of the truth: "The truth, he thought, has never been of any real value to any human being - it is a symbol for mathematicians and philosophers to pursue.

In human relations kindness and lies are worth a thousand truths. He involved himself in what he always knew was a vain struggle to retain the lies. ‛Don't be absurd, darling. Who do you think I love if I don't love you?'". Although he is, at least initially, "unaccustomed to lies", his marriage is a longstanding forum for the evasion of the truth. What follows from this is that Scobie's increasing concealment of his activities contains, in some respects, its seeds in his relationship with his wife.

Greene's undermining of Scobie as a detective begins with the inverted situation of others policing the policeman; he is constantly observed, gossiped about, scrutinized. But the subversion of his detecting power is also presented by mocking the duties he must perform, including searching a ship for diamonds: "To try and find a few diamonds in a liner of fifteen thousand tons was absurd: no malign tyrant in a fairy-story had ever set a goose girl a more impossible task, and yet as regularly as the ships called the cypher telegrams came in - ‛So and so travelling first class suspected of carrying diamonds. The following members of the ship's crew suspected.... ' Nobody ever found anything". His meeting with Yusef also furthers the picture of Scobie as the target of gossip as well as a policeman who is reduced to guesswork:

"Oh, I had heard that you were resigning, Major Scobie." "No." "We shopkeepers hear so much - but all of it is unreliable gossip." "How long will the rice shortage go on, Yusef?" "You know as much about that as I do, Major Scobie."

If Louise sometimes rises to the role of shrewd observer and even a jailer, it is Yusef who ironically recalls the Great Detective in certain comic respects; because he cannot read or write he stores all his information in his head - a parodic reminder of the cerebral ruminations of Sherlock Holmes - and his network of information is so formidable as to highlight Scobie's own woeful inadequacy as a detective. Yusef repeatedly warns Scobie that Wilson is spying on him:

"They have sent a special man from London to investigate the diamonds - they are crazy about diamonds - only the Commissioner must know about him - none of the other officers, not even you." "What rubbish you talk, Yusef. There's no such man." "Everybody guesses but you." "Too absurd. You shouldn't listen to rumour, Yusef." Yusef's reading of Scobie is accurate; the policeman cannot even detect as well as Father Rank, who hints that he perce ves the special agent's identity and also displays his own powers of observation in trivial matters in a dialogue with Wilson:

"You ought to have been a policeman, Father." "Ah," Father Rank said, "who knows? There are more policemen in this town than meet the eye - or so they say."

"Who say?" "Careful of those sweets," Father Rank said, "they are harmless in moderation, but you've taken four already."

Father Rank detects while Scobie hides secrets: the policeman and the priest reverse their expected functions. Father Rank unabashedly affirms that he is a gossip: "If a man tells me anything I assume he wants me to pass it on". On the other hand, Scobie, as the priest admits, is a person to whom people make "confession": "If people are in trouble they'd go to you, Scobie, not to me. They ask me to dinner to hear the gossip".

A detective's power is contingent on his vision; seeing becomes, quite literally, the root element in overseeing. Mark Seltzer, in discussing Henry James's use of the techniques of surveillance, notes that police fiction is "precisely the form that most insistently manifests the twin operations of vision and supervision, of spectatorship and incrimination.... In the figure of the detective, seeing becomes the mode of power par excellence". Greene suggests that Scobie's initial refusal to acknowledge Wilson's identity is a product of his own self-deception, as Louise tells her husband's nemesis: " | Oh, I think sometimes he's got a kind of selective eye-sight. He sees what he likes to see'". When Scobie teases Robinson over his preoccupation with medical books, the bank manager retorts that "a man's got to know what's wrong with him", which qualifies as a perfect critique of Scobie. Though he constantly reiterates the impossibility of comprehending someone else - "in the confusing night he forgot for the while what experience had taught him - that no human being can really understand another" - he fails to realise how this also applies to his own murky self-awareness. Thus the adulterous relationship with Helen takes him by surprise:

It seemed to him that he had not felt so much at ease with another human being for years - not since Louise was young. But this case was different, he told himself: they were safe with each other. He was more than thirty years the older; his body in this climate had lost the sense of lust....

She stood pressed against him with her hand on his side.... She raised her mouth and they kissed. What they had both thought was safety proved to have been the camouflage of an enemy who works in terms of friendship, trust and pity.

Even his sense of responsibility wanes at the point where he blames God for his dilemma: "Take your sponge of gall. You made me what I am". The inability to fully examine his own behaviour, and his unwillingness in the first half of the novel to accept Wilson's real identity, are part of the same pattern that ultimately leads to the murder of his servant, Ali - an incident which epitomizes the relinquishing of power as it relates to the limits of vision:

It seemed to Scobie that now or never he must ask what was Yusef's plan, but the weariness of his corruption halted his tongue....

"You must not worry, Major Scobie. I think your boy can be made quite trustworthy."

He said with relief and hope, "You mean you have a hold on him?" "Don't ask questions. You will see."

The irony of Yusef's comment that Scobie will see resonates firmly with the reader, for the murder opens Scobie's eyes to his self-imposed blindness: "Oh God, he thought, I've killed you: you've served me all these years and I've killed you at the end of them".

Eventually Yusef's warnings and Wilson's dogged questioning and open admission that he is watching him put Scobie on guard, and the last half of the novel records Scobie's grudging acceptance of the reality that he is being spied upon; finally he asks the Commissioner, "Am I the only one who doesn't know about Wilson?". His relationship with Helen has set in motion the mindset of a man trying to cover his tracks; as he leaves her hut for the first time after they make love, he has already begun to fashion in his own mind the undetectable crime: he planned the moves ahead: he embarked for the first time in his life on the long legalistic arguments of deceit.... He looked carefully everywhere for signs of his presence: he straightened a mat and hesitated over an ash-tray. Then at the end of it all he had left his umbrella standing against the wall. It seemed to him the typical action of a criminal.

The fact of pursuit, so dominant in other Greene texts, reveals itself to Scobie in a scene at the club: "Scobie looked across the table at Helen.... Again he was aware of Wilson looking fro.m one to another of them, and Scobie drew desperately at his mind for any phrase that would end their dangerous solitude. They could not even be silent together with safety". Increasingly Scobie feels life "closing in on him".

The inevitable result of this perceived pursuit is his deep suspicion of the people around him; everyone seems like a detective to the beleaguered suspect: "The door creaked gently open behind him. Scobie did not move. The spies, he thought, are creeping in. Is this Wilson, Harris, Pemberton's boy, Ali...?". The word "trust" is the axis around which all else revolves in Scobie's mind. Yusef's conception of trust is that "You must always know more about them than they do about you", a definition that ruthlessly connects all human feelings and interactions to the dynamics of power; as he demonstrates in the case of Ali, the most "trustworthy" person is one who can never again speak. Ironically, this is Scobie's self-perception as well; once dead, he feels he will no longer plague God: "I can't go on, month after month, insulting you.... You'll be better off if you lose me once and for all". Thus Scobie feels a kinship with his pursuer, Yusef, a trust based on their sharing a life of deceit: "Now he felt an odd yearning towards his tormentor... as though concealed there was his only companionship, the only man he could trust. At least his blackmailer knew him as no one else did: he could sit opposite that fat absurd figure and tell the whole truth". Scobie's illicit activities prompt his pervasive concern with how things look to others, and yet he is often blind to the fact that he is a bad deceiver; at the club he muses that he and Helen have evaded the detection of others: "Scobie thought with a tremor of self-disgust, how clever we've been: how successfully we've deceived the gossipers of a small colony. It oughtn't to be possible for lovers to deceive so well". He does not realise what others know and the extent to which he has been observed; returning one night from Helen's hut he meets a knowing Wilson:

"Scobie," Wilson exclaimed and the man turned. "Hullo, Wilson," Scobie said, "I didn't know you lived up here."

"I'm sharing with Harris," Wilson said.... "I've been taking a walk," Scobie said unconvincingly. "I couldn't sleep." It seemed to Wilson that Scobie was still a novice in the world of deceit. In addition to this, Yusef informs Scobie that Helen's boy is also in the Syrian's employ, and that he is now in possession of a compromising letter that Scobie has written Helen: "The formal voice suddenly stopped and the old Yusef implored again, |Oh, Major Scobie, what made you write such a letter? It was asking for trouble'". For Louise, Scobie's outlook is transparent - "He has a terrible sense of responsibility" - and she has even known of his affair all along, as she admits after his death:

"Did you know all the time - about her?" Wilson asked. "It's why I came home. Mrs Carter wrote to me. She said everybody was talking. Of course he never realised that. He thought he'd been so clever." Scobie's adultery, in fact, is public knowledge; in the end even his suicide, carefully planned so that "no one must even suspect", is uncovered after Wilson inspects the diaries in a prototypical piece of police work: Wilson said, "Have you noticed that he's written in pieces about sleeplessness - afterwards?"

"How do you know?" "You've only to compare the colour of the ink. And all these records of takini his Evipan - it's very studied, very careful. But above all the col7our of the ink." He said, "It makes one think." She interrupted him with horror,

"Oh no, he couldn't have done that." Ostensibly it would seem that Wilson is left with the last word on the subject of Scobie: "His secrets were never very secret".

But The Heart of the Matter, as does much of the author's work, allows for the conflicting impulses of pursuit and evasiveness, charting both the undermining of Scobie's policing authority and the consistent spying on his activities, and yet on the other hand insinuating his resistance to being appropriated. The ability of Scobie and other Greene figures to remain impervious to efforts to detect theme - specially in the metaphorical sense of maintaining a deeply guarded self or inner life that defies perception or is opaque to others and thus remains free" - needs to be understood in several different contexts, depending on the nature of the pursuer.

I should like, therefore, to analyse briefly how Greene depicts large areas of disconnection between the characters in the world of the text - with a specific focus on how this signifies Scobie's undetectability in the eyes of man - before addressing the more problematic and complicated issue of his potential to challenge his divine or literary creator. One of the primary themes that the novel uses to convey the inherent difficulty in tracing any character is that of the fundamental unreliability of writing. Throughout The Heart of the Matter there are examples of written communications that are distorted: letters are mispelled or lost or stolen; cables informing Scobie about the illness and subsequent death of his daughter are sent in reverse order; official government telegrams are contradicted by other telegrams; Scobie's diaries are terse and cryptic; as Yusef says, "Words are very complicated". The idea of writing concealing or distorting its own meaning pervades the novel, as Scobie indirectly exhibits:

He had written down against the date October 31: Commissioner told me this morning I am to succeed him. Took some furniture to H. R. Told Louise news, which pleased her. The other life - bare and undisturbed and built of facts - lay like Roman foundations under his hand. This was the life he was supposed to lead; no one reading this record would visualise the obscure shameful scene in the garage, the interview with the Portuguese captain, Louise striking out blindly with the painful truth, Helen accusing him of hypocrisy.

The cables Scobie receives from Louise about the death of their daughter also exemplify the distortion of writing: "I got one cable just after breakfast.... The cable said, Catherine died this afternoon no pain God bless you. The second cable came at lunch-time. It said, Catherine seriously ill. Doctor has hope my diving. This was the one sent off at five. ‘Diving' was a mutilation - I suppose for ‘darling'". The cables in their proper order would have broken the news gradually, but instead they are darkly comic; "diving," intended as a term of endearment for Scobie, ironically suggests the condition of the dying girl. Scobie's letters to his wife while she is away are similar to his diaries: "He had to be accurate: he could comfort only by omission".

The exactness of the writing is almost absurdly tangential to the essence of his thoughts, and Scobie encounters the same kind of obtuseness when he reads Pemberton's suicide note; the two men are linked by the impenetrable records they leave behind: "Don't go and pay the money I owe - the fellow doesn't deserve it. They may try and get it out of you. Otherwise I wouldn't mention it. It's a rotten business for you, but it can't be helped. Your loving son. The signature was ‘Dicky'. It was like a letter from school excusing a bad report". The assault on writing and its aspiration to meaningfulness is again manifested in the note Helen's father sends to comfort her upon her husband's death; he little realizes that his words are projections of his own world view and have no meaning for Helen, as she tells Scobie: "He's very sweet, but of course he doesn't know a thing about me".

This breakdown of all forms of communication helps to supplement the novel's picture of human beings who are profoundly isolated from one another. Louise's assumption that her husband's fate is predictable - "It's no good even praying" - is quickly refuted by Father Rank, who asserts that the Church "knows all the rules. But it doesn't know what goes on in a single human heart". The impossibility of such knowledge signals the end of human detection, and Greene contributes to the disruption of such detection by implanting contradictory clues about the same character. Scobie cannot be categorized exclusively as a saint or as "a very sick man" ; his behaviour incorporates both clear-eyed perceptions and lies, to others and to himself.

We see Scobie as a deceiver and yet a stickler for truth, as a perceptive observer - his unearthing of the Portuguese captain's letter fixed to the cap of a cistern indicates a trained eye - and yet blind to the actions of others as well as to his own motivations (what Greene calls his "inordinate pride" - Heart xv), and as a man consumed by responsibility to the people around him and yet shifting the blame to God for creating him that way.

The Commisioner's somewhat affectionate appellation "Scobie the Just" may seem ironic in light of Scobie's later deceptions, but Yusef remembers that Scobie could have jailed him if not for a scrupulous regard for the truth: "You could have caught me if you had told your policeman to say something a little different. I was quite overcome with astonishment, Major Scobie, to sit in a police court and hear true facts from the mouths of policemen. You must have taken a lot of trouble to find out what was true, and to make them say it". The enigma of Scobie signifies the difficulty of interpretation, in opposition to detective fiction that dispels discord through a structure of problem solving. Scobie misreads the theological memoir A Bishop among the Bantus to a little boy in the hospital as "a kind of detective story", to satisfy the boy's thirst for adventure, but he makes sure to tack on an unthreatening ending in which "Arthur" Bishop, the "secret agent," successfully infiltrates a pirate ring: Bishop discovers all their secret passwords and hiding-places and their plans of raids, of course, so that he can betray them when the time is ripe".

Scobie thus instinctively grasps one of the cardinal principles governing the genre, that of narrative closure; the ending of a detective story is "less a resolution than an erasure: the answer to a riddle, the unmasking of a criminal, and, most important, the full explanation of everything that has happened in the preceding narrative". But The Heart Of the Matter's secrets and distorted correspondences prevent a simple resolution or unmasking of its mysteries; it is easy neither for the characters to detect one another nor for the reader to affirm an all-encompassing understanding of the characters, especially Scobie.

Scobie can be policed (in the sense of watched or regulated), but he resists being detected - literally "to be uncovered" - by his fellows, a trait that he shares with several of Greene's other protagonists. In Brighton Rock, for example, Pinkie's "young ancient poker-face... tells nothing" ; he is described as having "an air of removing his thoughts, like heavy bales and stacking them inside, turning the key on all the world". The cryptic inner life of Querry, the cipher-like architect of A Burnt-Out Case, remains hidden even in his moment of death: "ǀAbsurd,' Querry said, ǀthis is absurd or else...' but what alternative, philosophical or psychological, he had in mind they never knew". His incompleted speech is an ambiguous seal on "an ambiguous man", and satisfies Greene's desire to create an enigma: "I feel X later changed to Querry must die because an element of insoluble mystery in his character has to remain".

Many of Greene's novels thus call into question our capacity to interpret the world around us or even each other; an initial series of observations or impressions about a character quickly yields to the fact that man is mysterious, as Leon Rivas, the revolutionary priest of The Honorary Consul, remarks: "I have never met a simple man. Not even in the confessional, though I used to sit there for hours on end. Man was not created simple". Often man's clouded or distorted insights are contrasted in the text with the vantage point of God, who possesses infinite wisdom.

Fowler, in The Quiet American, skeptically links the very limitation of human perception to the impetus for a religious faith: "Perhaps that's why men have invented God - a being capable of understanding". His sentiment is echoed by Maurice Bendrix, who theorizes that "when we get to the end of human beings we have to delude ourselves into a belief in God, like a gourmet who demands more complex sauces with his food". But this kind of outlook notwithstanding, Greene often depicts a powerful divine agent that is experienced by certain characters in the form of an almost tangibly immanent presence, invisibly monitoring their activities.

In The End of the Affair, to cite but one instance, both Bendrix and Sarah Miles lay claim to having an exclusive understanding about why the affair ended, but neither one is privy to complete knowledge, which is reserved for an omniscient force; the novel illustrates what Greene calls God's plot-making, a divine "narrative" that conflicts with a linear structure leading to a conclusion - of which detective fiction is an example - that typifies man's ordering of reality. God transcends the boundaries of temporal knowledge; as the priest in The Power and the Glory intimates, His is a point of view unconfined by time or space: "He thought of the immeasurable distance a man travels.... And to God it was only a moment. The child's snigger and the first mortal sin lay together more closely than two blinks of the eye".

Scobie's attitude to this divine hound fluctuates from a plea to remain connected after he commits himself to maintaining the tie with Helen - "Oh God, I have deserted you. Do not you desert me" - to frustration at God's easy submission to man's pursuit: "Scobie thought: God has just escaped me, but will He always escape?... It seemed to him for a moment cruelly unfair of God to have exposed himself in this way, a man, a wafer of bread, first in the Palestinian villages and now here in the hot port, there, everywhere, allowing man to have his will of Him". But if he is exasperated by what he experiences as God's accessibility, Scobie still cannot see Him, as he admits: "I've preferred to give you pain rather than give pain to Helen or my wife because I can't observe your suffering. I can only imagine it".

The presence of God approaches him like a silent observer that has emerged from the darkness: "The other voice... spoke from the cave of his body; it was as if the sacrament which had lodged there for his damnation gave tongue". The novel's pattern of placing Scobie in view while hiding his pursuer is thus subtly repeated in his relationship with God; this kind of dynamic recalls Jeremy Bentham's scheme for a Panopticon, a circular prison centered on a main watchtower in which fully visible prisoners are constantly monitored by invisible guards. This new form of punishment, what Michel Foucault calls "disciplinary" as opposed to "traditional" power, "leaves the domain of more or less everyday perception and enters that of abstract consciousness; its effectiveness is seen as resulting from its inevitability, not from its visible intensity.".

In such an enterprise, then, the detective or pursuer becomes an invisible but constant presence, continuously asserting his unseen but nonetheless formidable power. In Greene's work the most persistent manifestation of this inexorable but abstract detection are the "beating wings" of Brighton Rock or what Scobie experiences as the sudden movement of an external force which longs to reach him before he dies: "It seemed to him as though someone outside the room were seeking him, calling him, and he made a last effort to indicate that he was here". Whether one argues that his motivations are based on monstrous pride or an oddly sacrosanct fidelity, Scobie's suicide is a means of removing himself from the faceless gaze: "And you too, God - you are ill with me.... You'll be better off if you lose me once and for all.... It will be no use then sweeping the floor to find me or searching for me over the mountains. You'll be able to forget me, God, for eternity". Though Scobie insists that his final actions result from his aversion to insulting God with his lack of penitence, the burning desire to be out of sight is also clearly revealed in his words.

Given the substantial rendering in Greene's fiction of God's omniscience, Scobie's suicide cannot mean that he is actually concealed from divine vision, and yet the "other voice from the cave" gives the vague impression that such flight is plausible: "You say you love me, and yet you'll do this to me - rob me of you for ever. I made you with love.... And now you push me away, you put me out of your reach". What this represents is Scobie's own internalization of God, a Voice that he conceives of in a very particular way as being subject to man's challenge and repudiation.

Scobie's final utterance in this agonized debate - "you see, it's an impasse, God, an impasse" - reflects a defiance of divine wishes, at least insofar as he imagines such expectation; Scobie has assimilated moral theology in such a way as to turn religion, in Miguel de Unamuno's striking phrase, "into a kind of police system" . Though the text's pattern of subverting the temporal process of detection does not extend to a questioning of God's knowledge, Greene's fiction does speculate on a reciprocal interrelation between God and man, a mutuality that exists between creator and creation; this is espoused in The Honorary Consul by Leon Rivas: "The evolution of God depends on our evolution.

Every evil act of ours strengthens His night-side, and every good one helps His day-side. We belong to Him and He belongs to us". In a certain sense, then, Greene asserts the displacement of simple cause and effect and posits a deity subject to being shaped by man; the suicide can be construed in that light as a kind of policing of the divinity, who must now submit to Scobie's choices.

Finally, the other voice from the cave suggests not simply the negotiations that Scobie carries out with the divine overseer but, on another level, the constant supervision of the character by his author. The Heart of the Matter consistently demonstrates Flaubert's theory that "an author in his book must be like God in the universe, present everywhere and visible nowhere", as Scobie falls under the perpetual invisible gaze of both the eye of God and of Graham Greene. The novel strongly brings into focus the relationship between authority, literary creation, and a sense of divinity, an interlinkage that has been deftly illuminated by Edward Said; not only does "authority" connote the power to enforce obedience or influence action, "but it presents a connection as well with author - that is, a person who originates and gives existence to something, a begetter, a beginner, father, or ancestor, a person also who sets forth written statements". Scóbie's disappearance may thus be seen to have the dual aim of trying to rebel against both of his "creators," as Greene admits: All writers, even the worst, are led into assuming a role vaguely comparable to God's, for they create characters over whom they exercise almost total control. I should add, though, that a writer is even more like a double agent than he is like God: he condemns and sustains his characters by turns. Their relationship is so ambiguous that when the characters come to elude his control - as which Scobie in The Heart of the Matter - one doesn't know whom to blame.

A critical sentiment frequently expressed with regard to Greene is that he exercises excessive control over his texts, with the effect of making "the characters subservient to some story-line which is not created by them but by some power outside them". The goal of this tight rein is to manipulate the reader into accepting a certain theological or political doctrine, an assessment of the novelist typified by one critic's lament that in The End of the Affair Greene's management of the plot in the later stages "has the effect of detaching the characters from their established logic as personalities and forcing them to serve a function outside themselves" (Zabel 293-94). These charges do raise legitimate issues about Greene's work: "To what extent does the need to communicate the supernatural influence, determine or undermine a novelist's narrative technique?" (Sonnenfeld 308). But even Greene's admitted penchant for authorial intervention, what he calls "the traditional and essential right of a novelist, to comment, to express his views" (Collected 116), does not produce or guarantee an iron-clad control over or regulation of his characters, a situation that he acknowledges in terms that strongly parallel Father Rivas's theology: "The fact is, one is changed by one's own books. The writer plays God until his creatures escape from him and, in their turn, they mould him".

Greene's belief that Scobie was able to evade him may be an allusion to the fact that his intent in developing the character was to show the destructive consequences of pity, but the effect on readers was quite the opposite: "To them Scobie was exonerated, Scobie was |a good man,' he was hunted to his doom by the harshness of his wife". A further indication of

Scobie's lingering ambiguousness also can be located in the various roles that he has been assigned by critics. An early reviewer of The Heart of the Matter sees it as "a kind of moral detective story. The crime is ‛the worst a Catholic can commit' and the criminal ironically a professional hunter of men".

On the other hand, Gwenn Boardman suggests the possibility that the pursuit of truth in a detective story is "a search for ‛the heart of the matter' of religious experience as it is in Scobie's quest", implying that Scobie is actually the novel's detective. The specific issue of whether Scobie is the man the text is hunting down or the one solving its deepest puzzle - it would seem to me that he is plainly both - serves to reframe the larger question of how to understand him by the end of the novel; as I have indicated, the answer to such a question depends in large part on the relationship between the character and those pursuing him. The Heart of the Matter, with all the tenaciousness of its mechanisms of policing, points out the large gap between mortal knowledge and the mysteries of the human heart. And in confessing to Scobie's partial autonomy even from his author, Greene implies that fiction which is invested in tracking of the minutest kind still cannot totally account for an individual's destiny. Yet I do not believe that imbuing Scobie and other protagonists with an aura of mystery entails a true loss of artistic control on Greene's part, but rather underscores yet again a reciprocity between a creator and his creation, leaving Scobie's fate to recall Tennyson's Ulysses: "Death closes all: but something ere the end/ Some work of noble note, may yet be done/ Not unbecoming men that strove with gods."

Tale of Two Writers; Graham Greene and Isaac Bashevis Singer, the Two Greatest Storytellers of Their Time, Are Enduring Mixed Fortunes in Their Centenary Year.

Byline: NORMAN LEBRECHT

IT has taken me all my reading life to realise that the two novelists I have most admired were born in the same year.

The coincidence of their current centenary is no excuse for sentimental reflection on my part, but the more I reread their work, the more confluences I discover between two storytellers who never met nor admitted to reading the other.

Both have been victims of fluctuant taste. Isaac Bashevis Singer, who won the Nobel Prize in 1979, has fallen so far out of fashion that British publishers are no longer bothered to keep his works in print, nor to raise a bid for the latest tell-all biography by a French journalist, Florence Noiville.

Graham Greene, who was denied the Nobel after an incidence of sexual rivalry with one of the judges, is enjoying a centennial resurgence. His titles have been recycled in fresh paperback covers, his life has attracted half a dozen prurient memoirs and the final tome of a step-byfootstep biography by Professor Norman Sherry will hog the review pages come autumn. "Don't ask me, ask Sherry," he laughed, when I queried some episode in his past.

One of the privileges of journalism is that, with persistence, you get to meet everyone you've ever wanted to. I spent a day with Greene in 1984, roaming his wartime haunts, and a day and a night with Singer in 1983, talking beneath the stars on a magic mountain. Both were reputed to be difficult.

Greene had agreed to the interview at the pressing of his publishers, anxious to prod sales that had stagnated in his later years. Singer I caught at the peak of his fame in a period of boredom; his wife, Alma, would drag him for six weeks each summer to a soul-numbing Swiss resort.

I picked Greene up at the Ritz and took him to sit for a portrait by Lord Snowdon. In the car, he recalled that Snowdon had been his last appointment before he left the country in 1966, "one of few occasions when I was cheerful". He used to come back four or five times a year to see his family, but he no longer belonged. He leaped at my suggestion that we take a stroll around Greeneland, the backstreets of St James's where he plied a spook's trade in MI6 during the blackout. His memories were anecdote-free.

He talked of smells and sights, of physical sensations and questions of faith. We wound up in a dingy pub wrangling over censored Christological references in the Talmud.

Singer confronted me at the reception desk of his hotel. "From the Sunday Times?" he exclaimed. "A yeshiva bocher?" A whiff of the rabbinical academy must have pervaded my greeting. We sat outside in the Alpine night. Any quotation that I began in Aramaic he would complete immaculately and recite the next half-page, though he had not opened a religious book for half a century. He sought, as Greene did, a universal morality. Amid the chattering of crickets he gently ventured that "man is a Nazi to animals". I became, overnight, a vegetarian. No two writers belonged, I thought, to more different environments. Greene was born on 2 October 1904, son of a Berkhampstead headmaster, trained on green and pleasant fields, groomed for the establishment. His younger brother became director-general of the BBC, his nephew chairman of the British Museum. Singer saw light in a teeming Warsaw tenement on 14 July 1904, third child of an indigent freelance rabbi.

HIS elder siblings - Israel Joshua and Esther - achieved modest success as writers in New York and London (Esther Kreitman's unpublished stories, titled Blitz, were recently issued by David Paul); the rest of Singer's family perished under Nazi occupation.

Greene went to work for The Times.

Singer contributed to pinchpenny prints before following Israel Joshua to America. His English was horribly accented and barely colloquial. He wrote to the end of his life in Yiddish, a language most Jews deemed irretrievably dead. What united Greene and Singer was a fireside tradition that belongs to no time or place.

Singer said he owed his narrative impetus to Dickens and Dostoevsky: "There was a man. He lived in such a place. One day something happened."

Greene cited Dickens and Conrad - "a disastrous influence... I had to stop reading him." Both spoke of making the reader turn the page and return for more. Neither had much time for modern writers who placed character ahead of plot. Singer snorted ungratefully at my mention of Saul Bellow, who had introduced him to an English readership in 1953 with his translation of Gimpel the Fool in 1953. Greene, who praised Henry James, growled "perfumed writer" when I asked about John Updike.

Both my heroes claimed to be tonedeaf and each insisted he never listened to music. Both spoke in a dusty monotone, Greene hesitant and lisping, Singer squeaking when excited.

Yet both wrote with a sense of rhythm and a mellifluous line that would be the envy of any composer.

Singer's supreme masterpiece, The Slave, is assuredly the finest novella since Death in Venice.

His family sagas may be potboilers but his memoir, In My Father's Court, is an indispensable evocation of a vanished culture and the semi-autobiographical Shosha is a powerfully sympathetic portrait of a conflicted 1930s woman.

His posterity, or what presently survives of it, was marred by a movie.

Barbra Streisand's 1983 adaptation of Yentl, which Singer abhorred, is a travesty of his nuanced story of a girl who lived between the sexes, craving a man's rituals while preserving her feminine integrity. Two other films - the Golan/ Globus Magician of Lublin (1979) and Paul Mazursky's Enemies (1990) - sank with less trace.

GREENE considered himself a screen professional, a sometime film critic and screenwriter of The Third Man, Brighton Rock, Our Man in Havana and The Fallen Idol.

At the time we met he was selecting the 17 best adaptations of his novels for the Brighton Festival.

He relished the transition, yet Greene, like Singer, was traduced by film. Memorable as Trevor Howard was in The Heart of the Matter (1953), magnificently as Otto Preminger directed Tom Stoppard's script of The Human Factor (1980), neither film begins to convey the moral dichotomy that sunders Greene's characters into equal parts of good and evil.

The common legacy of Greene and Singer is an art that was driven not by action, which is Hollywood's ideal, but by a narrative of human suffering and transcendence in morally ambiguous circumstances.

Few writers today deal in such shades of grey. The

overuse of irony and satire diminishes suffering and denies transcendence. The gimmick and the grotesque command attention. Simple, spellbinding storytelling is critically undervalued. It will return. It always does.

Greene and Isaac Bashevis Sin ;er, the Two Greatest Storytellers of Their Time Are Enduring Mixed Fortunes in Their Centenary Year. Newspaper Title: The Evening Standard. Publication Date: May 24, 2004. Page Number: 53. COPYRIGHT 2004 Solo Syndication Limited; COPYRIGHT 2004 Gale Group

Life in Cold and Stormy Greeneland; Glass Act... Graham Greene Playing Host in the Fifties at the Height of His Fame.

Byline: Richard Greene

Graham Greene: A life in letters Little Brown pounds sterlingGreeneland was a term coined years ago to sum up the imaginative landscape ofGraham Greene; a landscape in which whisky-sodden old priests struggle withtheir loss of faith in the blazing sun while locusts gnaw at their diseasedtoes. There was always a danger that the heightened seediness of Greeneland wouldtopple over into farce. Greene himself regularly entered - and usually won -competitions in the New Statesman to parody himself, although he was sometimespipped at the post by his brother or sister. Entering a Graham Greene parodycompetition in The Spectator under the pseudonym 'Colin Bates' in 1980, Greenefailed even to reach the top five. Undeterred, he rejigged the parody - about aboy being won in a backgammon contest - and eight years later used it as thefirst paragraph of his last novel, The Captain And The Enemy.

Graham Greene died in 1991. Since then, a small publishing industry seems tohave grown up selling souvenirs from Greeneland; notably his authorisedbiography, finally coming in at an incontinent 2,251 pages, but also otherbiographies, for and against, slim memoirs by and about ex-lovers, a book ofhis letters to the Press and an unexpectedly enjoyable book of extracts fromthe Dream Diary he kept by his bed. This steadily growing mountain of theauthor's toenail clippings is now in serious danger of burying his works.

Or, to put it another way, the souvenir shop is taking over the island it isintended to celebrate: Greeneland is in danger of becoming a province ofDisneyland.

In the chain bookstores, great heaps of this volume of his letters are bound tobe pride of place on the table nearest the counter; on the other hand, if youwanted a Graham Greene novel, the assistant would spend a lot of time fiddlingaround on the computer before telling you that they'd have to order it inspecially. Richard Greene says in his introduction that Graham Greene onceestimated that he knocked off 2,000 letters a year.

Most of these must have been very humdrum.

When I worked on a Sunday newspaper diary column in the late Seventies, I wasstartled by quite how assiduously the Grand Old Man Of Letters, who had builtup a reputation as, of all things, a recluse, would comb the papers for anymention of his own name,and with what speed he would send off a letter,generally taking offence. It is a shame that more letters showing thispernickety, self-absorbed and touchy side of his character could not have beenprinted in this volume: the only two really poisonous letters included are tohis former friend Anthony Burgess in 1988 ('You are either a liar or you areunbalanced and should see a doctor') and, in 1964, to that great actor RalphRichardson, whom he accuses of wrecking one of his now long-forgotten plays.

'I feel that in the last weeks I have been very patient, but my patience is nowexhausted,' Greene pompously begins this letter. A string of threats andinsults follows: '...Alas you fancy yourself as a literary man, and I have aslittle faith in your literary ability as in your capacity to judge a play. Ihave found you - not for the first time - incapable of understanding even yourown part...The time has come to call an end to the selfishness, the lazinessand the obstinacy which has impeded nearly every rehearsal.' He concludes withthe threat of blackmail: 'I assure you that if you do not from now on speak thelines which I have written, I will see that the gist of this letter has a widecirculation - and I don't exclude the Press.' Both these letters are, ofcourse, exhilarating to read. The author's gloves are off; he has lost hiscustomary cool.

But virtually all his other letters, spanning the ages from 16to 86, are written with an almost forensic, and slightly creepy, detachment.Even when he is professing anguish in youthful love letters to his soonto-bewife, one has the sense of contrivance, of pretending-to-feel: 'I wish Iweren't in love with you. I've always enjoyed it before, even when I thought Iwas being miserable... I'm depressed, because I love you so frightfully.' Inhis introduction, the editor mentions Greene's famous claim that he playedRussian roulette by himself aged 19. He goes on to mention that Greene'sbrother doubted the story, as there were never any bullets for the gun inquestion. 'Whether the episode is factual or symbolic hardly matters,' observesthe editor. 'It explains with great aptness a key pattern of boredom andrisk-taking that characterised Greene's life.' But of course it matters: thereis no risk-taking at all in playing Russian roulette with an unloaded gun.

One must conclude from this, as from so many incidents mentioned in hisletters, that Greene preferred his danger vacuum-packed.

I'm afraid I feel this, too, about his celebrated anguished struggles with hisfaith. In 1950 he writes to the great passionate love of his life, CatherineWalston, with a cunning plan for skirting around the Roman Catholic rulings onadultery: 'Wherever we settled for any length of time, we would have two roomsAVAILABLE, so that at any time without ceasing to live together and love eachother, you could go to Communion (we would break down again and again, butthat's neither here nor there).' This strikes me as having more to do withaphrodisiac than anguish: a few weeks later, he suggestst: 'I think the onlyway to stay together for life is to go back & back to Confession & Communionafter every time.' He was later to describe himself as a Catholic Agnostic,which is really just a way of converting the action ofhaving-your-cake-andeating-it into a sacred doctrine. This fans the sense thatthere was always something of the pantomime about his

Catholicism: somethinglightweight and theatrical, and a little too noisy to be real.

His fixation with treachery - and with the Soviet spy Kim Philby in particular- also showed his propensity for juggling with personal morality. 'I neverbelieved in the prime importance of loyalty to one's country. Loyalty toindividuals seems to me to be far more important,' he writes in support ofPhilby. He never tackles the question of just how many loyal individuals Philbysent to their deaths.

This book works well as a condensed portrait of the successful literary life inthe 20th Century. We find him aged 20, posting off his first book to theliterary grandee Walter de la Mare; aged 25, he is attending a party withRudyard Kipling and the Duchess of Devonshire; aged 34, his novel Brighton Rockis attracting good reviews but modest sales; aged 45, he finds 'my books inevery shop. three different people writing books on me for three different publishers'. Thefollowing year, he has his first unsuccessful nomination for the Nobel Prize; aprocess that was to continue, on and off, for the rest of his life. In hismid-50s, he has become one of the most celebrated writers in the world, and isbusily reaping the dividends.

'I enjoyed myself at Charlie Chaplin's... I also had an amusing lunch with theQueen of Spain and the Infanta and now I have to dash off to lunch with thePolish Ambassador.' Along the way, Greene was tremendously supportive ofyounger writers, in particular Muriel Spark, R. K. Narayan and Brian Moore.Muriel Spark later wrote that he sent her pounds sterling20 every month, together with a fewbottles of red wine 'which took the edge off cold charity'. This was obviouslyadmirable, but his endless letters to them, generally thanking them graciouslyfor their new books, make for slightly repetitive reading. Only when he revealsa shaft of irritation: 'I'm going to be mercilessly frank - I was verydisappointed in a lot of it,' he writes to Mervyn Peake about a first draft ofTitus Groan, do things begin to perk up.

A Life In Letters will be bought by all those devoted travellers who can neverown enough postcards and souvenirs to remind them of the shady dives andcreepy-crawlies that are such a feature of Greeneland. They will undoubtedlyfind the occasional item to satisfy their sense of nostalgia. 'Whenever onekills something which has flopped on the floor the ants come and get to work,stripping the corpse and then heaving and pushing the skeleton to the door,'Greene writes to Dearest Mumma from Sierra Leone in 1942.

For the most part, though, the letters are too terse and lack colour: I wouldeven say they were disappointing, were it not his sense of disappointment thatattracted his readers to him in the first place

The Start of the Affair; He Wrote of Love, Lust and Betrayal - Which Is Why GRAHAM GREENE Was Not Only a Great Author, but One of Hollywood's Best Storytellers. Now, 100 Years after His Birth, BARRY NORMAN Reveals His Dark Cinematic Secrets.

Byline: BARRY NORMAN

Graham Greene? Greatest English novelist of the 20th century?

Could be. Worth arguing anyway, and no doubt, as we celebrate the centenary of his birth on October 2, it will be debated exhaustively. But, as those celebrations get under way, there is another side to Greene that should not be overlooked: namely that he had a greater influence on the cinema than any other novelist. What tends to obscure his influence on the medium is that, if you think Greene and then think film, the next step in the thought process leads you to his biggest success, The Third Man - whereupon you might well pause for a bit before remembering Brighton Rock and... what else was there?

Well, I'll tell you what else: to date, the number of films based on Greene's work has passed 40, and it won't stop at that. It is, after all, only two years since the remake of The Quiet American, starring Michael Caine - a much better version, incidentally, than the 1958 original-was released in the cinemas. I'd be prepared to bet that, even now, filmmakers of serious intent are thumbing through his books and wondering which studio might be interested.

Greene's own fascination with the movies began way back in the silent era in his home town of Berkhamsted, Hertfordshire. There, his father, the headmaster of a local public school, allowed him to visit the town's picture palace to see a Tarzan flick under the deeply misguided impression that this would be 'an educational film of anthropological interest'.

Probably to the boy's immense relief it wasn't, of course, anything of the kind, but the young Greene was hooked. From 1935 to 1940 he was a film reviewer for The Spectator magazine and none of the prevailing icons of the movies was safe from his acerbic pen. Mae West? 'A big-busted carnivorous creature in tight white sequins'. Irene Dunne, when singing to a horse (the things they ask actresses to do), 'She is the one without the white patch on her forehead'. Jean Harlow? 'She toted breasts like a man totes a gun'. Greta Garbo? 'A beautiful Arab mare', which might or might not be a compliment - depending on how a woman reacts to being likened to a horse, no matter how thoroughbred.

Nor were directors safe, either. The 39 Steps, in Greene's opinion, was 'inexcusably spoilt' by Alfred Hitchcock's 'inadequate sense of reality'. (He really hated old Hitch, which was why, many years later, he refused to help him out with the script of I Confess, in which a priest is wrongly accused of murder, a subject which Hitchcock thought might well appeal to a fellow Roman Catholic like Greene.) But, as other critics have discovered before and since, there was a limit to what he could get away with. In 1937 when writing in a magazine about Shirley Temple, the nine-year-old star of Wee Willie Winkie, he accused Twentieth Century Fox of procuring her for immoral purposes - presumably to titillate her admirers, who, he said, consisted of middle-aged men and clergymen. He didn't actually call them paedophiles but he might as well have done.

The studio sued for libel, and won. The magazine promptly folded. From the start of his career, clearly influenced by the cinema, Greene was writing crime and espionage thrillers - The Man Within, A Gun For Sale, Brighton Rock and

The Confidential Agent - all of which were turned into films. Greene didn't like director Fritz Lang's version of his later novel The Ministry Of Fear, published in 1943, nor was he keen on A Gun For Sale, made in Hollywood as This Gun For Hire, even though it turned Alan Ladd and Veronica Lake into stars, just as Brighton Rock made Richard Attenborough a huge success. In all these novels, or 'entertainments' as he called them to distinguish them from his more serious fiction, and their screen treatments, what was to become known as 'Greeneland' was gradually taking shape. Greene disliked the term but, when pressed to define it himself, sourly said it was, 'White men going to seed in outlandish places, guilt-ridden, on the bottle'.

But there is much more to it than that: it has to do with the struggle between good and evil, the search for God and the saving of one's own soul, all recounted with his Catholic fervour. And it is strongly evident in Roy and John Boulting's treatment of Brighton Rock, in which Attenborough played Pinkie, the vicious little gangster tormented, as a Catholic, by his awareness of sin. Brighton Rock was an immediate hit and, soon afterwards, producer Alexander Korda brought Greene together with the director Carol Reed to make The Fallen Idol, based on Greene's The Basement Room.

This, too, was a success - Greene won an Oscar nomination for his screenplay - and the writer and director embarked on what is unquestionably the greatest triumph in the cinema for either of them, The Third Man. In 2000, more than 50 years after it was made, it was voted the best British film of all time, an accolade which is difficult to dispute. Greene wanted it to be set in Rome or Paris; light, bright cities physically untouched by war, but Korda, who had money in Austria he wished to dispose of, overruled him.

Just as well, too, because with its background of the ruined beauty of bomb-blasted Vienna, The Third Man, whatever else it is, is a classic example of film noir, a genre of darkness and shadow in which almost nothing is what it seems and nobody can be trusted.

Orson Welles starred as the elusive Harry Lime and, true

to form, kept everyone hanging around until his salary was upped to pounds sterling60,000. In these days of pounds sterling15 million fees that may not seem much but, in 1949, it was a fortune.

Greene was paid pounds sterling9,000, with which he was able to buy both a yacht and a villa in Italy. The Third Man is one of those rare films which, with hindsight, you feel should have won every Oscar available, but it gained only one, for Robert Krasker's cinematography.

Even so, it was the apogee of Greene's adventures as a filmmaker, even better, he said, than his novella on which it was based.

There were, of course, many more movies of his books to come, among them Our Man In Havana. Hitchcock had wanted to make it but Greene refused to sell him the rights. In the end the film, scripted by Greene himself, was directed by Carol Reed. It was the third and last of their collaborations and starred Alec Guinness, Noel Coward and Ralph Richardson.

By then (1959) Reed, Guinness and Richardson had all been knighted, leaving Coward to bemoan that 'three nights in Havana' was altogether too much.

Perhaps the whole project was altogether too much, because it was the least successful of the Greene-Reed collaborations. Shortly afterwards, Greene became disenchanted not so much with the cinema as with the way his work was translated to the screen.

Earlier, he had been impressed by the 1954 version of The End Of The Affair, inspired by one of his own many love affairs, in which the heroine, seeing her lover apparently dead in an air raid, promises God that if He will spare the man she will give him up - and is true to her word. It is, perhaps, Greene's most overtly religious book and he described it as 'the least unsatisfactory' of the adaptations of his serious novels. But, before then, he had been deeply unhappy with The Heart Of The Matter, which starred Trevor Howard, because the crux of the story - the suicide of the Catholic policeman, Scobie - was deliberately made obscure so as not to offend the Catholic church. Greene was absolutely livid with the 1958 version of The Quiet American, not because the eponymous protagonist was played by the inadequate Audie Murphy, but because the writer and director, Joseph L. Mankiewicz, had changed it from an anti-American to an anticommunist story.

To his credit, Greene, who would certainly have benefited in increased book sales from a successful cinema run, ruined the film's box office chances by furiously denouncing it in a letter to The Times. Films of his books continued - Travels With My Aunt, The Human Factor, The Honorary Consul - and, in 1967, he wrote the screenplay for The Comedians, set in Haiti under the sinister dictator Papa Doc Duvalier. With a cast headed by Richard Burton, Elizabeth Taylor, Alec Guinness and Peter Ustinov, this should have been a sensation.

Instead, thanks to Peter Glenville's lumpen direction, it was a flop. So Greene began to turn away from the movies. He came to the conclusion that 'my books don't make good films', which is arrant nonsense. It's true that not all the movies turned out as well as they should, but that's a complaint that could have been made by any number of great writers from Jane Austen to Evelyn Waugh.

In any event, Greene's books led to two undoubted cinema classics in Brighton Rock and The Third Man. More recently, after Greene's death in 1991, two remakes - Neil Jordan's The End Of The Affair, with Ralph Fiennes and Julianne Moore, and Phillip Noyce's The Quiet American - have yet again proved the enduring power of Greene's writing.

Cherish him by all means as a great novelist, but let's not forget that he was also the most cinematic writer of the last century.

ADDICTED TO DEPRAVITY; Special Report; Voracious Affairs. A List of Favourite Call Girls. Even Fantasies of Seducing the Queen. Why Was Graham Greene So Hooked on Immorality?

Byline: CHRISTOPHER HUDSON

THE novelist Graham Greene entered into his lifelong

duel with death at an early age. Bullied mercilessly at Berkhamsted School, where his father was headmaster, he sat up one night trying to saw open his knee with a penknife.

When that failed, he tried swallowing toxic substances: eye drops, hay-fever drops, bleaching powder, even deadly nightshade leaves.

When none of them killed him, he took 14 aspirins and plunged into the school swimming pool. His legs felt like lead but he did not drown.

All his life he sought out dangerous places and flirted with death, as though at war with himself. Yet he was so secretive that only a few people were able to penetrate the mask and see him in the round.

The mask was that of the worldfamous author. Along with Evelyn Waugh, he was perhaps the preeminent English novelist of his generation. No one else wrote so powerfully about the presence of sin and guilt in a secular world which nowadays scarcely recognises the concepts.

Yet the more we learn about this most Catholic and moral of writers - born 100 years ago this month - the more he turns out to have had as immoral a life as can be imagined.

He had a voracious sexual appetite. Although he was married for 64 years, he slept with numerous prostitutes and conducted a sequence of brief affairs in addition to keeping four long-term mistresses.

He was also an enthusiastic user of drugs. On a visit to China in 1957, he shocked officials by announcing, at every place he visited: 'There are two things I want: a pretty girl to sleep with, and to know where to get some opium.' His search for a personal damnation, for which there could be no absolution by earthly priests, was part of his death wish. As he once told a friend sardonically: 'I had to find a religion... to measure my evil against.' His cousin Ave, to whom he proposed marriage in the mid-1920s, believed there was a streak of madness in the family that might account for this deviant behaviour.

Graham's eldest brother, Herbert, had a weak hold on reality, and his mother never told him about her own father, a clergyman, who spent most of his life in an asylum. Nevertheless, the rest of his siblings all distinguished themselves, including Hugh who became directorgeneral of the BBC.

As a young man, Greene secured a place at Oxford University where he cultivated an air of worldly boredom. He later claimed to have alleviated the tedium by playing Russian roulette.

He found other diversions, too. In 1925, he took up with a pleasant, softmannered girl named Vivien Dayrell-Browning, a devout Catholic convert.

He deluged her with letters, and - to overcome her fear of sex - even offered her a celibate marriage.

EVEN though they married two years later, Greene had no intention of staying faithful. He had cultivated a taste for casual couplings with London call girls. He once compiled a list of the 47 prostitutes he could recall using in the 1920s and 1930s. Their nicknames give a flavour of the sexual practices they specialised in: Russian Boots, 'Flagellatee', Black Pants, Nurserymaid, Dentist's Assistant, and Tall Blonde & friend. On a separate sheet, he listed vignettes of more recent encounters that had ended with him leaving money on the mantelpiece: 'Girl by mirror', 'Beautiful bottom in S. Kensington', 'Circus girl in Cranbourn St', 'Monique', 'Girl off Chester Place', 'Fish tea in Nottingham', 'Absolute stray', and 'Girl who tried to keep me'.

No wonder his friend Peter Glenville observed: 'His sexual stamina always astonished me because it was endless.' Another friend, Michael Meyer, said: 'I always thought that Graham had a rather schoolboy attitude to sex - never for a moment gay, but fascinated by mild divergences from the norm... I remember him suggesting that we find a brothel where two women could put on a lesbian exhibition.' Despite such peculiarities, it was for Vivien's sake that Greene converted to Catholicism. He did so, in the same spirit that he had joined the Communist Party at Oxford or travelled to dangerous places - out of an unquenchable hunger for new experiences.

By joining a Church which transmuted the problems of right and wrong into the certainties of good and evil, he found the subject matter for his literary career. HIS first published novel, The Man Within, rapidly went into six impressions and was translated into five languages. But the next two novels were failures, and for a while the Greenes struggled. They retreated to a tiny cottage in Oxfordshire, where he wrote a biography of the late 17th-century libertine Lord Rochester, a kindred spirit whose sexual deviances knew no bounds. The book was too explicit to find a publisher for another 40 years.

Happily, Greene's next book, Stamboul Train, was a great success, and earned enough money from the film rights to give him the freedom to travel. Vivien was by this time pregnant with their first child (much to the dismay of Greene who initially considered putting the baby up for adoption).

But he had no intention of allowing family life to intrude upon his predatory sex life. Early in her pregnancy Vivien's mother died. Greene persuaded her not to go to the cremation in London on health grounds, and went alone, spending the afternoon with one of his favourite prostitutes whom he called 'O'. Years later, when she had become aware of her husband's persistent promiscuity, Vivien said: 'Some of the people he picked up were quite frightful... I think all of his judgment of character went into his novels. He told me: "All that is good in me, all that's anything worth having in me, is in the books. What's life is just what's left over." ' Most of his friends and lovers would have disagreed. Greene did not live through his books; his books lived through him. They feed off his most intimate experiences.

The Heart Of The Matter, for example, is all about his marital problems and his crumbling relationship with his first long-term mistress, Dorothy Glover.

A short, stoutish woman in blue glasses, she was a part-time book illustrator and decidedly homely in looks. But Dorothy evidently had a powerful sexual attraction for Greene which was lost on friends who met her - all except for his brother Hugh, who briefly became her lover, too.

Dorothy was Greene's lover, friend and drinking partner until the late 1940s, and they remained friends until her death in 1971.

His affair with her once saved his life. One night in 1941, while Vivien and their two children were evacuated to the country, a stick of bombs fell on to his Clapham Common house and gutted it. Greene escaped certain death only because he had spent the night at Dorothy's home.

As the war progressed, Greene ended up in the job which suited him best, the Secret Intelligence Service. He was sent to Sierra Leone, where he spent his time writing books, visiting whorehouses and checking on the occasional agent.

On a later posting to Portugal, he became close friends with his bureau chief, Kim Philby, later exposed as one of Britain's most notorious traitors.

After the war, Vivien desperately hoped he would return to being a husband and father. Yet she, inadvertently, was the cause of him meeting the greatest passion of his life. In 1946, a wealthy socialite named Catherine Walston contacted Vivien to say that Greene's books had persuaded her to convert to Catholicism and to ask if he could be her Godfather in her new faith. Catherine was married to Harry Walston, one of the richest men in England and a prominent Labour MP, but when Greene met her he was instantly besotted by her vivacity and staggering beauty.

Like Greene she loved to break the rules. As a hostess she would come down to dinner in jeans, and when her guests followed suit the next night she would appear in a full-length evening dress. She'd had many affairs before, which her husband had tacitly accepted, but this one was on a different scale. She and Greene escaped to her private island, Achill off the west coast of Ireland. She wore a red dressing-gown for the journey which Greene later told Vivien was the sexiest image of a woman he had ever seen.

Initially, Catherine found her new faith sexually exciting. She enjoyed seducing priests, and joined Greene in a light-hearted plan to commit adultery behind every high altar in Italy. Such libertinism was by no means unique: Greene had once fantasised about seducing the Queen.

In Catherine, he had found a woman who enjoyed the kind of sexual experimentation he had previously encountered only with prostitutes. In the early 1950s, she even dressed up as a boy and went with Greene to a high-class brothel in Venice, where he was working on a film. For Greene's wife, it was a devastating betrayal. But because of Vivien's faith and her children, she was loathe to protest.

On one occasion, Greene and his mistress even arrived at the door of Vivien's home and insisted on spending the night together. Vivien duly cooked them dinner and made their beds in the morning.

There can be no doubt that in Catherine, Greene had found true fulfilment.

He once wrote to her: 'I want you and nothing but you for the rest of my life.' But over time she began to find his devotion suffocating, and despite his pleas was not going to leave her husband.

As he had done as a schoolboy, Greene sought escape by flirting with suicide, adding 24 aspirins to half a pint of whisky. He awaited death with something close to contentment, but all that came was a deep sleep.

AS THE 1950s wore on, he confronted the unbearable reality that Catherine was distancing herself from him out of a deepening religious guilt. The Catholicism which had brought them together was now parting them.

He took refuge in travel, drink and drugs. In Vietnam, researching The Quiet American, he would smoke five to ten opium pipes a night.

Eventually, the pain subsided enough for him to enjoy a four-year affair with a gloriously pretty Swedish film star, Anita Bjork. He remained married to Vivien but never returned to her.

In 1966, he settled permanently in Antibes in the South of France for tax reasons. Shortly after parting company with Anita, he took up with the woman who would be his companion for the rest of his life - Yvonne Cloetta.

She was married to a French consular official, and Greene, who had not been close to his own children when they were young, enjoyed playing the surrogate father to her two daughters. But in his heart, he still remained devoted to

Catherine Walston. When she died in 1978, he received a most extraordinary letter.

It was from Harry, her cuckolded husband, who wrote: 'You should have no remorse... You gave Catherine something that no one else had given her..

. it developed her into a far more deeply feeling human than before.' His absolution was in part fuelled by the fact that Harry had been conducting a 30-year affair with Greene's agent in France, Marie Biche.

Greene lived out his last days in Antibes with Yvonne Cloetta. It was with her by his bedside in the spring of 1991 that he lost his final duel with death.

His insatiable sexual appetite had remained undimmed. In the words of his biographer Norman Sherry: 'Everything I know about Greene tells me he retained an interest in sex even during his last terrible illness.' Greene knew that in the eyes of his God, such promiscuity was the route to eternal damnation. But without that knowledge, he could never have become one of the greatest writers of his age.

It's Thanks to Graham Greene I'm an Addict

Byline: SEBASTIAN SHAKESPEARE

SOPHIE DAHL has revealed the 10 books that shaped her life and inspiredher to take up writing. Her choices range from Zadie Smith's White Teeth (whicheased her homesickness in New York) to Alan Hollinghurst's The Line of Beauty(she aspired "to be half as good as Alan Hollinghurst"). The books that shapedmy life were by no means the most consoling, or the best books I have everread, but they certainly coloured my tastes and outlook.

When I was accompanying my mother to South America on a cargo ship aged seven,I decided there was more to life than staring at the sea day after day. So Ipicked up my first novel, Travels with My Aunt by Graham Greene. Henry and hisaunt gallivant around the world encountering a series of memorable characters.As Henry became addicted to his new life of adventure, so I became addicted toliterature.

Gerald Durrell's My Family and Other Animals transported me to another worldCorfuand his portrayal of scorpions, toads, ladybirds and glow-worms was farsuperior to any Disney production. It was only after reading Tarka the Otter,by Henry Williamson, that I realised literature could move you to tears. Muchlater I discovered it could also instil a sense of foreboding. George Orwell's novel 1984 shaped my fear of the future when I was a teenager.His vision of a totalitarian state resembled rather too closely my own schooland stirred me to revolt against authority.

Borges's Labyrinths proved that fact could be combined with fiction tospell-bending effect: his stories about time, illusion and infinity were moremagical than any mood-enhancing narcotic in my teens. The seduction scene inThe Day of the Jackal by Frederick Forsyth opened my innocent eyes to thecharms of the French language"Viens, primitif " were the two sexiest words I would hear in any tongue foryears to come. Thank you, Freddie. Unlike my school contemporaries I enjoyed Charles Dickens'sGreat Expectations and shivered in Magwitch's shadow. Karel Capek's Letters from England made me see England with fresh eyes, as aforeigner. He observes that in England streets are not where anything happensbut they are just used to rush home. I naively used to think magical realismwas the preserve of the Latin Americans but then I read Czech novelist BohumilHrabal's I Served the King of England and realised the baroque imagination hadits origins in Europe.

And all fiction flows from that most baroque of creations Don Quixote, about aman who reads too many books and loses his sanity, imagining he is a knighterrant. As Emerson said, there is creative reading as well as creative writing.Books shape us all, whether you are a reader, or a writer. or both..

Why british thriller Writers of the 1930S, such as Eric Ambler and Graham Greene, offer a far better exploration of the nature of freedom than any other novelists

By Julian Evans: Throughout February, Quentin Skinner, regius professor of modern history at Cambridge, delivered the Ford's Lectures in British History under the title of

"Freedom Representation and Revolution, 1603-51". In the 17th century, according to Skinner, a particular view of freedom gained ground in England. Our liberty, to be true liberty, must be based on more thai our ability to exercise our rights and liberties withoui interference from a discretionary power. (That, according to Skinner, is merely negative liberty.) It must rather be based on our having the status or standing of independent persons, not subject to another's will.

This not so innocent distinction helped cause the English civil war of 1642-51, and the new view of liberty legitimised the setting up of the English Republic. It was despatched in the counter-revolution; the version of freedom we have inherited is that negative, counterrevolutionary one, enshrined in Thomas Hobbes's Leviathan (1651). Our Leviathan is the monarch, to whom we are still beholden for our rights and liberties. This quite unjustifiable state of affairs becomes a lot less remote in applied terms: under her representative Tony Blair, according to the mildly spoken Skinner, our executive is not nearly responsible enough to the legislative. It is, in effect, an elected dictatorship.

When the feeling persists in a democracy, as it does in ours, that we are not truly free, a revival of the view of those 17th-century critics of the crown is overdue, though we should perhaps be careful how we understand our loss of freedom. We inhabit a democracy, yet our expectations have nearly ceased to be of a democratic kind. They are more to do with economic mobility.

The novel has been predicated on its involvement with individual, often political, freedom ever since it lost its religious sense, roughly a century ago. Here one tends to think of Sartre and Camus, and their conspicuously impractical agenda. In fact, by the 1930s, British novelists were way ahead of European existentialists. Freedom has seldom been more coherently and excitingly explored than in the British thrillers of that decade. Graham Greene's It's a Battlefield are key works; so are the pre-war novels of Eric Ambler, Uncommon Danger(1937), The Mask of Dimitrios (1939) and Journey into

Fear (1940). The Thirties thriller, with its protagonist cut loose from society, operated a readily understandable code that placed him in a rapidly mutating equation of good and evil.

The ordinary heroes of Ambler's fiction — stringers, writers on holiday, language teachers, stateless persons, all ensnared accidentally and resentfully in a world of menace — are psychologically convincing. Ambler was among the first to notice that glace-haired foreign spies were not always villains. His Russians, for instance, were often sympathetic; it was the agents of capitalism who had to be watched. (Ian Fleming's James Bond fails as a seeker of freedom: he is merely the agent of Leviathan.)

Ambler's novels are prophetic. In his second, Uncommon Danger, a freelance hack named Kenton finds himself up against agents of the Pan-Eurasian Petroleum Company, men who will not stop at murder to destabilise the Romanian government and gain control of the Bessarabian Oilfields. In The Mask of Dimitrios, his hero Latimer remarks that "Good Business and Bad Business were the elements of the new theology". What Ambler had identified was a new field of conflict that would determine how free we are: not personal patriotic, but personal-economic. To his heroes, dignity — and therefore freedom — lies in discovering that the world is dominated more by financial interests than political, and that accepting the smallest amount of cash for the wrong motive can relieve you of your honour. In person, these beliefs turned Ambler into an uncomplicated English anarchist.

When I spoke to him, shortly before his death in 1998, he said: "I don't really think I believe in democracy. Except in wartime, when it's in short supply." Ambler's natural successor, the only thriller writer of any consequence who is interested in freedom, or in the importance of the human act, is James Buchan. In a series of potent, complex novels, he has written about the cold war , the City of London (High Latitudes) and post-revolutionary Iran . In this last book, the hero John Pitt is taken as a spy, tortured, then released to fight as the last and most useless conscript against Saddam's army. Buchan's story, in the ideal tradition of the thriller, is a Bildungsroman that turns Pitt from a spoilt, dreamy youth into a man of humanity, battered and improved by experience.

There, perhaps, lies the reverse of Professor Skinners coin. For us 21st-century westerners, enjoying both unprecedented material wealth and an ideological passivity originating in our unwillingness to disturb that level of comfort, it may take another war to rediscover what true liberty means. Or, at least, another English revolution.

Bibliography

Allain, Marie-Francoise. The Other Man. New York: Simon and Schuster, 1983. A series of interviews with Graham Greene.

Allott, Kenneth, and Miriam Farris. The Art of Graham Greene. London: Hamish Hamilton, 1951. This book on Greene remains one of the best, despite its essentially thematic approach. The chapter titles are chosen to illustrate Greene's "obsessive" subjects: the terror of life, the divided mind, the fallen world, and the universe of pity. Given their rather narrow focus, the readings are remarkably penetrating and cogent.